TYRANTS AND MOUNTAINS

By the same author

MY TRAVELS IN TURKEY
MAN WITH A LOBELIA FLUTE
THE WHITE PUMPKIN
REBEL PEOPLE
THE LAST DAYS OF WHITE RHODESIA
THE ROCK OF THE WIND
RETURN TO POLAND

TYRANTS AND MOUNTAINS

A Reckless Life

DENIS HILLS

JOHN MURRAY

© Denis Hills 1992

First published in 1992
by John Murray (Publishers) Ltd.,
50 Albemarle Street, London W1X 4BD

The moral right of the author has been asserted

A catalogue record for this book is available from the British Library

ISBN 0–7195–4640–0

Typeset in 12½/12½ Bembo by Colset Private Limited
Printed and bound in Great Britain at the University Press, Cambridge

*In memory of
my parents and Dorothy,
and for my sisters
Carol and Rosamund*

Contents

Illustrations

(between pp 118 and 119)

MONTE CASSINO

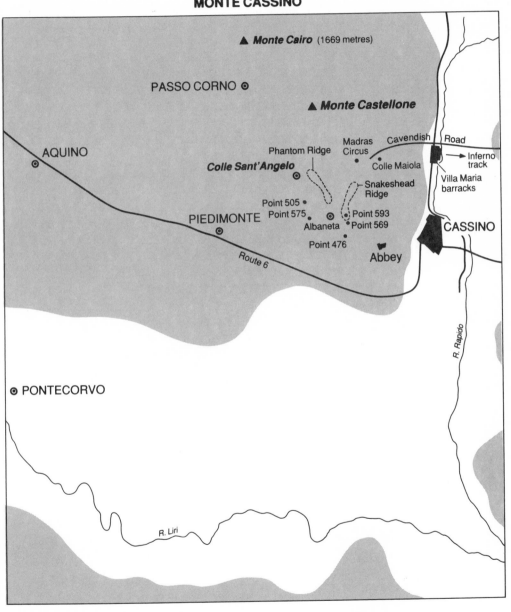

TURKEY & IRAN

Chapter 1

Childhood and School

I was brought up in Moseley, a middle-class suburb of Birmingham where my father was for many years manager of the Moseley branch of the Midland Bank. He was the son of a popular local sportsman in Warwick who had died young of gangrene after his leg was amputated following a rowing accident, leaving his widow and children with no pension and very poor. My mother came from a farming family, the Hurlstones of Heathcote Farm near Warwick.

One of my first memories is of leaning out of my push-chair and grabbing an apple from a greengrocer's stall. Graham Greene – true to his later self – remembered a dead dog lying in his pram. I also saw a dog, two of them. They were stuck together, a six-legged prodigy, and some navvies were laughing and throwing stones at them. I have scarcely any memories of the First World War, since I was born in 1913. I remember a medal that was struck in memory of the sinking of the *Lusitania* passenger liner by a German torpedo with severe loss of life, and the outcry against 'Hun barbarism' – it seems to me that anti-German feeling, in a greater or less degree, has been a part of the English psyche ever since those days when the Kaiser drew his shining sword. I remember a hospital for convalescent wounded who wore bright blue uniforms and sat in invalid chairs in the garden of a converted Moseley manor – I was warned not to stare at them as some had horrifying facial injuries. There was gossip about Zeppelins and I scanned the sky for them; and there was the excitement of Armistice Day when I was sent to buy a special edition of the *Birmingham Post*. I had no war-like relations to tell me stories about the Hun except for an uncle, a captain in the Royal Warwickshire Regiment, who told me he had

1

once taken cover from enemy fire behind the body of a corpse ('I got covered in maggots').

Of the farm where my mother's parents once lived I remember the date 1666, when the house was built, cut in the stone-work near the entrance; and I have a dim vision of fields with haycocks, of horses, the smell of stables and straw and baking bread, a huge blackened cooking range in the kitchen and solid wooden furniture. By then my grandmother was already a widow, living in a gas-lit Victorian house in Leamington Spa. There was a silver riding whip in the hall, several chiming clocks, and creaking stairs. She was a small, haughty woman dressed in black and liked sitting in her garden under an apple tree on a wrought-iron seat bought at the Great Exhibition of 1851. My three aunts had freckled hands and heavy trailing skirts and lived to a great age – the secret of their longevity, I was told, was to rest their legs on special stools. I was taken sometimes to a tiny church at Wasperton, near Heathcote, surrounded by orchards. It had a crumbling pitched roof and a graveyard in which the Hurlstone and Oldham family tombs lay side by side. The Oldhams, my grandfather's family, were neighbouring farmers – they and the Hurlstones hunted, rode and attended church together, and employed Irish reapers as seasonal labour. The lettering on the older tombstones was almost illegible and encrusted with moss. The stones are still there, and have not been uprooted by vandals to make room for a trimmed lawn or a car park.

My father was a gentle, sensitive man whose hair had turned snow-white before he was thirty. He was for long a mystery figure. He rarely took me out – perhaps he was too busy. For in addition to his banking hours he was a senior Mason – he had an ornate apron on which trinkets were pinned and he studied a secret catechism of rules and ritual. He was also a past president of the Moseley bowling club and the leading tenor in the church choir at St Anne's, in which police sergeant Thomas sang bass. Grandma Hills lived with three unmarried daughters in an old house in Warwick bordered by a canal. The painted barges and the great muscular horses that pulled them along the tow-path filled me with restless thoughts.

Being the youngest, I was spoiled, and this must have encouraged an inherently wayward and impulsive nature. I grew up to think of my three sisters as swots; they read a lot and took exams which they invariably passed. I sometimes smacked their chilblains. (Chilblains in winter were considered normal for girls, who were weaker than boys!) My brother Charles, who was eight years older, introduced me to stamp collecting, wood carving and bicycling. British Empire countries issued wonderful sets of postage stamps with pictures of camels, tigers, kangaroos and palm trees.

I learned pot-hooks and spelling at a Moseley kindergarten where the pupils were mostly girls with ribbons in their hair. One of them, Mollie Oakes, asked me to kiss her. My mother, when I told her of this, forbade me to speak to Mollie. Mollie's father, she explained, was 'only a common clerk'. I didn't want to believe this, as social posturing meant nothing to me and Mr Oakes was a jolly fellow who used to give me Gold Flake cigarette cards with pictures of cricketers and footballers. One of my friends was the milkman. He let me ride in the float among the milk churns and hold the horse's reins. The coalman, however, scared me. He humped the heavy jute sacks on his back and his black sooty face made him look like the devil.

Later, at my first private school, which I attended until I was nine, I found I was good at cricket and wrestling and could look after myself in a fight with street boys. These were the sons of local artisans who attended council schools, whistled at the tops of their voices and ran errands for shopkeepers. My private school, Lonsdale House, belonged to two spinsters, Miss Jones and Miss Tiplady. My class teacher was Miss Juggins. She drove to school in a pony and trap and wore high-laced boots stained with horse manure. Once I arrived at school with a swollen nose and blood on my jacket. When Miss Tiplady rebuked me I explained to her that I had been 'fighting for the honour of the school'. My answer pleased her.

Owing to my father's preoccupations I was closer to my mother. She had attended a finishing school in Düsseldorf (the old building was still standing when I looked for it in 1953) and had been trained as a schoolteacher; for a time she taught at Malvern Girls' College. People admired her as a formidable and talented woman. She had once turned on a young suitor who was pestering her at church and told him to 'Go away, you brute!' A boy known as Fatty Goodacre used to bowl a cricket ball at me and I sometimes struck it into neighbouring greenhouses. When a policeman called to make inquiries about the damage, my mother would mollify him with tea and scones. She was highly literate. Attracted by the many books in the house I became an avid reader and when not slogging a cricket ball or climbing fruit trees I pored over Hans Andersen and Grimms' fairy tales in bed on summer evenings. Once, excited by the Grimms' two-headed ogres, I crawled in my nightshirt from my attic window on to the roof and had to be coaxed down by a policeman.

A friendly German from Bremen, Herr Hans Graf, used to give my mother a weekly magazine, *Berliner Illustrirte*, and copies of *Watermanns Journal* and, when he died, a magnificent leather-bound set of Goethe, Schiller and Uhland. It was these books, with their strange Gothic script and coloured drawings of helmeted Prussian dragoons with lances and of mad Anabaptists walking naked through the streets of Münster, together with my father's serialised history of the Boer War – plumed generals and bearded Boer commandos in frock-coats on horseback – that fired me with dreams of travel and adventure. The war artist Caton Woodville was a master at drawing Imperial battle scenes. Isandhlwana, Spion Kop, Majuba Hill and the Gordon Highlanders waiting in kilts on a kopje to be slaughtered, were immortalised by him among deeds of British valour. A focus of my fantasies was a print of Millais' picture of young Walter Raleigh listening spellbound to an old seaman as he points towards the sea and the Spanish Main.

When I stayed in Leamington Spa I sat for hours listening to the band of the Royal Warwickshire Regiment playing outside the Pump Rooms. Grey-haired men with silver-knobbed canes used to bring their wives to enjoy the old marching tunes. They lived in quiet leafy roads named after the Victorian royal family and I imagined that they had spent colourful lives serving the Raj in India among snakes and sepoys. I was told to treat these old sahibs with deference, as their tempers had been ruined by curry. Their wives had complexions like crinkled brown cardboard.

The next stage in my growing-up was at my prep school, The Woodroughs. It was an idyllic place housed in a big cream-coloured mansion and had a playing field ringed by trees with a white cricket pavilion and practice nets. We learned Latin from Kennedy's 'Shortbread-Eating Primer'. One of the first words I learned – *strix, strigis*, a screech-owl – I have never forgotten, though I never came across it again in any Latin text. Mr Plattnauer, a short bullet-headed man with a barrel chest, took us for gym. A music mistress taught us to sing 'Men of Harlech', 'Marching through Georgia', 'The British Grenadiers', 'The Miller of the Dee', and 'Oh God, our Help in Ages Past' – we had no ambition to be choir-boys and our voices screeched. There was one coloured boy in the school, a jolly little Jamaican called Bennion. Because of his dark skin we called him 'Dirty' Bennion, but everyone liked and petted him as a sort of mascot. An Irish boy, Gibbon, with flaming red hair and a large bottom, was the school bully; and there were two Jews. One of them (Fanny Marks) sat next to me in class. He had a weak bladder and was said to wear a pee-bag and to polish his prominent nose with emery paper.

The headmaster Mr Hawkes loved cricket, which he had played for his college at Cambridge; and in my last year, when I was twelve, he introduced rugby football in place of soccer. I was so keen to shine at rugby that one day, though I had been put to bed by the doctor with mumps, I sneaked out of the house with my striped shirt and boots to play in a match. As a result, I was told later, some other boys caught the mumps from me.

One of the masters at The Woodroughs, W.L. Shorting, had a powerful silver-painted Norton motor-bike and opened the batting for Worcestershire during the summer holidays; alas, he never made many runs in those days of marvellous professional bowling partnerships such as Kennedy and Newman (Hampshire), Macaulay and Waddington (Yorkshire), Parker and Mills (Gloucestershire) and Parkin and Tyldesley (Lancashire), though it was 'Tich' Freeman of Kent, a tiny pin-toed fellow who looked like Punch, who was the great destroyer of batsmen. When I did the hat-trick in a school match I decided that cricket was the most important thing in life and whenever possible I used to hurry to the county ground to watch Warwickshire. Though so much has vanished from memory, the faces and performances of the cricketers of the mid-Twenties are still fresh in my mind.

I sat in the cheap seats on a raised bank above the river Rea – a dirty trickle – with a stone bottle of ginger beer and listened to the rough language and barracking of the crowd. Speaking through bad teeth, with an ugly Brummie twang, they were almost incomprehensible to me. At the time of the coal miners' strike (1926), when the visiting Glamorgan team was stonewalling, there were shouts and cat-calls, 'Get back to the bleedin' pits, Taffy!'

From my bench on the boundary line – I eventually wangled a membership card and was permitted to sit in the Members' stand with the gentlemen and their ladies in summer hats – I watched every movement and gesture of the players. One of my favourites was Billy Quaife, a tiny, dapper man; he and Fanny Walden of Northants were the two smallest men playing county cricket. Quaife had a waxed moustache that he had worn since Edwardian days and was a very slow scorer. In his farewell match at the age of 56 he scored a not-out century against Derbyshire. Another hero was Harry Howell, the fast bowler. He and the gangling Warwickshire captain, the Hon. F.S.G. Calthorpe, once skittled out Hampshire for fifteen runs, and yet Warwickshire lost the match. When he retired Harry Howell became landlord of The Sun public house, and he died falling down the stairs. Tiger Smith the wicketkeeper was another character. He was bandy-legged, sweaty and hairy and had huge broken fingers. When I gave him my autograph album to sign he said with a grin, 'I'll do yer a big 'un' and scrawled his name across the whole page. Those were happy summer days under cotton-wool clouds that drifted gently over the brick chimney pots of Edgbaston and the duck pond in Cannon Hill Park.

As for soccer, I listened on a crystal set to that sensational moment in the Arsenal–Cardiff City Cup Final (1924) when an error by the Arsenal goalkeeper gave the Welsh tribesmen victory. The best team in the Midlands was Aston Villa, with Billy Walker. But because of the rough crowds I was rarely taken to watch a professional match. From the age of ten I regularly watched the Moseley rugby team at the Reddings. Coventry, Leicester and Northampton were the strongest Midlands sides, while the Oxford and Cambridge University teams provided brilliant international players. I saw the All Blacks with Nepia the Maori at full back. The Harlequins and Blackheath, being London clubs, had prestige. Welsh teams like Pill Harriers and Abertillery had a reputation for rough play ('Bloody coal miners with broken finger-nails', a spectator told me). Rugger players were of lighter build than today's gladiators. Perhaps there was less emphasis on technique and on carefully worked out tactics and more on 'guts' – on hard running and tackling and on the sheer joy of playing. Penalty kicks were rare; it was shameful to be penalised. Players did not make a fetish of body-building and keeping fit. The Moseley scrum half I remember as a small man with one lung who used to take his wife, who dressed like a tart, to drink at The Fighting Cocks.

About this time I was getting more and more mischievous and rebellious. I resented the straitlaced behaviour expected of Moseley residents and enjoyed defying them. In a small way I became an inveterate law-breaker, the boy who when dared to break the rules would always take up the challenge. 'Trespassers Will Be Prosecuted' notices were an irresible temptation to climb every forbidden fence or wall, 'to see what was on the other side'. Apple stealing, exploring gardens and prohibited property, shinning up drain pipes and climbing roofs became my speciality. With my close friend, 'Warty' Bailey – I gave all my accomplices ugly nicknames – I picnicked in the deep grassy cuttings of the LMS railway and turned Moseley station upside down while Harris the station-master was at lunch and the porter (Hawk Nose) drinking in The Trafalgar Arms. Sometimes we crouched in the sooty tunnel as trains came thundering through with a gush of steam and sparks and the glow of furnaces lighting up the faces of the firemen. I had a strong body (legs especially), scarred knees, curls, an innocent face and a lisp. 'How is it possible', the shocked Mrs Gardiner who kept the sweet shop said to me, 'that such a good man like your father should have such a wicked son!' As an accomplice Bailey was a perfect foil, and intensely loyal (we still meet in a pub at Kingston, where he is the revered senior vice-president of the debating society). To this day, sixty years later, he has retained an impeccable concern for old friends that would put most of us to shame.

An exciting event that fired my imagination was the arrival in Birmingham of a troupe of mounted Cossacks who gave brilliant displays of acrobatic horsemanship. The men wore full Cossack uniform with cartridges secured in pockets across their chests. They jumped through hoops of fire and rode under the horses' bellies. But it was reading that moulded my dreams of escape and adventure. After the books prescribed for 'well brought-up children' (Dean Farrar's *Eric, or Little by Little*, *Robinson Crusoe* and *The Swiss Family Robinson*), all of which contained a moral, I latched on to the bracing yarns of Captain Brereton and Captain Marryat, of Henty, Percy Westerman and Jeffrey Farnol. They created stereotypes in my mind which, though experience has modified them, have stayed with me for life. Here were one-eyed pirates and sea-dogs; hooded monks stoking the pyres of the Spanish Inquisition; Sur Rajah Dowlah and the Black Hole of Calcutta; fakirs lying on nails, Gunga Din, Zulus and Fuzzy Wuzzies, and the cattle rustlers of Zane Grey. I read the *Gem* and *Magnet* and the school stories of Talbot Baines Reed, Gunby Hadath and Wodehouse. Hadath started one of his books with a quotation that I copied out: "'Tis the hard grey weather/Breeds hard English men'. On a winter's day with the cold rain pelting down, the words gave me a feeling of comfort. Sexton Blake's mysteries were too far-fetched. I abandoned him for Sherlock Holmes and the exploits of Brigadier Gerard. My parents approved of Conan Doyle and I borrowed his books at a penny a time from a newsagent in Ladypool Road. I and my acquaintances were always short of money. We spent our coins on buns and Spearmint chewing-gum; a nasty trick was to rub the sticky mess into a boy's hair.

Meat and my mother's heavy puddings, steamed or baked with thick crusts, gave me vigour and I had no serious childhood illnesses. The family doctor (who bore the ominous name of Dr Moriarty) was a choleric Irishman who bandaged my cuts and lacerations with dry lint dressings which he would later tear off with a violent tug, together with the suppurating scab and blood. I didn't mind sitting in his waiting-room as he had old numbers of *Punch*. Here was the adult world making a fool of itself – flappers, monocled men with prominent front teeth, riders falling off their horses in the hunting field. At eleven, after acute pain, I had my appendix removed in a nursing home. Waking up from the anaesthetic in the night I heard the clatter of the nurse's medicine trolley in the corridor and called out, 'Any rags, bones or bottles?' This remark was held to my credit. I was proud to learn that my appendix had been a very big one; but the operation has left me with a formidable scar.

It wasn't until I was twelve, shortly before I left the Woodroughs to become a pupil at King Edward's School in Birmingham, that I first learned about the sexual act. I was bicycling home from blackberrying near Henley-in-Arden with a boy called Lee (his father was a civil servant in India) and he told me that babies were the result of parents coupling together. I found the idea unbelievable, so grotesque and funny in fact that I almost fell off my bicycle. Just imagine, I thought, all those grave and respectable grown-ups grappling together among the bolsters! I couldn't conceive of my own parents doing such a thing, let alone the austere Revd. H. Greaves who took us for Bible lessons and never smiled. Until then I had a vague notion that babies were created in answer to prayer, and my sisters had once told me that they were brought by angels who dumped them ready-made on the parents' eiderdown. Now, like Adam, I had lost my innocence. But I decided not to brood over this revelation.

King Edward's School was a large grey building with a grimy façade, in the centre of Birmingham next to New Street railway station. The station was covered by a soot-stained glass roof and the acrid smoke of locomotives thickened the air in its neighbourhood and blackened the school windows and our clothes. In retrospect it seems wrong to have made schoolchildren grow up on such an unhealthy site. Finding myself among the small fry in a famous day-school of 500 boys, I had to learn new rules. No one bullied me, though there was a tow-haired lout called Hinks whom I found it safer to avoid. School started with morning prayers and a hymn. The prefects stood to the right of the headmaster, Cary Gilson, a grave, heavy-set man, remote and grey-bearded, with hooded eyes; the masters stood against wood-panelled walls bearing the names of boys who had won scholarships, prizes and honours at Oxford and Cambridge – there were scores of them. When the school rugger or cricket team had beaten a rival – Bromsgrove, Trent, Denstone, Worksop and an Oxford college were among the fixtures – the players were discreetly clapped as they took their places. Envious of these athletes, I determined to excel at games and the first thing I did was to learn one of the basic skills of rugby – the art of tackling an opponent low. It is a technique, by the way, that seems to have been replaced in much modern rugby by high tackling and scragging. For a small boy this was a test of courage, or 'guts' as we called it: the thrill of toppling a heavier and stronger player by diving straight at his knees.

At cricket I found I could bowl faster and straighter than the others. But I had to fill out physically, and Sergeant Moore the gym instructor, who had a steel left arm as the result of a war wound, took me in hand. Today, when I think of a gym, I remember the pong of sweaty vests drying on hooks. Later, in Africa, I noted the warm musky odour of class-rooms, and in Turkey the rancid boots of soldiers; more pungent than all of these was the garlic and goat of a Romanian country bus.

Lessons were not a problem. I enjoyed Mr Strong's history periods. They were in the mould I was already familiar with from Henty, Charles Kingsley and Stevenson. Mr Strong used Warner and Martin's *History of England* with its catalogue of English triumphs over the Spanish, the French, the 'lesser breeds' and, latterly, the Kaiser. History was seen through personalities and dramatic events – Cromwell and Kirk's Lambs, the South Sea Bubble and the War of Jenkin's Ear, Marlborough, Clive and Wolfe, the elder Pitt's gout, Trafalgar, Balaclava and the siege of Lucknow. It was taken for granted that the English with their frigates and their 'thin red line of 'eroes', though slow starters, always won. The Americans who successfully defied England during their War of Independence were really emigrant kinsmen who had settled overseas.

I travelled daily to school by commuter train with other boys and we – an élite distinguished from *hoi polloi* by our school uniforms and superior accents – behaved badly, locking the carriage doors against other passengers and scragging each other. Soon after it had left its grassy suburban embankments the train plunged into the slummy factories and warehouses that surrounded the city centre. The smoke and soot turned one's collar grimy in a day. One of the senior boys who used the train was Enoch Powell. He was pointed out to me as a boy to stay clear of – 'an unfriendly fellow – talks to no one'. Powell had a pale face, was never without his cap, carried an armful of books (Greek texts?), and kept to himself. His penetrating blue eyes, furrowed brow and set mouth discouraged familiarity, and he was reputed to be cleverer than any of the masters. He didn't play games but was sometimes caught up in the train scrums where we behaved like savages. Once we debagged a boy, drew a face in ink on his bottom and thrust it out of the window with a pencil stuck in the anus. 'Man smoking!' we cried as we overtook another train – its passengers stared back in horror. On another occasion we debagged a city clerk because he wore pointed shoes and used brilliantine and we suspected that he had been informing on us to the railway authorities. After his father made a complaint five of us had to appear in the juvenile Magistrate's Court and were fined five shillings each for assault. The *Birmingham Post* gave us a headline: 'Schoolboy Justice'.

During my first three years I was regularly beaten. Indeed, I must have broken a school record, for I was caned (six strokes on the bottom) about twenty times by a dozen different masters. Some of them – soft-hearted men – seemed quite loath to cane me, but gave in to the fashion. Piggy Sneath, a clergyman with a round belly and squeaky voice, showed unchristian malice as he swung the yellow bamboo. Pink 'Un went red as he adjusted the curve of my seat for a clean blow. Tanky Bell was the most unpredictable – and the most lovable. He was old and fiery-faced and lost count of the strokes, spraying me with a shower of blows on the back of the knees and thighs. Receiving the cane without wincing, and showing the weals to one's friends, were a sort of bravado (to examine one's wounds one had to crouch over a mirror). Above all I found the rite of flagellation preferable to detention, which would have kept me from the rugger and cricket field. It did not occur to us that a master might find a perverse or erotic pleasure in beating a boy. It struck me as odd, though, that one of the masters, a bachelor with a severe Roman profile, kept a special gym shoe to hit our bottoms with. Despite my bad record I didn't dislike the masters; even Piggy Sneath was only an irritable version of Mr Quelch. And some masters had a warmth of manner and the gift of talking to us as adults that made it impossible not to co-operate with them.

My friend Bailey was by now a boarder at Bromsgrove School. We met during holidays and continued our trail of mischief. One Christmas we filled a whisky bottle with urine and left it with a message and a poem at the door of the charge office at Moseley police station. The poem was dedicated to 'The Policeman who Passes in the Night' and had some literary touches:

> . . . The clump of ebon boots that dully shine
> With daily rubs, the woollen-panted back . . .

At fifteen I was playing for the school rugby and cricket teams. In my first game we beat Bromsgrove at cricket and then in a club match I straight away bowled my old prep school master W.L. Shorting, which was an unforeseen and embarrassing moment. I missed one school match, at Bedford, through being kept in detention by Pink 'Un. In my first season at rugby (I played in the centre) we again beat Bromsgrove and were leading against Denstone when Eustace our captain failed to get up after being tackled. Foam was dribbling from his mouth and it seemed he was having an epileptic fit. The incident was unsettling. But in retrospect our wiry robustness seems unbelievable. After tearing about in mud and rain or sliding through snow we would get into a hot bath and then go out into a bitter wind for a draughty tram ride to our homes.

I scraped through matriculation, and then to everyone's consternation I won the school history prize. The subject of my winning essay – 'The Role of Great Men in History' – had appealed to me because I admired men of action, and I had lately been reading Thomas Carlyle, whose heroes included Muhammad, Cromwell and Napoleon. Moreover, I thought it would be amusing to pit myself against the swots. At seventeen I moved up to the sixth form and with three other boys I was encouraged by Ian McMaster, the senior history master, to work for an open history scholarship to Oxford.

About this time I had my last brush with authority, and was lucky to get off lightly. Rusty Webb, one of the 'two worst boys in Moseley', was given a few pounds and a steerage ticket to Canada and told to clear out by his family. He left Bailey and me a ten-shilling note to drink his health. Lured by the bright-red cherry impaled on a toothpick, we ordered gin and 'It' at a pub. After three rounds I stood up in the bar and began to deliver a harangue on birth control – I had been reading Dean Inge on eugenics. 'Tear off the rubber macintosh!' I cried to the few gloomy customers. Bailey and I then retreated. Alas, we had attracted attention, and when, on some crazy whim, I whipped off a man's hat and threw it over a cemetery wall a policeman appeared on a bicycle.

After a chase in pouring rain I thought I had lost him. But no – he was waiting for me in a side road and took me to the cells to sober up. Bailey, who was not to blame, was being sick in a hedge and was helped home by a Good Samaritan. The magistrate in the morning said, 'I am surprised that a boy of your education and promise should behave in such an unruly manner.' He fined me ten shillings. I learned later that the Revd. R.S. Lound had had a word with the police about me. 'The boy has high spirits,' he is reported to have said, 'which properly used are the very qualities of leadership.' The humiliation of this incident jolted me. It was time to start growing up. And when the school made me a prefect (more consternation!) I found I had been effectively disarmed. It was not until forty years later that I heard of Rusty Webb again. An obituary in *The Times* of 10 March 1972 said that he had died at sea off Port Stanley, alone in his sloop. Four years previously he had sailed single-handed – and unnoticed – round the world, and once, when his boat sank on a reef, he had patched the twenty-one holes himself and sailed on. Little knowing, Moseley had nurtured a hero.

Ian McMaster walked with a stick. He had a high, domed forehead and a gentle manner. He asked me several times to tea with his beautiful clever wife who in restrospect reminded me in her appearance and dress of Virginia Woolf. He lent me books: Maurice Hindus's *Red Russia*, Tawney's *Religion and the Rise of Capitalism*, McDougall's *Psychology of the Crowd*. Hindus's enthusiasm for the Soviet Union's massive – and according to other observers, inhuman – economic and planning drive I found unsympathetic; Tawney implanted a prejudice against the usury, greed and commercial acumen of a Protestant northern capitalist society (my own!); McDougall's comments on crowd hysteria I was able to relate to what I had already glimpsed at large football grounds. In the second-hand bookstalls tucked away among the grim surgical appliance shops and the pubs in John Bright Street I discovered Fichte, Treitschke, Count Keyserling and Bishop Dibelius to complement my mother's library of German classics. I think reading these authors must have helped me to satisfy the examiners at Oxford; for one of the questions to be discussed in the scholarship paper – 'The citizen's first duty is to the State' – was familiar to me from the Prussian philosophers. The essays of W.R. Inge, Dean of St Paul's and a friend of Kipling, were another find. 'The Gloomy Dean' was an Anglican patriot: a pessimist with aristocratic tastes. In his popular journalism he lamented the nation's declining morale, the unbalanced birth rate, and relations with Germany. Clergymen, he pointed out, live longer than Black Country glassblowers and barmen, but alas the proletariat breeds faster than the gentleman and England, he prophesied, would eventually sink to the status of a third-class nation, like Sweden. Later I learned by heart the words with which he ended his book *England*: 'I have laid bare my hopes and fears for the country that I love. This much I can say, that never even when the storm clouds appear blackest have I been tempted to wish that I was other than an Englishman.'

Up till then the history I had read for Higher School Certificate dealt largely with British Imperial expansion and enterprise. Froude, Seeley and Trevelyan were graphic chroniclers of Anglo-Saxon dominion. The books we now had to study under McMaster and his junior colleague Copeland were by comparison arid. Analysing Tudor constitutional history, the Star Chamber, the acts and documents that underlay the growth of Parliamentary government in England, was part of the process of acquiring 'scholarship', but they were less entertaining than Macaulay's bloody annals of Monmouth's failed rebellion. However, we were encouraged to choose our own random reading. C.G. Coulton's *The Mediaeval Village* (1925) has left me with an indelible picture of our oafish ancestors, their boorishness and squalor. This passage, describing a French peasant, has always haunted me:

As Aucassin rode along an old grass-grown road, he raised his eyes and saw on the way a great fellow, wondrously hideous and foul to behold. He had a shock of hair blacker than coal-dust, and more than a hand-breadth between his two eyes, and thick cheeks with a huge flat nose and great wide nostrils, and blubber lips redder than roast flesh, and great hideous yellow teeth. He was clad in hosen and shoes of cowhide bound round with linden-bast to above his knee; he was wrapped in a threadbare cloak and leaned on a great knotted staff . . .

And what about the cruel punishment for crime among those hairy Calibans? – partially burying a man in a field, and then driving a plough over him 'to plough his heart out'. I also came across A. L. Rowse's first book, *Politics and the Younger Generation*. The author has since confessed that he finds the book unsound, though I cited it in my Oxford scholarship paper. Today's student must feel overwhelmed by the sheer mass of specialised academic literature that now litters his path. In those days we tended to read widely rather than intensively.

Still, my chief joy continued to be on the playing field with its competitive edge of victory or defeat and its code of companionship and fair play. In my last year I captained my school (as well as the Warwickshire public school teams) at both cricket and rugby, and I also played for clubs: all this during the happy days of summer and long light evenings or on fresh wintry afternoons of hoar-frost and mud. Every cricket match had its delight: bowling with the new ball, driving through the covers – once when my parents were present I struck a four that just missed my mother's ankle. Under the white flannels one felt the surge of youthful muscular power and agility. And there was the ritual of the game: the umpires' white coats, the moving numbers on the score-board, the sight screens and the sawdust, the affection of team-mates. No one disputed the umpire's decision. There were no Red Indian howls of triumph.

On the rugby field one remembers the short, sharp bruising encounters with players from rival schools, who always seemed to be a little heavier or older: dropping on the ball amid charging boots, fierce, low tackling, the precision of a passing movement that ended with a wing-three quarter haring for the corner flag. Some matches I remember well – perhaps because we won them. Marking Prince Obolensky, for instance, an elusive runner who played for Trent College, and later for England, when he once ran diagonally across the field to score the winning try against the All Blacks; and flattening Archie Warr of Bromsgrove, a stocky, hairy boy built like a small bull – he too played for England. Then, after a match, the shared bath-tubs of hot muddy water (we had no showers) and Elliman's Embrocation and Sloan's Liniment for strains and swellings: Sloan's had to be used with care – a single drop spilled on the testicles made one jump like a scalded cat.

It was through playing village cricket with adults that as a young boy I first got to know the good humour, the fairness and kindly character of the true English sportsman. I started playing for a family team run by Mr Thomson's small factory (Normansell) which made fireside accessories (pokers, tongs, fenders, coal scuttles) for families battening down for the winter over a coal fire. Every Saturday Mr Thomson packed his three sons, his wife (who carried the hamper) and some of the factory hands into his open Vauxhall and drove us to challenge a local village. Once we played the staff of Hatton Lunatic Asylum. The patients cheered every run. One patient, I noticed, spent the whole afternoon marching briskly up and down. 'He must be very fit,' I said to the wicketkeeper. 'You should feel sorry for him,' he answered. 'The man got sunstroke when he was a soldier in India and imagines he's still on guard duty.'

When the game was over Mr Thomson would drive us back to his home, where a huge Stilton cheese stood in a room filled with Cotman landscapes. Later I was to play country house cricket and turn out for Moseley Ashfield. Today when I pass through the village of Wootton Wawen, a few miles from Stratford, I remember the tufts, cow pats and hoof marks on its cricket field. We changed at The Navigation Inn which had a river boat painted on the signboard. The ale (Flower's) was said to be the best in Warwickshire. I am angry that I am too old to be there now, thumping the village grocer's best ball over the hedge. My old friends in Mr Thomson's team have long disappeared. Keith, the wicketkeeper, collapsed while climbing Snowdon. Tay was killed when his bomber was shot down over Germany. Tom Haydon, who was Europe's second-best table tennis player, bequeathed his skills to a daughter, Anne, who became Wimbledon tennis champion.

I was just eighteen when I took the train to Oxford to sit for an open scholarship in history. I had chosen Christ Church as my priority and was given rooms in Peckwater Quad. I dined in hall with other candidates, facing Holbein's swaggering Henry VIII. J.C. Masterman, a handsome history don and all-round sportsman (hockey, cricket and tennis), later to be a key figure in wartime Intelligence, interviewed me. He was pleased with my games record, which would, I knew, be a strong point in my favour as a scholarship candidate. He asked me about Ian McMaster. How old was he? 'Middle-aged.' 'What do you mean by "middle-aged"?' 'About thirty.' Masterman laughed. I was an *ingénu*. But I needn't have worried. I was awarded a history scholarship by Lincoln College worth £100 a year – about half the amount needed to live modestly during my terms of residence – and I was now free to enjoy the rest of my last year at school before packing my trunk for the Turl.

This was an idyllic period. I had leisure to laze in the prefects' room among the hymn books and faded photographs of old teams, and to read novels. One assumes that the prefects were a good choice: Martineau became a bishop and P.G. Mason headmaster of a famous school. Enoch Powell had not been made a prefect – he was a solitary, and too wrapped up in himself to contribute to the communal life of the school. I caned a boy only once, 'for insolence', but as an experiment; the victim readily submitted to bend over 'on condition you don't hit too hard'. I had of course to guard against hubris. Jim Byrne, the kind and humourous captain of the Moseley XV (his father had played full back for England), said to me one day, 'Watch yourself, Hills. It was only yesterday that you had cradle moss sticking to your bottom.'

Despite a growing awareness of girls, I remained, like my school friends, in a state of sexual innocence. It was accepted that girls were inferior to boys, and boys who hung round girls were thought to be sissies. The girls who attended the female wing of King Edward's in a uniform of gym dresses, black stockings, ribbons and brimmed hats were in any case like one's own sisters – unapproachable. Tomboys, however, were tolerated. They wore long scarves and brogues and cheered from the touch-line or at cricket matches. I played tennis with one strapping Saxon girl whose father became a property tycoon. She was succeeded by a girl with large brown eyes. When I squeezed her among the midges in a Moseley private park she felt as frail and tender as a butterfly. Later there was a slightly older girl who worked in a ladies' beauty parlour and had a handsome blonde Greek head. I persuaded her several times to walk with me to the grounds of my old prep school and embraced her in the cricket pavilion. Like most of my undergraduate friends I arrived at Oxford virginal, appallingly repressed (neither condition was thought to be abnormal), inexperienced but not prudish, and in rude health.

Another mark of my immaturity was that I was fifteen before I saw the sea. I went with Bailey and his family to a boarding-house at Sheringham, and we behaved badly, nailing a bloater to the underside of the dining room table; it was still there when we left and smelling strongly. We also interrupted a brass band concert. With a bag of soft tomatoes we concealed ourselves on top of a cliff exactly above the band and audience below, and let the tomatoes drop – there was no need to aim, the tomatoes splashed unerringly on their targets, and within less than a minute we were sprinting off into the gorse. Bathing costumes in those days were secured by shoulder straps over the shoulder, and a beach attendant would call bathers to order if they let the garment fall to the waist. The fishermen mending their nets were as dark as Spaniards and wore ear-rings.

A camping holiday in Scotland left memories of mud and rain, of a bull poking its head through the tent flap near Inverness, the wild green hills of Pitlochry and a cold wind blowing off the sea at Oban. This raw northern landscape, the sheep roaming freely across lanes, the silvery burns and conifer forests and the savage echoes of Glencoe gave me new images to enrich my enjoyment of Stevenson and Burns. On a later camping trip to Devon, jumping naked from a deserted cove into a blue sea shining with broken crests gave me an indescribable feeling of free-dom: no clothes, no busybodies with brass buttons, the smell of ozone and seaweed and joy in one's health and agility – the future stretched ahead into a cloudless infinity.

Chapter 2

Oxford and the Blond Beast

M y rooms at Lincoln, when I went up in October 1932, looked out
onto a square of immaculate grass, with the buttery and hall on
one side and the chapel on the other. A bust of John Wesley, a former fellow of Lincoln, stared from a ledge. I had a coal fire, a tiny
bedroom with a water jug and basin (no tap) and a scout, Tom, who
kept his brooms in a cubby-hole under the stairs. The college func-
tioned under a well-worn routine: morning lectures (voluntary) and two
weekly tutorials, a frugal cold lunch of salad and cheese (commons)
and, for most undergraduates, games in the afternoon. As a scholar it
was sometimes my turn to read the lesson at early morning chapel; once,
rather rashly, I chose that hilarious passage about Moab being a wash-
pot, which didn't please the Rector, J.A.R. Munro, a cold stern man
with a white beard, and a regular worshipper. Coming back from rugger covered in mud was an ordeal as the college provided only half a
dozen bath-tubs in a draughty outhouse and one of the cubicles was
usually occupied by Swaminathan. He took a long time over his ablutions, and would lock himself in like a frightened virgin while he soaped
himself. The college lavatories were a row of doorless cubicles known
as The Fleet. Here we squatted and gossiped before lectures. Some of
the foreign undergraduates thought this a barbarous custom.

At the end of my second term I decided to abandon history and
read Modern Greats (Politics, Philosophy and Economics). The history
school covered nothing later than European diplomacy up to 1914 and
I was more interested in post-war politics and international affairs than
in the Council of Trent. I wanted to study the trends behind the skeleton
of facts and dates. But I was not lucky with my tutors: the Dean (Cox)

who took me in philosophy was a dull, pipe-smoking bachelor without wit; my gentle economics tutor was frail and blind and it was difficult to make contact with him.

I had no difficulty in making friends. I played cricket and rugger with the hearties and found entertainment, eccentricity and malicious charm among the aesthetes. One of my first acquaintances, Jean-Pierre Reinach, was a shy intellectual Jew from Paris, grandson of a notable French savant. Reinach seemed lonely and lost. He despised rugger ('a game for savages'), gave me a set of Dürer and da Vinci prints to hang on my walls ('you live like a peasant'), and was delighted when I took him on the river in a punt and he could gaze at the 'beautiful English girls under the willow trees'. He was killed parachuting into France in 1942.

Stanley Jackson, another Jew, attracted me because he was one of the ugliest men in Oxford. His father had been a kosher butcher, his widowed mother lived above a Chinese laundry in Charlotte Street; they had come to England as poor immigrants from Poland. He was older than most of us. Cynical and sophisticated, he wore a long, narrow-waisted black overcoat – the sort favoured by gigolos. Jackson stimulated me, but his influence was disturbing and in part harmful. During our walks on Headington Hill he chipped away at my adolescent loyalties. He ridiculed the 'monastic discipline' of Oxford – 'Oxford treats us like half-baked seminarians' – and spent his weekends in London with his girl friend, returning on Sunday night by the Flying Fornicator from Paddington. There was an element of risk in the affair, for she came from a country family and her brother, who was at Trinity, had threatened to flog Jackson with a hockey stick if he saw them together. Nevertheless the Cheltenham-educated lady and the East End Jew were to make a happy marriage together. While he was at Oxford he published a crib for law students (*A Manual of International Law*) which earned him a few pounds. When I last heard of him, he had made a name for himself as a journalist and biographer. His most recent book, *The Sassoons*, is a successful paperback.

Other friends were Michael Nathan, David Thomson and Alexei Sabouroff. Michael Nathan (he later changed his name to Wharton) came from Bradford, 'the place where woollen underpants are made'. He was frail and faunlike, with thick black hair and slightly almond-shaped eyes. People used to go to his rooms to drink brandy or Pimm's ('with a dash of Kiwi shoe polish to add flavour and colour') in a fug of joss-sticks, and then go rowdily into the night to disturb the peace. Michael was a mocker. His sly, wicked sense of humour, expressed in wry phrases, was a gift that in later life he has used with great effect as the *Daily Telegraph's* Peter Simple. In those days, Michael had no time for Empire builders ('nigger bashers'), or the homilies served up by J. B. Priestley, whose broad Yorkshire accent he mimicked. But I didn't really care for the incense, the Mozart, the brandy and the hangovers. At bottom I was a hearty. Michael's later metamorphosis into a Blimpish sort of Tory with strong right-wing views – his support, for instance, of the White Rhodesian cause at a time when the liberal world was baying for Ian Smith's blood – surprised and pleased me; but his new persona was less to the liking of his old friend David Thomson.

David Thomson was a big blundering fellow with a sonorous voice who wore thick glasses. His sight was very weak and he was seen to stumble over prams when walking along the High. He was generous and impulsive and free of the English caste snobbery that most Oxford undergraduates suffered from – as a boy he had done farm work with field labourers in Scotland (a time he vividly described in *Nairn in Darkness and Light*), whereas I had scarcely ever talked to a working man. David and I sometimes drank beer in the Nag's Head, galloping into the night when we saw the proctor and his bulldog approaching. David's poor eyesight made him vulnerable, and was a worry to his friends. In my second year he was knocked over by a car ('I never saw the bloody thing') and was taken to Radcliffe Hospital with concussion. After Oxford our ways parted; and I did not see David again until the seventies, when I traced him to a basement room in Camden and, looking through the window, spied his head, now white and woolly, bent over a coal-scuttle. By then he was a well-known writer.

Alexei ('Vodka') Sabouroff, a history scholar from St Paul's, was the son of a well-known Tsarist diplomat. He was a dilettante, bone idle, extravagant and far more erudite than any of us. His favourite reading, he claimed, was the *Encyclopaedia Britannica*, Proust and Talleyrand's memoirs. Sabouroff had a broad, pale Slavonic face and sybaritic tastes – brandy, cigars and expensive dinners. He liked good-looking undergraduates whom he would gently corrupt with hospitality and dinner at The George. The company of women distressed him. 'Talleyrand was right,' he said to me. 'What is marriage but two bad tempers by day and two bad smells at night?' Sabouroff was not popular among his contemporaries. In the gossip column of our college magazine, the *Lincoln Imp*, Michael Nathan was quoted as saying, 'Count Sabouroff and I are celebrating tonight the anniversary of our last hair-cut, you know.' A gang of hearties eventually ducked Sabouroff in a fountain. 'He screamed like a girl,' someone told me, 'and vanished from Oxford.' Not long afterwards he was found dying in a London street. Had he lived he would have shed, somewhere, a brilliant light.

D. F. Karaka, a Parsee from Karachi, lived in the rooms above me. He was the first coloured undergraduate to be elected president of the

Oxford Union. Before he achieved this recognition he used to call on me late at night in a garish dressing-gown and discuss his woes. Karaka had a heavily pockmarked face and a chip on his shoulder. The Englishman's superior airs, he said, made him feel like an outcast. He longed to be admired by the best people. It wasn't easy for me to explain that it was his own colour-consciousness, his flamboyant manner and the violence of his views – he was a passionate opponent of British Imperial policy in Asia – that alienated people. At Oxford we were used to the type of Indian student who, however brilliant, showed respect for our institutions and didn't wear a black pork-pie hat or excel at ballroom dancing. I tried to console him. Why not turn out for the college hockey team?

Lincoln was a small college (150 undergraduates) with a strong quota of Rhodes scholars and a dozen Jews who were mostly studying law. I have not followed their careers. But none of them, I think, will have ended his days sleeping in a cardboard box amid pigeon droppings under a railway arch. David Lewis, a Canadian Rhodes scholar from McGill University who had brought his wife with him, was politically mature but strongly left-wing. I enjoyed debating with him; and it was Lewis who warned me, after my first visits to Germany and Austria in 1933–34, not to be taken in by the Fascists. He eventually stood as Labour candidate for the presidency of Canada but lost the election to Pearson. Some of our American Rhodes scholars had odd names: Igel (hedgehog in German) and Schimmelpfennig (mouldy penny). Another American, George Tilley, after spending his first year in a state of morbid celibacy, suddenly plucked up the courage to address a swarthy, middle-aged lady who used to sit alone in the Odeon cinema café listening to the saxophone player. She turned out to be an Armenian and despite her forbidding manner and slight moustache she gave Tilley 'hours of bliss on her ottoman'.

Parties and society meetings took up much of one's time but I spent most afternoons playing rugby and cricket, punting and walking. The last rugby match I played in before coming up to Oxford had left a pleasant memory. The Old Edwardians were playing Sale, which had a strong team. I was marking Claude Davey of Wales, the best centre three-quarter in Britain. To my astonishment I managed to burst through his tackle, run through to the full back and pass the ball to my wing, who scored. We won the match, though Sale had the indestructible Sever, an England player, on the right wing. Sever had an iron-hard body and stopping him in his stride was like flinging oneself at a bear. Oh! for the lost joys of those moments when mind and muscle and athletic gifts were in perfect co-ordination.

I played in the Freshmen's Trials and for the Greyhounds. Unfortunately the level of games at Lincoln was abysmal. Lincoln was not a fashionable college, the fixture lists were poor, and the University side was always studded with international players. By the end of my first year my old enthusiasms had begun to ebb and I was developing other interests.

All my Oxford friends, with the exception of Jackson, seemed to be virgins. Sitting at a coal fire over anchovy toast we sometimes unburdened ourselves of our secrets. We were romantics. An affair with a woman whom one respected implied patient courtship, vows, roses and trysts. As an introduction to 'real' sex it was thought advisable to experiment with a skivvy, a waitress or a nurse – or perhaps with a foreign girl, French or Belgian. University undergraduettes were out of the question. They were too earnest, too dedicated to a career. They wore black stockings, homely blouses and jerseys, and rode bicycles with a basket for books fixed to the handlebars. At sherry parties one was expected to discuss with them the London theatre or the French Impressionists.

One day Leslie Cutcliffe, with whom I had spent a fortnight walking across Exmoor and along the Devon coast, took me to tea at his parents' home in the Broad, where his father ran an English-language course for foreign students. There I found three German girls eating walnut cake. They had ravishing smiles, they were coquettish, they had splendid figures, and there was no need to discuss Picasso with them. I took such a fancy to these sirens that I made an instant decision to visit their country. This decision – to travel abroad – was to mould the rest of my life. It has turned me into a wanderer. By the end of the term I had arranged to spend two months of the long summer vacation with a German family near Berlin.

The first thing that I noticed about the Germans as I sat in the train taking me via Cologne and Magdeburg to Berlin was that they were keen eaters. My fellow passengers carried rye bread and sausage sandwiches which they carefully unwrapped from grease-proof paper and munched to the last crumb. Railway stations smelt of sweet cigar smoke. At halts where the train did not stop, station-masters stood to attention as it thundered past. Workmen carried satchels and wore caps like tram drivers. I had an impression of discipline, orderliness and loud voices; young people had pasty complexions.

The Mark family was waiting for me in Eggersdorf, which was a small dormitory village twenty miles to the east of Berlin on the main railway line to Warsaw. It stood on sandy soil in a clearing surrounded by pine and birch woods. Herr Mark was the headmaster of the village school. He had grey hair that stood up vertically from his scalp, a large pink face, and glasses. Three of his sons and two daughters were living at home. Heinz was studying philology at Berlin University. Ernst, who had a harelip, was an engineering student at the Technical High School. Friedl, the youngest, was a schoolboy and member of the Hitler-jugend. The two girls were waiting for someone to marry them. Wilhelm, the eldest son, owned the village hardware shop. Frau Mark was the model Hausfrau: mother, cook, needlewoman and confidante. Herr Mark insisted on silence at meals. As meat was expensive we were given large helpings of potato salad, and stewed berries with sour milk.

I was given a spotless white bedroom with a *Federbett* – a large red feather-quilt buttoned up inside a sheet (no blankets) – and a picture of a naval scene from the battle of Skagerrak (Jutland) which, I was to learn, counted as a German victory. After a few days Herr Mark took me firmly in hand. 'You are *schlampig* (slovenly),' he said. He sent me to his son's shop to buy a leather purse – 'no German carries money loose in his pocket'; a bell for my bicycle – 'you are breaking the law'; and a pump – 'no sensible man rides without a *Pumpe*'. Every afternoon he gave me German lessons in his little sandy garden amid the hollyhocks and rhubarb and the humming bees. Sometimes he would open his atlas and point to the town of Gnesen (Gniezno in Polish) which was in the old territory of West Prussia. Herr Mark was a native of Gnesen and had been forced to leave when West Prussia was handed over to the Poles by the Treaty of Versailles. 'Herr Denis,' he would say, 'the day will come when we will seize back our lost provinces with the sword', and he would stare angrily at the express train that thundered past his garden on the way to Warsaw. For him the Treaty of Versailles was a '*brutales Diktat*', and the German people would never rest until its unjust territorial provisions had been dismantled.

Herr Mark warned me against the local girls – 'the pretty ones are *Huren*, whores'. He loved *Ausflüge* (picnics) – it was one of the first words he taught me, together with *tüchtig* (thorough), *arbeitsam* (hard-working) and *pünktlich* (punctual). He would dress up in his knickerbockers and a special cap and take me to lake Müggelsee, the Bismarck Tower, or to a beer garden; or I walked with him through the woods near his home to gather mushrooms and fallen cones for kindling. The dark forest impressed me with its files of tall silent trees – 'like grenadiers on parade', I managed to say to him in German; the simile pleased him. In the long summer evenings I played handball on the football field with the local team. A detachment of SA (Storm Troopers) also used the field, for drill. After marching up and down they went into the Friedrich der Grosse Inn to bellow songs. The inn stood in the shade of a giant oak which, I was told, *der alte Fritz* had planted himself. A favourite song was *Volk an's Gewehr!* (To Arms, People!). The Storm Trooper's uniform was a brown shirt with a swastika armband, breeches and jackboots, a leather belt with clasp and a peaked cap. Most of the men were railway or postal workers, clerks and minor officials. Many were middle-aged with beer bellies. The older men wished to be friendly and bought me beer. 'The *Engländer* are gentlemen', they said, lifting their glasses. 'We are blood brothers – why, you look like a German!' I don't remember them mentioning the Jews; perhaps Heinz had warned them to keep clear of the subject. *Bolschewismus* was the enemy; and, like Herr Mark, they had a low opinion of the French (*Halbneger* – a mongrel nation with negro blood), the Italians (*Zigeuner* – gypsies) and the Poles (*Dreckpolacken* – Polish rubbish). When criticising the British a common slur, which I was to hear many times, was that we were a nation of 'business people with no heart' – *Geschäftsleute ohne Herz*. Xenophobia, I have learned, is endemic wherever people cluster together as tribes within national state boundaries surrounded by rival neighbours. The Germans at that time not only had the bitterest memories of defeat in war, the loss of land, military occupation, inflation and the trauma of vast unemployment; they had the additional frustration of knowing that only fifteen years earlier, with the Tsarist empire reeling, they had been balked of victory at the last minute.

On day-trips to Berlin by S-Bahn I had meals with Heinz and his friends at the university in Unter den Linden; the entrance was adjacent to the Tomb of the Unknown Soldier, facing the statue of Frederick the Great on a horse. The students struck me as older and more mature than my Oxford contemporaries, and poorer. Their clothes were worn but pressed, and they carefully counted their change before putting it into their slotted leather purses. Some students had duelling scars that had slashed their cheeks or serrated a nose. At an open-air students' rally which I attended near the Siegesallee the speaker harangued us with Nazi slogans. Assailed by choruses of Heil Hitler! and a forest of raised arms I felt that the Turl, with its harmless tradesmen selling rowing scarves and my college half-empty and asleep in the summer vacation, inhabited a different world.

Using my tiny Lilliput pocket dictionary I memorised scores of German words and phrases and worked through the political columns of Dr Goebbels' *Völkischer Beobachter* with its bold headlines in heavy Gothic script. I was too shy to sit in the elegant cafés on the Unter den Linden and preferred sausage-and-beer stalls. There was a certain attractive grossness about the middle-aged Berliner with his thick boar's neck, his cigar *Stumpf* and rasping voice, and the whores who hung about shop and hotel entrances. They had formidable busts, wore brimmed hats and jewellery and smoked through cigarette holders. 'So ein schöner Junge,' they would call out to me, taking a step forward. 'Was machen Sie so allein?' or 'Komm, Liebling.' Remembering Herr Mark's wagging forefinger and my empty pockets, I walked past holding my Lilliput dictionary and found workmen to talk to instead. Some had been soldiers. 'The English Tommy was a good sport,' one of them told me. 'One Christmas Day we left our trenches and played football together. Then an officer came, and we had to start shooting each other again.'

Heinz was wrapped up in his philology studies. He was preparing a thesis on Dickens' use of slang, but made heavy weather of Dickens' wit. He was by no means committed to the Nazi movement. Yet to avoid compromising himself he was careful not to criticise the Führer. I got on best with Ernst, and spoke often with him in his attic room after the others had gone to bed. Ernst had openly rejected Nazism and because of this he was ostracised by many of his colleagues at the Technical High School. His badly repaired harelip afflicted his palate and voice and the disfigurement had turned him into a loner. 'The logical end of the Hitler movement', he told me, 'will be war.'

I could see for myself that the pressure of Hitler's ideology had not left Herr Mark's family unscathed, and that elsewhere its intrusion into private lives was upsetting relations between hitherto normal people. Herr Mark was a man of straightforward virtue. But as a Prussian patriot of the old school his ambition was to see Germany recover her lost eastern territories, by force if necessary. Wilhelm, the eldest son, whom I didn't trust, made sure that his 'Heil Hitler' greeting to his customers was loud and incisive. Friedl was too young – 'He understands nothing,' said Ernst. Friedl carried out with alacrity the tasks given to him by his section leader and class teacher. One of them was to march up to twenty kilometres with a rucksack filled with heavy stones. His favourite reading was war stories about German *Heldentum* (heroism).

The dry northern air and sandy soil, the cool sharp nights, the conifer woods which smelled of burnt toast, the gleam of lake water, gave me a feeling of vitality. The Mark of Brandenburg was an ancient landscape that had been settled by hard, thrifty men – Huguenots and Protestants – who had sown potatoes and rye, set up industries, bred soldiers, scholars and pastors, and transformed this poor border territory into a centre of Prussian power. Wherever I went swimming in the lakes I saw young Germans flexing their muscles, rowing, cycling, setting off on foot tours, training their bodies. The older generation of Germans was often fat and bald. The new generation was Spartan. I was expected to race with them when swimming and to join in their gymnastics on the sandy beaches.

Towards the end of my stay with the Mark family I cycled with Heinz to the small Baltic island of Rügen. It was a fortnight's hard work: hours of pedalling, no dawdling, early nights, and butter milk (no beer) to slake thirst. We put up at youth hostels with wooden beams and earth closets, explored the cobbled streets of Prenzlau, Stralsund and Swinemünde, and weaved our way through gigantic hedgeless tracts of yellow corn. Harvesting in Pomerania had already begun. The lanes were blocked with loaded farm wagons and threshing machines drawn by powerful horses; the labourers smelt of schnapps. One day we stopped at a small *Junker's* estate: fine riding horses, shapely daughters, ponderous furniture and family photographs of women with bustles and officers in spiked helmets. The farmstead was surrounded by a long wall and outbuildings that reeked of pigs and dung. Looking at the flat faraway skyline one felt engulfed in an endless sea of rye and wheat sprinkled with cornflowers.

We crossed to Rügen by ferry. The small golden island, embedded in sand and woodland and a clean blue sea, fell away in dazzling white cliffs scoured by a strong breeze. Tourists were few. The young Germans we met at hostels were superbly sun-tanned – the men like Vikings. And they were vain. They wore hairnets in bed, gargled after every meal with Odol mouth-wash (carried in small phials), greased their rippling muscles with ointment. They had immaculate back-packs with kettles, army-type water bottles and rolled blankets; and they seemed so practical, so self-assured, that they made me feel envious and effete. With such young men at its disposal the German nation, I thought, need fear no one. I didn't know it at the time, but Isherwood and Spender had recently shared a holiday in Rügen. Their diaries and letters show how attracted they were to the young Germans' cult of sex and nudism in the sun, of the bronzed athlete and sun-drugged paganism. Their love–hate relationship for the Germans was to last for many years; and Spender still broods about it.

Before I left Eggersdorf I had arranged to spend the last weeks of my vacation in Vienna with the family of Artur Weiss, an Austrian university student. I took the train via Dresden and Prague and found myself in an old-fashioned flat in Clusiusgasse in 9 Bezirk. The Weiss family, I discovered, was Jewish, but they did not strictly observe the traditional rites. Herr Weiss was a failed businessman. He spent most of his time in a chair near the balcony window listening to the street cries of hawkers and sellers of bread rolls, milk and fish. Frau Weiss, dark and smiling, was born in Budapest. Her *Mehlspeisen* (pastries and pancakes) were delicious, and she fussed over me ('You have a cough'). Molli the daughter was at a secretarial college. Artur, for a Jew, was idle and easy-going. He had two passions – the opera and swimming – but barely enough money to accompany me to football matches or to the Dianabad with its artificial waves. At the opera we queued for cheap standing places in the gallery. On Sundays Artur put on his plus-fours and we joined in the *Corso* – a ritual parade of citizens who strolled up and down the Ring greeting friends and flirting.

Unemployment was a dismal problem in Vienna. Over one-third of the workforce was without jobs and it was a common sight to see scores of men playing cards on the banks of the Danube to fill in the idle days. Austrian politics were brittle and confusing, with tension and hopelessness feeding on the depression and fermenting under the surface. Dolfuss, the diminutive 'pocket Chancellor', was a brave, stubborn little man with a distinguished war record as an officer on the Caporetto front. Conservative elements praised him as a good Catholic and anti-Socialist. His main supporters were Count von Starhemberg's strongly Catholic Heimwehr force – its banner was a crutched cross – and Major Fey, its leader in Vienna. But he was detested by the Social Democrats and by 'Red' Vienna's working class. Finally, there was growing pressure from young Nazis, particularly round Innsbruck in the Austrian Tirol, for the return of the South Tirol from Italy.

I found the medley of nationalities in Vienna fascinating. The capital had a strong flavour of the Balkans and the Slav world, and of Jewry. Hungarians kept restaurants. Romanian gypsies provided music. Czechs and Poles were often cobblers and tailors with basement workshops. Conspicuous were the Orthodox Jews with their ringlets, beards, kaftans and high Russian boots, and their fur or round flat caps. They stood in groups at street corners and in market places, spoke Yiddish, gesticulated, and turned away when they sensed I was watching them. They reminded me of moth-eaten eastern patriarchs, as though the Old Testament had tipped them out into the Ringstrasse. Some of the younger Jews had the pallor of people who live in cellars or airless garrets. 'They live on onions and dried fish,' Artur remarked to me. 'They are mainly Jews from Galicia, not Vienna-born. They breed crooks and geniuses.'

The physical vitality of the young Germans, their enthusiasm for a national cause and their discipline, had impressed me. If this was one side of Fascism, it wasn't entirely bad. The undercurrents – the anti-Semitism, the aggressive songs and behaviour of the Storm Troopers – were sinister. But would they last? At Oxford we had no crusading spirit: patriotic sentiments were considered bad form – even laughable. We knew of course that the Empire was the solid rock on which we stood and that it paid our bills and opened windows to future careers; but we were not crusaders. When I discussed my German experience with Michael Nathan and David Thomson, they mocked my enthusiasm. They said I was a Fascist.

To learn more about the Germans I started in my second year at

Oxford to read Heine and Rilke. I browsed through Spengler's *Decline of the West* and read Fallada and Remarque. Hans Fallada's *Kleiner Mann Was Nun?* had made a stir in Germany. It was a moving, rather mawkish picture of a young German couple struggling against the poverty and injustice of the economic depression. I also read Goethe's *Die Leiden des Jungen Werthers*. Meanwhile I went the round of clubs and societies, attended meetings of the Anglo-German Society and heard a bland address by Harold Nicolson, who seemed something of a snob. That evening, unfortunately, I had downed a sconce (a big tankard) of buttery beer in Hall. Its effects made me noisy and I had to leave the meeting before it was over.

Mr Cutcliffe's English-language classes had by now attracted fresh beauties from Germany and Sweden. They were a distracting influence on undergraduate studies. Blonde and blue-eyed, like porcelain dolls, the Swedish girls remained, alas, cold and controlled. The German ladies, having warmer hearts, would thaw sufficiently to permit an embrace on the tow-path or in the garden of The Trout Inn. I went to German films: Peter Lorre in *M*, based on the notorious Düsseldorf child murders where the killer announces his presence by whistling a haunting tune, and a child's balloon is seen drifting over a yard; *Mädchen in Uniform* – its Lesbianism escaped me at the time; and *All Quiet on the Western Front*, based on Remarque's book. I saw this famous anti-war film, which carried the same message as Robert Sheriff's *Journey's End*, with a German chemist from I G Farben who was visiting the Dunlop tyre factory in Birmingham (perhaps he was an industrial spy). Reinhart found the film offensive. 'Its defeatist message', he said, 'no longer fits in with the new German mentality. War has its heroes as well as its sheep and cannon fodder. Our small German army', he went on, 'is a model for all. Its standards are so high that if a recruit has had just one dental stopping he will be rejected.' This was a grim thought: all those perfect teeth grinning under coal-scuttle helmets.

During the Christmas vacation I spent a few days walking up the Rhine, starting at Köln. The wintry landscape was rimmed with snow, the fields dark and dead, the Rhine grey, the highways busy with industrial traffic. I felt foolish ambling along a metalled road wearing a raincoat, and by the time I reached Koblenz I knew I was not going to enjoy myself. Bonn, however, brought me an adventure. I met Magdalene in a wine bar. She was on a shopping visit from Remagen. She was fair, with a large firm body, and wore a hat with a veil. After hours of footslogging I was in rude health. With a pounding heart (no proctors, thank God) I signed a hotel register as 'Mr and Mrs MacDonald'. When I had undressed she sprinkled me with eau-de-Cologne – perhaps I was sweaty after my stint on the road – and called me 'Mein kleiner Löwe'.

In the night we clung to each other like two animals seeking warmth, and next day she gave me a handkerchief and a rosy apple. I feel now that I was lucky. Some people's sexual initiation can be a disaster: an act of seduction by a woman old enough to be your aunt, or a squalid encounter with a drab. As I ate the rosy apple I felt not guilt but elation.

During this second year at Oxford I realised that I would never shine at economic theory or the moral philosophy of T.H. Green or Bradley. Hume and Hegel required much abstract and logical thinking; and I had no head for economic statistics. Kant's *Critique of Pure Reason* as expounded by Mr Cox, the Dean, between puffs at his pipe, remained a conundrum. Professor Zimmern's painstaking examination of the legal complexities of the Geneva Convention taught me nothing that I wanted to remember. I didn't take to G.D.H. Cole, who wrote for the Left Book Club, wore a red tie, and believed in a planned Socialist economy. So I neglected the set books and, when I was not playing cricket, went punting on the Cherwell – how glorious it was to jump into the cool black water or to glide between hanging willows at the end of a long wooden pole. I sometimes visited Parsons' Pleasure. On this damp grassy bank naked scholars paced up and down like ageing shepherds in a stage pastoral. Regular visitors included a clergyman with a cherubic face and round pink belly who read aloud from a book of sermons. One day the University heavyweight boxing champion, Clouston, emerged naked and muscular from the changing room, causing a flutter among the recumbent nudes. He had a Chinese dragon, like a totem, tattooed on his chest (he was probably the only undergraduate in Oxford to boast a tattoo) and came from a rustic parsonage near Bletchley where ennui was driving him mad. I read later in a newspaper report that when Clouston went down he joined Mosley's party and was arrested by the police for causing an affray. Another regular visitor had the improbable name of Jasper Stembridge. He introduced himself to me as the senior geography master at Denstone and author of a series of textbooks. I felt uneasy as he lay naked on the grass beside me, for he made some flattering remarks about my shape and invited me to stay a weekend with him. I declined.

Major Yeats-Brown, late of the Bengal Lancers, arrived on the Oxford scene in the summer, looking for recruits to support Mussolini's Corporate State. He was extremely glamorous. He had led an adventurous life and written an attractive book (*Bengal Lancer*) about his escapades. Mussolini and Fascism, however, were associated in Oxford minds with castor-oil and flogging, and few undergraduates took the major seriously. Once I went to the October Club to hear H.G. Wells. He was a tubby, red-faced man with a disappointingly thin, reedy voice that was difficult to hear. He was in full flow when there was a crash and banging at the door and a party of Fascist Club undergraduates (led perhaps by Clouston) burst in and interrupted the meeting.

For the idle who had given up going to lectures there was Elliston's for morning coffee – Michael Nathan would buy a packet of Balkan Sobranie and we would go there together. In the evening, if Sabouroff offered to pay, there was The George. Pubs were out of bounds, and the proctor and his two bowler-hatted 'bulldogs' would prowl the lamp-lit streets ensuring that the disciplinary regulations were enforced. This meant, for instance, that out of doors we had to wear (or carry) our gowns, refrain from holding a girl by the arm, resist the impulse to climb the Martyrs' Memorial, and not get caught in the Clarendon bar – if spotted and challenged by the bulldog ('Are you a member of the University, sir?') there would be a fine to pay in the morning.

One of Oxford's most frustrating though no doubt necessary regulations was that as soon as Big Tom had sounded the last stroke of midnight the colleges locked their gates. If you were not back by then the only recourse was to climb in over a wall. This required agility and nerve – two qualities I had in excess. Several times, coming back late from a party or dinner, I had to shin up the old stone wall that backs on to Fornication Lane – the dark little alley which separates Lincoln from Exeter and smells of cooking and stale kitchen air. Alas, I grew overbold, and towards the end of the Hilary term, aflame with Michael's grog, I didn't properly secure the rope I was using to lower myself from the Bursar's window, and fell like a sack into the Turl. I lay dazed for a few moments. Then I heard running boots and saw a soldier. He bent over to look at me and began to hammer at the gate to rouse Chambers the porter. Sober now, I ran to The Mitre to bathe my lacerated face, leaving the 'props' – the Bursar's stick and Gladstone bag, part of my act in the role of College beadle – behind on the pavement. When all was quiet I climbed back from Fornication Lane to my rooms and in the morning my new scout, Arthur, got a raw steak from the kitchen to put over my bruised face. To no avail. Someone had identified me and I was rusticated for the final days of the term.

The incident, though trivial, should have rung a warning bell. My rebellious instincts were getting out of hand. In the summer term I injured my bowling arm – a bad case of tennis elbow – and after playing my last game for the college, in which I took eight wickets against Thame, I had to face the rest of the summer with a stiff and painful arm. To get over my disappointment I borrowed a bicycle, and though I could use only one arm, set off on another journey through Germany.

It was July 1934. I bought a ticket for Hamburg and wheeled my bicycle on to a Russian cargo ship at East Surrey docks. I had a rucksack and a few clothes strapped to the carrier and hoped to get as far as the Swiss border via Hanover and Frankfurt. Most of my fellow passengers were left-wing 'cultural' tourists going to Leningrad and Moscow, part of a regular pilgrimage which the British intelligentsia was making at this time to Russia. They thought it odd of me – almost shameful – to be visiting Nazi Germany. Was I a Mosleyite? I noticed that they didn't care much for the Russian food served by stout stewardesses in white aprons with enormous hips: the sour cucumber soup and pickled herrings, the pancakes and coarse bread, the glasses of weak lemon tea. An Oxford friend had given me an introduction to Rita, a Jewish girl in Hamburg, and she put me up in her flat for a few days. Rita was worried. Anti-Semitism was growing rapidly. Jews were being discriminated against, dismissed from their posts, ostracised, and sometimes insulted in the street. I was able to confirm this, for when I took Rita to the cinema a group of young Germans recognised her as a '*Jüdin*' and jeered at her.

In those days the country towns of Germany were small jewels of architecture unravaged by war. The narrow cobbled streets of Lüneburg, Soltau and Celle winding between high-gabled timber-framed houses, the squares with weathered statues and a fountain facing a church and a brightly painted *Rathaus*, had an air of peace, continuity and thrift. Hanover then was a stylish old town where, it boasted, the best *Hochdeutsch* was spoken. It was proud of its coat-of-arms, a Hanoverian white horse, and of its associations with the British Royal family and the British Army, in which Hanoverian foot soldiers had served. Since then, wartime destruction has changed its face for ever. The great gaps torn by Allied bombs in its ancient façades have been rebuilt, as in nearby Brunswick, in utilitarian steel, concrete and glass cubes, with garish lighting and signs.

From the flat north German plain I turned south-east from Hanover into the wooded hills of Thuringia. One evening after dark, as I was pushing my bicycle up a hill, bells began to peal down in the valley and lights appeared like glow-worms among the trees. The bells tolled with a slow rhythm; along the paths came people holding oil lanterns. 'Hindenburg is dead', they told me. 'We are going to the *Pfarrer* (priest) to pray for him.' Field Marshal Hindenburg was a hero to the Germans. His victory at Tannenberg had crushed the Tsar's invading Russian army in 1914.

On the morning of Hitler's funeral oration I took a seat in a beer garden in Nordheim. It was crowded with families. When everyone had eaten, the waiters cleared away the plates, the bar was closed, and the hoarse and penetrating voice of the Führer burst through a loudspeaker. In his panegyric Hitler identified himself with Hindenburg. Like Hindenburg, he said, the Nazis stood firm in defence of Germany against the enemy in the east – Russian Bolshevism. As propagandist oratory the speech was effective. But it was a piece of casuistry. For years Hindenburg had detested the Austrian corporal and the unsoldierly rabble he had built up from the scourings of Bavarian pot-houses. It was only at the end of his life that he had been persuaded to accept Hitler as Germany's new leader. Most of the listeners in the beer garden must have known this. Now it was too late to argue. Hitler had usurped Hindenburg's halo for himself.

The small towns of Thuringia thrusting up their spires among wooded hills had a fairy-tale setting. The timbered façades, the high-pitched gables and steep roofs decorated with scrolls and figurines and mottoes, belonged to the magic world of Hans Andersen and Grimm. The bakeries smelt of fresh rolls and great *Vollkorn* loaves like dark puddings. The butchers sold sausages thick as truncheons. The inns shone with polished wood. Painted clocks with moving figures struck the hour from towers. Even the swastika flags and bunting that hung everywhere had a sort of pride and gaiety – as long as you could forget their association with the tramp of marching men. It was the *Romantik* of the German landscape that enchanted me. Eichendorff in his lyrics had written about it:

> Es rauschen die Wipfel und schauern . . .
> Es redet trunken die Ferne
> Wie von künftigem, grossem Gluck!

> The hilltops rustle and tremble . . .
> And far-away voices sing drunkenly of happiness.

Like Eichendorff I had fallen in love with the fields of ripening corn, the great farm horses, the smell of hay and midden heaps, the farmer and his wife bending over a furrow, the tow-haired children with their school satchels and flying pigtails, the woods where I got off my bicycle and fell asleep on pine needles. Though I was always hungry I couldn't afford to eat much. A lump of *Speck* (bacon fat) smeared with paprika, strong cheap cheese (*Mainzer Stinkkäse*), rye bread, cranberry jam and buttermilk saw me through till evening when I ate *Bockwurst* or *Eisbein* in an inn and talked to the guests. Every inn had its *Stammtisch* – a special table reserved for the favoured few – and a copy of Julius Streicher's *Der Stürmer* hanging on a hook. The *Stürmer* was a scurrilous rag, a sort of vicious schoolboy's joke. Its gross cartoons of Jews showed them as hideous Oriental bagmen or tycoons with bottle-noses cuddling blonde

Aryan maidens. A copy of it also hung in a locked glass case in every village square.

At Eisenach, under the Wartburg, I sat on a wall near the Bach statue and watched a rally of schoolchildren in the square. The girls wore white blouses, gym skirts and socks. Their fair hair was braided into pigtails or pinned into buns. The boys, tensing their half-developed muscles, were in shorts. A brass band was playing marches. Swastika flags hung from poles and balconies, and every shop and kiosk had a picture of the Führer in uniform. It was a scene I was getting used to, yet it gave me a growing feeling of unease: for there was something unnatural about the innocence and solemnity of the schoolchildren. They were being hypnotised and I thought of Ernst Mark's warning, 'The Nazis are preparing for war'. The overweight musicians in brown shirts playing the Badenweiler March, the paper flags with hooked crosses waved by small children, the speaker with his talk of *Blut und Boden* (Blood and Soil), weren't part of a pageant; they were a threat.

From the Harz I followed the river Main to its junction with the Rhine, near Frankfurt, where I stayed in a cheap boarding-house in the Judengasse. This was a mistake. The Judengasse was in a rundown part of what used to be the old Jewish ghetto and I was tormented in the night by bedbugs. It was the first time I had met these small, silent brown creatures that hide in the plaster and woodwork of doss-houses and swell horribly as they feed on your blood. In Frankfurt I came across, for the first time, the squalid side of Germany – shabby working-class districts with stained walls and threadbare washing draped over little balconies; children with runny noses and makeshift toys; morose, short-tempered men who had no jobs; the smell of overcooked cabbage and shared latrines. There were Jews in the streets, but no one in kaftans and Russian boots.

From Tübingen, Hegel's old university, an ideal place, I imagined, for study and wine drinking in its setting of woods and vineyards, I turned to Freudenstadt in the Black Forest, hoping there, in my mood of romantic elation, to surprise a wood nymph eager to be embraced or a woodcutter eating stewed rabbit in a marzipan cottage.

On the road I fell in with other wayfarers, among them roving carpenters (*Hamburger Zimmerleute*) who wore flared black corduroys, black jackets and wide-brimmed hats and went from village to village doing odd jobs as part of their apprentice training. They carried their tools in shoulder bags and had large, bony hands. There were bands of *Wandervögel*, too. They were not drop-outs but earnest young people who sat round camp fires and sang folk songs to the accompaniment of a guitar or a small accordion. Roaming for them was an adventure, a chance to learn about their own homeland and *Volk*, to sing its songs and to sleep rough under the stars. They had scarcely any money and lived on hard sausage, bread, fruit and buttermilk. Hitler, they told me, had given the Germans new hope for the future. Soon there would be jobs (*Arbeit und Brot*) for everyone, in construction projects and public works, road building and land reclamation – and military service too. One of them, a student, pointed to the vale below us in which there was a white church, a group of barns and some striped cattle standing knee-deep in a brook, and said to me; 'This is my *Heimat*. For this I would fight to the death – but for nothing else, not for a woman or a priest, let alone a politician.' Then he added, 'Perhaps you don't have such crazy thoughts. As an Englishman you have phlegm. And you have your colonies.'

From Freudenstadt I turned back along the Rhine valley through Kehl, Speyer and Bingen to Cologne. Kehl stands on the German bank of the Rhine and faces Strasbourg on the French side. Walking across the Rhine bridge from Kehl to Strasbourg I found myself heading for a French machine-gun trained on the approaches. This gave me an odd sensation, as though I were a fugitive or a criminal coming to an enemy country; and I had indeed a feeling of guilt, for I had concealed my small hoard of German money in my sock as it was forbidden to take marks out of Germany.

Then, not far from Speyer, after dark, I lost my bearings in dense woodland and was about to settle down for the night in a hollow under a pine when a man emerged from the trees with a creaking bicycle and a tiny lamp. He insisted on taking me to his home. Kurt was a pay clerk in a bone-meal factory. It had an abominable smell and was brand-new, as were his job, his young Swabian wife, and his little house with its vegetable patch. 'For all this,' he told me as he sent his wife out to buy two cigars, 'I have to thank the Führer.' But I could see he had a struggle to live. I counted the articles in his uncarpeted living room – there were eight in all: two chairs, a table, a divan, a clock, a wedding photograph, an iron stove and a radio. The radio was one of the standard sets which a newly-married German couple was entitled to buy for a few marks. It ensured that, day in, day out, they would hear nothing but the government voice. Kurt and his wife also showed me their copy of Hitler's *Mein Kampf*. The book was presented free to all newly-weds though, as I learned later, Hitler earned huge royalties from it since the municipalities had to pay for each copy.

My last memories of Germany were of marching children, Brown Shirts, beer gardens with bands, and terraced vineyards. Even the Lorelei had a Nazi banner on it. My money was almost finished and for the last few days, as I headed back for the Dover ferry, I lived on a large

Westphalian rye loaf and apples which I took from wayside trees and orchards. After Germany, Belgium seemed a dull country. Rolling over to sleep among the cabbage plants, in a sea of green vegetables pricked by spires, I felt I had left Eichendorff behind.

My first essay in travelling rough had taught me two things about myself: I didn't mind discomfort; and I relished the unexpected – both traits, I may add, that have stayed with me for life. The spell cast by the German *Romantik* was also powerful medicine. I had submitted myself to a strong cultural shock and to the voice of a propaganda machine whose message – a revived Germany – was being accepted with earnest enthusiasm by young German people. In an article I wrote for the college magazine I rather rashly over-stated my new enthusiasm, and quoted this passage from a French writer: 'Sac au dos, jeunes gens et jeunes filles, se mirent à parcourir les montagnes et les plaines germaniques, dressant leur tents au hasard des paysages et des rencontres. Ce mouvement prétend libérer la jeunesse de l'atmosphère étouffante de l'époque au moyen d'un retour à la nature.'

David Lewis replied to my article. He made fun of my 'Nietzschean philosophy of the blond beast'. The true aim of politics, he said, 'was to get rid of the brutal maintenance of a decaying Fascist–capitalist order and to establish a classless society.' Michael Wharton must have remembered this. In his memoir *The Missing Will* he mentions that I was 'at first attracted by the Nazi movement, though not', he adds mildly, 'for long'.

At the beginning of my third year I gave up my rooms in college and moved into digs on Headington Hill. This was to prove a serious mistake; but I reasoned that if I saw less of my friends I would have more time to read for my finals. I also asked the Dean for permission to spend a term at Heidelberg. I told him that I was thinking of taking up journalism as a career and that 'National Socialism was the most significant event in current European politics'. My request shocked Mr Cox. His eyes blinked and he took his pipe out of his mouth while he considered my brashness. 'Mr Hills,' he said disapprovingly, 'one does not come to Oxford to prepare oneself for a career. It is enough that one is at Oxford.'

'Old fossil', I thought as I descended the creaking wooden staircase. But at long last I was allotted a tutor to take me in politics. Miss Headlam-Morley was a distinguished historian and gave me a reading list of books on the Treaty of Versailles that dealt with the principles of self-determination on which the peace terms were based, and with the new territorial and minority problems they created. Miss Headlam-

Morley was severe and ladylike. She wore a long tweed skirt and stood with her back to the blazing coal fire warming her haunches like an alderman while I read out my weekly essay. After a few weeks I realised that I would never elicit much light or response from her.

At the end of the term I decided to spend three weeks in Saarbrücken where a plebiscite was due, under international control, to decide the future of the Saarland. Just before I left I played for my club the Old Edwardians against Moseley at the Reddings in the annual Boxing Day fixture. This was a match the Old Edwardians dearly liked to win and I mention it because it has left a happy memory. It was a windless, frosty day, the ground was firm, and in the first half I managed to cut right through the Moseley defence, draw the full back, and pass to Chips Elgood on the wing, who had a clear run and scored in the corner. We won the match; and the sensation of muscular power that surged through me as I outpaced the Moseley players is still fresh in my mind. I think it is excusable to remember such small, satisfying moments. They are a comfort, in view of all that is to come – the deterioration of the body, the stiffening joints and the humiliation of no longer being nimble enough to chase after a bus.

Under the Versailles Treaty the rich coal basin of the Saar was given to the French to exploit for fifteen years under League of Nations administration. The territory was to decide its future by plebiscite on 13 January 1935. Nazi organisations had already been active in the Saar and Hitler was demanding its reunion with Germany. To keep the peace an international force of over 3,000 men, including a British contingent, was sent to supervise the plebiscite arrangements.

I arrived in Saarbrücken just after the New Year and booked in at a hotel. There was an English sergeant in the bar in highly polished ammunition boots. He was slightly drunk and trying to get off with the barmaid. I watched his technique in amazement. He kept his eyes glued on the barmaid's legs and whenever she bent down he made a crowing noise like a cock. The sergeant told me he came from Leicester, and I lent him a pound. When I called at the barracks next day to retrieve my money he was not to be found. The presence of an international peacekeeping force gave a certain glamour to the plebiscite, and it was good to see British Army trucks bowling along the alien streets. The Italian soldiers wore the biggest helmets. Throughout the week before the poll the bars were crowded. True to their reputation for efficiency, the Germans had commissioned special trains to bring back from Germany over 50,000 former Saar residents to register their votes. Everyone I spoke to was confident that the Germans would win a famous victory. 'It will be a smack in the face for the French,' they said, 'even though they will still hold Alsace-Lorraine.'

I met Simon, a young American, in a bar and invited him to sleep on the floor in my room. He was wearing a Russian fur cap and padded coat and had spent some months in Russia studying the collective farm system. He was an ardent Communist and introduced me to the local Communist party cell. The members were sitting in a smoky room drinking beer and cognac and were delighted to see an Englishman. Polling day passed off without disturbance. The result was a triumph for the pro-German party. There was a 90 per cent turn-out of voters, and a phenomenal 98 per cent voted for the return of the Saar territory to Hitler's Germany.

When the result was announced everyone poured into the streets and I found myself wedged in a dense scrum gathered outside the *Rathaus* to cheer von Papen, Hitler's representative: flushed, triumphant faces, arms outstretched in the Nazi salute, deafening choruses of 'Sieg! Heil! Sieg! Heil!' It was my first experience of crowd hysteria, of harmless citizens transformed within moments into a mob of excited and aggressive animals: thick arms scything the air, hoarse cries and shining eyes. It was frightening and ominous. Some of the people there may have been remembering that, not long since, the French had been occupying the German Rhineland with black Senegalese troops 'in order to deprave the German women'.

The Communist party was banned immediately after the result of the poll. I went with Simon to a hall where its members were holding their last meeting. Their leader gave a short farewell address; and Simon and I joined about twenty Communists on a last defiant march through the streets – though in my case it was more out of curiosity than defiance. Snow had been falling and there were not many people about. Soon we heard a siren. An open police bus (no doors) drove up at speed and a police squad jumped out wielding truncheons. We all scattered. As a rugger man I had no difficulty in nipping up a wall, where I perched watching the affray. The raised arms and men stumbling in the snow were like a film scene. When the street cleared I began walking home (Simon had vanished) and ran into Sefton Delmer of the *Daily Express* who had arrived too late to see the incident, but wanted to file a story for his paper. Delmer took me to his hotel room. He introduced me to a half-dressed girl and gave me champagne in a tooth mug. Delmer had been up at Lincoln as a student so we toasted the college. I realised later that I must have taken part in the last Communist march on German soil.

Before I left for Oxford Simon and I took two German girls to a restaurant. Walking home through an empty park we stopped to look at the lights of the town. They were shining through a forest of swastika flags; and one of the girls said, '*Die gemütlichen Zeiten sind vorbei* – the comfortable days are over, and we shall all be singing soldiers' songs again.'

I returned to Oxford three days late for the beginning of the term and was scolded by the Dean, who showed not a flicker of interest in my excursion to the Saar. Soon after this my troubles began. I had too many friends and went to too many parties, and I found it increasingly difficult to get back to my digs on Headington Hill before the clocks struck midnight. By bicycle it was a long haul from Carfax, pedalling up the steep gradient in wind and rain. After two or three late arrivals my disapproving landlady looked at me with an expression like an angry chow. Her previous lodger, Michael Foot, she said, had been 'such a quiet and well-behaved gentleman'. After another and rather drunken arrival – I vomited into my chamber-pot in the night – she and her husband reported me to the college. I was summoned to the Rector and in a few brief words he sent me down (his icy calm repelled me and I was too proud to say anything in my own defence). The Rector not only cast me out; I was stripped of my scholarship too.

But the pill wasn't entirely bitter. I was given permission to continue working for my exams at home and to return to Oxford to sit for my finals in June. A tutor would read my essays, which I was to send by post. The ghosts of Descartes and Kant, Hegel and Cassel, with Rousseau in a fur bonnet at their head, now mocked me as I laid out my books in my parents' house. No more rugger (a pity, as I was captain of the college team), no cricket, no amusing friends, no blonde Swedish girls, and what was worse, the disappointment and dismay of my parents. When my father went to see the Rector after he had decided to send me down, he told him, 'Your son behaves like a Communist'. The Bursar's secretary, when I went to pay my battels, was kinder: 'It's your handsome face that got you into this mess.'

Chapter 3

Hitler's Greater Reich

I n August 1935, with Schools behind me, I was free to set off on a
journey to satisfy my curiosity about the German minorities (*Auslands-
deutsche*) who were living in the border territories that surrounded
Hitler's Reich. I had a rucksack, blanket and raincoat and expected to
be away for three months. Mr Record, editor of the *Birmingham Post*,
promised to pay me three guineas for every 1,500-word article I could
put together on my experiences. I intended to start with the German-
speaking Austrians of the South Tirol, which the Allies had handed over
to Italy at Versailles, then go on to visit the Germans of Czechoslo-
vakia, Memel (Lithuania), Danzig and West Poland. The future of
these *irredenta* seemed vital to any prospects of peace. Their aspirations
were attracting increasing world attention as Hitler rammed home
his demands for the territorial revision of the Versailles *Diktat* and the
reincorporation of the 'lost' lands into the bosom of Greater Germany.

At Innsbruck I stayed with a young Austrian, Vieider, whom I had
first met in a pub in Birmingham. He was newly married, and had
turned his flat into a boudoir under pink lights. Vieider was an ardent
Nazi. 'As a Tiroler,' he said, 'I have sworn to help Austria recover the
South Tirol from Italy.' He told me that many of the local youths were
Nazis and that the movement was especially strong among sportsmen
and mountaineering and skiing clubs. 'White stockings worn under
Lederhosen (leather shorts) are often the sign of a Nazi.'

The first stage of my journey was to walk over the Brenner pass from
Innsbruck and descend to Brixen (Bressanone) on the Italian side. It
rained hard. Wet and miserable, I wondered how many days, let alone
weeks, my shoes would last. A few weeks earlier an American had

preceded me on an elephant, riding in the footsteps of Hannibal – the elephant, however, had soon given up, with blistered feet. I noticed much military activity on the Italian side of the pass. Gun emplacements, hidden by wattle screens, were being blasted into the steep rock faces and every village was a billet for small wiry soldiers with feathers in their hats and blue puttees. On the third day during a hail-storm I was beckoned by some road workers to take shelter in their shed. As I took off my rucksack a dozen morose faces puffing at soggy cigarettes stared back out of the gloom. One man was using a sliver of broken mirror no bigger than a thumb to shave with. They were Austrians. What was the cost of bread and tobacco in England? they asked. Did bachelors have to pay a special tax, as under Mussolini? They complained bitterly about Il Duce's preparations for war against Abyssinia. 'We shall be conscripted to fight negroes. They castrate prisoners.' (' – And boil their bones for soup,' I added). Meanwhile, the foreman told me, the Fascist government had been flooding the Austro-Italian frontier with soldiers. 'They're said to be on manoeuvres. The truth is that Mussolini doesn't trust Hitler. He's afraid of what Hitler might get up to if the frontier is left unguarded while our army is away in Africa.' A stream of deserters, he said, was already making its way over the mountains into Austria to avoid being called up for Abyssinia. Later, in a tavern, I learned from two young men that an Austrian Legion camp had been set up in Württemberg where deserters were being accepted and trained as soldiers under their own flag. (The camp was in Urach and I was to visit it a year later.)

As I descended the valley to Brixen I was struck by the thoroughgoing policy of Italianisation. Every *Gasthaus* had become an *albergo* and the landlord's Christian names rendered into Italian, likewise all shop and public signs. The Italian officials who ran the railway and post offices insisted on speaking only Italian even when Tirolese peasants were unable to make themselves understood except in German. I attended a service in a mountain church which was held in Italian though the worshippers were local villagers.

My impressions, and I was still very impressionable, strongly inclined me to sympathise with the Tirolese. Their traditional costumes and Sunday finery were a replica of those worn by their kinsmen over the border. They spoke the same dialect, and in Andreas Hofer, hero of Tirol's war of liberation against Napoleon, they shared the same national martyr. As an Englishman I was in any case prejudiced against the Italians. Italian submarines had been provoking the British navy, the Fascist Italian state was challenging us as a colonial rival in Africa, and Mussolini was defying British diplomacy and the threat of economic sanctions in his pursuit of glory against The Lion of Judah ('bombs bursting like roses', as his

airman son was to boast). In those days the British press caricatured
Mussolini as a bull-frog with a loud mouth. Encouraged by the cartoon-
ist Low with his caustic drawings of Hitler and Mussolini, the British
public felt that by compelling a nation of 'macaroni eaters' to march
the goose-step, the barrel-shaped Italian leader was making an ass of
himself.

From Brixen I took a *Bummelzug* (slow local train) to Lienz in the
Salzburg province. The train plodded slowly through mountain valleys,
puffing past steep fields strewn with haycocks and wide-eaved chalets,
and crossing racing brooks. I sat with peasants in a big wooden compartment like a guard's van. What hands the men had – great bony hands
with thick scarred fingers in which they gripped curved pipes with
a metal lid hinged over the bowl. The men wore *Loden* jackets with
embroidered facings and big horn buttons. They had trailing moustaches
and a pungent smell. The older women had faces like dried walnuts and
wore two or three petticoats. They gave me lumps of sausage, and I
liked them. They were, I thought, true peasants. From their small plots
and Alpine meadows they provided bread, milk, cheese and meat, wine
and sour *Most* (cider), and they filled festival nights with yodelling songs
and the mad music of fiddle and clarinet. I would have liked to learn
more about them and to dance with the girls in a barn among the drying
corn cobs and the midden heaps.

I spent a day or two in Lienz and remember only the mountain
mist and an exhibition of paintings by the Austrian artist Egger-Lienz
whose work had found favour with the Nazis as a healthy and simplistic
representation of noble rustic virtues. The paintings were of heavily-
muscled farmers scattering seed over the fields or steering a plough,
and of flaxen-haired women clasping babies and sheaves of corn against
their breasts. These bucolic stalwarts were said to please Hitler. But
they weren't real peasants. They were kitsch. The real people had
been my companions on the *Bummelzug* with their twisted hands, their
tobacco-stained teeth and awkward bodies.

From Lienz I travelled to Passau at the confluence of three rivers,
the Danube, Inn and Ilz. I recall only a jumble of sunlit stone walls and
quaint houses and a paprika goulash in a crooked hostel. From Passau
I went on to the old Austrian frontier fortress town of Braunau which
faces the Bavarian outpost of Simbach on the other side of the Inn. Hitler
was born in this small, sleepy place. His father Alois (whose family name
was sometimes spelled Hiedler) had been a customs officer there. Up
to a year before my visit, Braunau had been a place of pilgrimage for
Nazi sympathisers from Germany. But since the murder of the Austrian
Chancellor Dolfuss by Nazi thugs in July 1934 – they let the wounded
man bleed to death – the Austrians had sealed off their frontier with

Germany, the bridge across the Inn joining the two countries was closed to traffic, and visitors to the Gasthaus Josef Pommers where Hitler was born were being turned away. No photographers, no Hitler salutes, were allowed and I could find no picture-postcards of the inn or of the Führer in any of the shops. The inn was a three-storey building in the old Salzburger Vorstadt next to an Austrian army barracks. Although it was closed, I found the innkeeper and a companion sitting at the back in a sunny courtyard bright with flower boxes. Bedding hung from the windows to air and a cow was grumbling in a shed. The innkeeper gave me a mug of sour cider. 'Hitler *Most*,' said his companion, grinning. 'It's special!'

Having decided that I was harmless, the innkeeper told his maid to take me upstairs to see the room where Hitler was born. I was startled to find that it had been decked out as a shrine. The plain wooden bed was dominated by a huge portrait of the Führer in uniform. His army photographs and pictures of the Berlin *Sieg* (Victory) hung on the wall. The table-cloth was knitted in the form of a swastika, and there was a visitors' book. 'Even the walls are painted brown', the maid reminded me with a smile. I noticed that she was wearing a red, white and black beaded necklace, the Nazi colours.

The complexity of Austrian politics struck me afresh when I walked past the Alpine Jäger battalion barracks next door to the inn. At the entrance a recent memorial slab had been placed to 'the martyred hero Dolfuss'. 'It was at this Kaserne', said the inscription, 'that Dolfuss handed in his papers and retired from the army on 4 November 1918. Although he is dead, the spirit of the Chancellor lives on.'

Later I joined a group of Austrians smoking their curved pipes by the river wall as they looked across the Inn to Simbach and the forbidden land of Germany. On the Simbach bank two hundred yards away a single swastika flag was flying from a tall pole. There was no doubt about its message. It was a provocation, a challenge, and an invitation to the Austrians to throw in their lot with National Socialism and share the glories of Greater Germany. As a foreigner I was allowed to walk over the bridge to Simbach. There were groups of Storm Troopers idling in the streets, many swastika flags, a copy of *Der Stürmer* displayed in a frame near the *Rathaus*, and Nazi literature in shops and kiosks. The German press was attacking 'the political Catholicism and Jewish financial interests' which were preventing Austrians from voting for the form of government they would prefer. A plebiscite – one of the Nazis' most successful political devices – would result, it was claimed, in a victory for National Socialism as overwhelming as in the Saar.

In Braunau the Austrian newspapers were equally vehement in attacking the Nazis. They strongly denied German accusations that Austria was 'the servant of the Vatican, the pensioner of Mussolini and the milch-cow of Jewry'. Austria, said one Viennese newspaper, was 'the protectress of cultural and religious toleration, a mission which she could only fulfil in independence of Germany'. To me, an outsider, it seemed irrational that the two neighbouring communities should be kept apart by an absurd little bridge. They both lived in the same rustic backwater. They shared a common landscape and a common rural life. They spoke the same dialect. But the relationship had an ominous imbalance. Germany possessed the power and the magnetism. Austria had little but charm.

I stayed for three days, swimming and sunbathing on a small pebbly beach cooled by the Inn. Some young Austrians befriended me. They had no jobs and felt that Austria would not prosper until it threw in its lot with Greater Germany. Several of their acquaintances had slipped over the border into Germany as recruits for the Austrian Legion. From the river I could see the tall spire of the *Pfarrkirche* (parish church) keeping its peaceful watch. The cobbled lanes smelt of hay, sour wine and pastry shops. Bedding hung from white-framed windows. The mad corporal who had been born among these country smells in Josef Pommer's tavern had not yet shown his hand.

From Simbach I took a slow train through the red-tiled villages of Oberbayern to Nürnberg. The old walled city with its Gothic stone carvings and turrets was bursting with a huge influx of Nazi officials, delegates, Storm Troopers, Labour Corps and Hitler Youth who had come to celebrate the annual Nazi Party Rally (*Parteitag*). The crowds were in holiday mood, boisterous and festive as though at an *Oktoberfest*. There were enormous queues for lodgings, for beer and sausage, for roast chicken and souvenirs. The week-long rally was held in the Zeppelin stadium, followed by torchlight processions through the streets. The opening display was a parade of 54,000 Labour Corps youths shouldering burnished spades. Stripped to the waist, sunburnt and corded with muscle, they goose-stepped past Hitler, who took the salute standing in his car. The drill was perfect, their bodies toughened by months of Spartan diet, road- and bridge-building, harvesting and reclaiming land. The cheering and march music was continuous, one military band relieving another every few minutes. For those who admired disciplined youth the spectacle must have been impressive as well as worrying. What was this ballet of muscular young robots leading to?

I had been lucky to find a room in a tiny house in the Altstadt where everything was old and crooked – the beams, the floors, the window frames. The toilet was a scrubbed wooden box placed over a cess-pit. The owner, a butcher, had a buxom Bavarian wife with massive arms and bust. On the third day I was reading in my room when she came in with a dust-pan and without warning seized me in an iron grip. 'We are alone,' she panted, squeezing me against her great bosom. 'Let us make love.' I was at a loss. She was too large. It was the wrong time of the day. Her husband might burst in with a cleaver. It was humiliating to be hugged to death, and I had to use all my strength to break away from her. She withdrew grumbling into the kitchen. When I saw her again her husband was back. She was rolling pastry, and gave me a demure smile.

In the Zeppelin stadium another impressive performance was given by picked army units who put on a display of weapon handling (using artillery, mortars and troop carriers). The exercises were carried out at great speed and with perfect co-ordination. But on a yet more memorable occasion Hitler reviewed his Storm Troopers – the *Sturmabteilungen*. Thousands of brown-uniformed men had been assembling in the stadium since the early morning. Many of them were middle-aged, they were not in the best condition, and it was a hot day. As they stood in ranks waiting for Hitler, discipline was relaxed and they opened their knapsacks and began to eat and drink. The parade had turned into a picnic. Then just before Hitler arrived the loudspeakers announced '*Achtung!*', and instantly the brown host of munching men was transformed into a sea of bottoms as everyone bent down to pick up his rubbish. Hitler mounted the tribunal to the sound of his favourite Badenweiler March. I could see Goering glittering with decorations like a fat prince; Hess rigidly erect, eyes staring from under thick eyebrows; Goebbels, small and slightly limping. Hitler started his speech quietly. Then he began to roar and threaten, and when, like a common ranter, he attacked Bolshevism, Jewish traitors and western diplomats, I sensed waves of exultation sweeping through the 100,000 people who packed the stadium. Their mood had turned belligerent. I felt that I was being personally browbeaten, that I was among enemies.

When it was over a mighty cheer filled the stadium and everyone stood up to give the Nazi salute. I was in a quandary. Should I raise my right arm like everyone else? No, that was asking too much. A man standing behind me tried to force my arm up. I pushed him away. Another man with a shaven head called me a '*Schwein!*' Then the crowd broke up and I followed a group of people to catch a closer look at the Führer. He was standing on a balcony, and as I studied his face I saw a fleshy nose that seemed slightly crooked, repaired teeth under a dandy's moustache, and a pasty complexion. Hitler was said to have 'magnetic eyes'; but his face was plebeian, and the top-boots and uniform did not disguise an unathletic body that was podgy round the hips. What won people over to him, I think, was his rude and powerful voice, the defiant message and its brutal phrasing, and the contrived settings in which he mounted the stage: the glaring lights and torches, the flags and bands and the calculated cynicism with which little girls with pigtails were made to present him with posies. Before I left, I got into another scuffle when a man with a thick neck called me a '*Scheisser*' for not giving the Hitler greeting. I had to fend him off. Perhaps I was being discourteous to my hosts. But I couldn't identify myself with this fairground mob. And I couldn't salute a bully.

The rally marked a significant step in the growth of Nazi anti-Semitism. The cheering and oratory culminated in the announcement of the notorious Nürnberg anti-Jewish laws (15 September 1935) which stripped Jews of their civil rights and condemned them to a ghetto existence. Every day Nürnberg was swamped with anti-Jewish and anti-Red literature. The Ludendorff press had printed thousands of scurrilous pamphlets including the 'Song of Levi'. The front page of *Der Stürmer* – Julius Streicher's *Käseblatt* or cheese-rag, as some called it – showed a skull grinning behind the face of a Jewish 'murderer and race defamer'. Notices outside Jewish shops warned customers to keep away and gangs were waiting to insult anyone who tried to enter. I looked for Jewish faces in the streets, but saw none.

Next to specimens of 'Aryan Art', a bizarre exhibition of 'Degenerate Jewish Art' was being displayed in a gallery, with a proclamation signed by the Bürgermeister: 'Here you may compare Jewish with German art and see for yourself what corruption entered German morals before Hitler's purge.' The 'Jewish' pictures, assembled from various collections, were indeed a repellent choice. They showed caricatures of the human body that recalled Grosz's most brutal sketches: horribly maimed war cripples, blinded, with metal limbs and claws; a man smoking a cigarette through a hole in his cheek. The 'Aryan' section of the exhibition was given over to portraits of mothers with children, smiling German landscapes and a blond Egger-Lienz peasant scattering seed. The visitors looked duly impressed. From their remarks it was clear that they interpreted these 'degenerate' canvases not as an attempt to reveal the horrors of war but as cynical mockery of the wounded and the brave.

Despite the belligerency of the party propaganda line, people in bars and restaurants went out of their way to be friendly to me, and Storm Troopers treated me to beer. These were ordinary Germans, rather drunk and overbearing, full of good cheer and anxious to fraternise with an Englishman. Wiping the beer froth from his lips a man would put me through the following catechism: 'Was machen Sie hier bei uns? Ach so, Sie sind auf Studienreise. Und was halten Sie vom neuen Deutschland? Sauber und in Ordnung, nicht wahr?' What are you doing here? Ah, a study-tour. What do you make of the new Germany? Clean and well ordered is it not?

I would tell him truthfully that I had met with kindness and hospitality.

'Das stimmt wohl. Wissen Sie, wir Deutschen und Ihr Engländer sind Bruder – blutsverwandt. Schauen Sie, junger Mann, Sie sehen genau wie 'n Deutscher aus (You know, you look just like a German. The Germans and the English are blood brothers). Wenn Sie wieder zuhause sind erzählen Sie allen Ihren Freunden wie schön und wundervoll das neue Deutschland ist. Wir dürfen nie wieder Krieg gegen einander führen. Na nun, Prosit Herr Engländer (When you are back home tell your friends that the Germans and the English must never fight each other again).'

Then someone would recall once more, 'that Christmas Day in the trenches when your Tommies invited our soldiers to play football.'

These were simple men. They meant well. It was festival week. I was still at the learning stage, picking up impressions. The time to evaluate them would come later.

My last memory of the Rally was not of the boozy back-slapping, but of two parades. One evening Storm Troopers from all over the Reich staged a torchlight procession through the town centre. Many of the marchers had beer bellies and some were anxiously dividing their attention between keeping in step and protecting their hands and faces against sparks from their torches. Julius Streicher marched at the head of his company of SA, a bullet-headed man with a brown face, a dark moustache and glittering eyes. He was so short that he could scarcely reach to shake the Führer's hand where the latter stood, on a raised platform. Streicher got a special cheer from the crowd and (he was a schoolmaster) from the children.

The parade of the SS Leibstandarte (Hitler's personal bodyguard) through the Altstadt was in a different class. Every man was at least six feet tall. As they tramped in their black uniforms past the little houses familiar from Dürer's engravings they seemed to be moving slowly, with great strides, but it was not easy to keep up with them. Their wooden faces were half-hidden by black helmets and the sweat was running down their chins. As a piece of military ceremonial these giant Praetorian guards were magnificent. The end product of *kadavergehorsam* (blind or corpse-like obedience), they looked almost inhuman. By the time the Rally was over, I had more than enough material for an article for Mr Record.

From Nürnberg I went east to Eisenstein, at the foot of the Grosser Arbor on the Lower Bavarian–Czechoslovak border, and began to walk

north through the great green folds of the Bohemian forest in the
direction of Pilsen. It was a country of dense trees and clearings, of ramshackle villages, tinkling cow bells, duck ponds and angry geese which
snapped and hissed at my legs. Children were everywhere – running
to school (some followed by goats), herding cows barefoot in the
meadows, chasing each other with sticks. Every village had its Gasthaus zum Wald and a wooden kiosk where men bought cigarettes loose,
two or three at a time. I ate Bohemian dumplings, gherkins and sour
cabbage, and chewed *Knackwurst* during the day. In the inns I had
to join in German folk songs and give my rendering – accompanied
by an accordion – of 'It's a long way to Tipperary'. The German population was considerable and German was widely used. Czech looked
incomprehensible. It lacks vowels and to my ear sounded clipped and
harsh. I often dropped into churches – none was locked – to rest in
a pew. I liked the smell of stale incense, the votive trinkets and paintings. For a wanderer in these woods a church was a welcome shelter –
weather-proof, solid and reassuring.

At Pilsen I got tight on the famous local beer – perhaps, at its source
among the native springs, it was an especially strong brew – and completed the journey to Prague by train. I had begun to look travel-worn,
and avoided the smart cafés. Mr Record, however, had sent me a few
guineas through the post office and I stuffed myself with red cabbage
and bilberries. From Prague I went to Eger, and then Karlsbad, where
I started walking north towards the Iron Mountains (Erzgebirge) that
divide Bohemia from Saxony. Soon I was in the foothills of the range.
I climbed another height and lost my way among rotting trees. Far
below I could hear the sound of falling water. It was growing dark.
Then I saw a small bent woman with a bundle of faggots, and she guided
me to a hamlet where a grey-haired widow was sitting in an inn parlour
with a work-basket. She gave me supper and told me that many Germans lived in the district, mostly skilled craftsmen who made furniture,
toys and glassware. 'We live poorly, and Hitler has promised to help us.'
She set some red wine before me. 'It's my son Karl's birthday', she said.
'Where is Karl?' I asked. 'He was posted missing in 1917.'

I disliked Chemnitz. Its gloomy grey buildings were hung with black,
red and white flags, and swastikas. A group of SA men passed me on
the pavement shouting abuse at the Jews: '*Deutschland erwache! Jude
verrecke!*' So I went to a cinema and sat among Reichswehr soldiers
watching the iron-faced mountain guide Luis Trenker courting death
with Leni Riefenstahl among the Alpine peaks of Piz Palu. Next day I
took a train to Königsberg, from where I planned to travel along the
Baltic coast to Memel.

Königsberg then (it has since been swallowed up by the Soviet Union) was a fine old Prussian Hanseatic city and port with solid red-brick churches, numerous bridges, markets and warehouses and miles of cobble-stones. I was happy to find a room in the Immanuel Kant-strasse. At Oxford I had spent weeks puzzling over Kant's philosophical propositions. Now I felt a perverse loyalty to my old tormentor.

I went into an elegant café which had a string orchestra, heavy plush furniture and trays of rich cakes. A matronly woman spoke to me. Was I a Dutchman or a Swede? She looked surprised when I told her I was an Oxford student. How could an English gentleman be so shabby? I explained that I was travelling rough, 'like Eichendorff's Taugenichts', and I quoted the wanderer's lines from Heine: 'Weiter, weiter son-der Rast, Du darfst nicht stille stehen'. The woman liked this and bought me two poppy-seed cakes. She then asked me to write down this ditty:

> Oh wenn deine Mutter wüsste
> Wie es Dir in der Fremde geht –
> Strumpf' zerissen, Hemd kaputt,
> Und durch die Hosen pfeift der Wind.
>
> Oh if your mother only knew
> How you are faring in a foreign land –
> Torn stockings, ragged shirt,
> And the wind whistling through your trousers.

Meeting this woman lifted my morale. My worn clothes had merited a line of poetry. In the evening I went to a symphony concert at the opera house. The foyer was full of military-looking men with short hair and straight backs. The women were magnificent, with splendid shoulders, strong hips, graceful limbs and rosy Aryan faces. They had startlingly clear eyes and wore their thick flaxen hair coiled in buns. I looked with envy at their escorts. With such Brünhildes, I thought, a country was worth fighting for.

I sailed in a small coastal boat along the Kurische Haff to Tilsit, where I look a slow train of tiny wooden carriages that puffed into Lithuania. The conductor made his way along the outside of the coaches, walking along the footboard while the train was still in motion. I watched several passengers leave the moving train by jumping out on the blind side into a field. Presumably they had no tickets.

Memel (Klaipeda, in Lithuanian) was a charming Hanseatic port of weathered brick and steep gables decorated with *Fachwerk*. It was already October and a cold north-east wind was blowing. People were putting on padded coats and fur hats. The election for the government of Memelland (the Diet) had just been convincingly won by the German parties. They collected twenty seats and the Lithuanians were left with the remaining five – proof that the territory was overwhelmingly German. During my five days' stay the Germans I spoke to were in an aggressive mood, looking forward to the time when Hitler would incorporate them in the Great Nazi Reich.

I put up at a rough inn used by country folk. The maid, a stocky girl with red hands, warned me that the guests were noisy and drunk. I could hear them through the walls – groaning, arguing, rinsing their mouths, hawking and spitting in the wash-basins. The latrine, of the 'long drop' type, was foul. Near the railway station I found a big muddy market-place packed with light wooden peasant carts made of removable planks. Their owners were sitting on grain sacks among staling horses. They reeked of schnapps. A German businessman who took me to hear a White Russian restaurant band told me, 'Memelland is a poor country. The Lithuanians are illiterate, thick-headed peasants. It will be different one day when we become part of the German Reich and share its economic strength.'

On my last evening I was sitting in a small tavern with some late guests when it was raided by the police. Three policemen burst in waving *Gummiknüppel* (truncheons). In the scrimmage glasses and chairs were overturned, and one of the guests, with whom I had been drinking, hurried me away and gave me a room for the night. I had blown out the candle and was half-asleep when a girl got into my bed. Perhaps it was *her* bed. A glimpse of her face in the moonlight showed wolf's teeth and a mop of coarse ash-blonde hair. Over the top part of her body she was wearing a prickly woollen vest like a fisherman's jersey. Her breath smelt overpoweringly of garlic and schnapps. She was so displeasing that I moved to the edge of the mattress. She prodded and kicked me with her feet, swore, and fell asleep.

Before I left Lithuania I walked through the countryside near Kretinga (Grottingen), about fifteen miles inland. The roads were rutted and muddy. A string of carts passed me, the drivers hunched on a plank over the horses' rumps. The little town of Kretinga was built round a wide cobbled square lined with tumbledown shops and stores owned by Jews. There was a large, flat-roofed yellow synagogue. In the lanes Jews were pushing wheelbarrows or carrying sacks. 'They may look like poor pedlars,' a Lithuanian told me, 'but they're rich.' Kretinga was my first glimpse of a small-town Jewish community in eastern Europe. In such *shtetls*, dotted throughout the Jewish Pale from the Baltic to the Black Sea, Jews had for centuries found asylum after their flight from the Rhineland to escape Crusader persecution and the Black Death. The Jews of Kretinga were the poor relations who had stayed behind when more enterprising kinsmen had emigrated to Vienna, Berlin and Frankfurt in the nineteenth century. With the advent of Hitler, all were doomed.

I returned to Tilsit and took a train to Danzig. This old Hanseatic grain port and its restive German population stood at the head of the Polish Corridor and had earned a reputation as a political trouble spot. Its purpose as a Free City was to ensure that the Polish hinterland had direct access to the sea, and the Treaty of Versailles had given Poland administrative rights over it. Unfortunately for the peacemakers, its people were overwhelmingly German, its legislative assembly was composed of Germans and the Nazi party already controlled a majority of the seats. The Polish Corridor itself, Poland's lifeline to the Baltic, was by its nature a piece of provocative map-making. It cut straight through former German territory, separating East Prussia from the rest of the Reich. The Corridor was a problem that wouldn't go away and there was a joke about it. A prize was offered for a learned book on the elephant. The German produced a treatise on the elephant's anatomy; the Frenchman described the elephant and its love-life; the Englishman wrote 'Elephants I have Shot'; the Russian examined the elephant's soul; and the Pole wrote a polemic on 'The Elephant and the Polish Corridor'.

During the short journey from the East Prussian frontier to Danzig the coaches were locked and there were several police and customs controls. An elderly German in my compartment was scathing about the inconvenience. 'We are on German soil,' he said, 'yet they treat us like spies.'

I found a cheap room in a working-class quarter of Danzig and explored the city. Its traditional Hanseatic style, its wealthy patrician houses and solid red-brick Protestant churches seemed thoroughly North German. Storm Troopers and Hitler Youth were marching about with flags. No one seemed to be talking Polish. My landlady, however, was half-Polish and she detested the Nazis. The *Blockwart* (concierge) responsible for her block of flats was a Nazi spy, she said, prying into people's political opinions. When SA men with swastika arm-bands rattled *Winterhilfe* collecting boxes on her doorstep, she turned them away. The building where she lived was damp and poorly lit, the woodwork rotting, the communal lavatory often choked. She lived on soup, potato pancakes and butcher's offal, drank schnapps, and grumbled.

One evening I found myself by chance at a Nazi meeting-place in a restaurant. A party of Storm Troopers came in and went behind a curtain into an adjoining room. I sat and listened. First, someone made a speech. '*Volksgenossen,*' said the voice, 'the Führer has not forgotten us in Danzig. We await the signal when we shall rejoin our brothers in the Reich.' They then sang '*Volk an's Gewehr!*' and started on *Heimat* songs. The speech and the songs were not merely a challenge; they were a war cry. And it seemed to me, as I sat over my beer and sausage, that any politician or diplomat who still believed in the long-term survival of Danzig Free City (and of the Corridor) was blind to reality. The reality was a Germany thirsting for revenge, highly disciplined and organised, determined to enforce its will, and contemptuous of its neighbours.

I was now ready to return home, with a last stop at Eggersdorf to see the Mark family. My train had to pass through Gdynia, Poland's new port a few miles west of Danzig at the head of the Corridor. On impulse, as the train drew up at Gdynia station, I hopped out with my rucksack and told the ticket collector that I would be breaking my journey for a few hours. I didn't tell him that I had no Polish visa.

I ate tripe and sour cabbage at a restaurant, then sat outside on a bench. As I was pondering what to do next, a policeman came up and asked to see my passport. As I had no visa he took me to the charge office, where the police must have taken me for a vagrant seaman, for they pushed me down some steps into a cell. It was pitch-dark and I couldn't make out my cell mates; from time to time there were thuds as other law-breakers were bundled – some dragged – down the steps to join us. While they quarrelled and retched I leaned against the wall. At least I had a roof over my head.

In the morning the cell was emptied and I was left alone till evening. I was given bread and glasses of tea. After dark other offenders were brought in. One of them, a German seaman, was set on by the others. I dragged him into my corner for his own protection. Next day he rolled me a cigarette and we were both escorted to a magistrate's office. The official wore grimy detachable white cuffs and used a scratchy pen – but he was helpful. I was fined a few shillings, given a week's transit visa, and sent to the British Consul. Mr Jeffreys was amused, not angry. After all, I had not been mixed up in a sailors' brawl, and he loaned me £5. For me it was an experience, and it was experience that I wanted. Mr Record, however, had other views. 'You have no business to get into such scrapes,' he wrote to me when I sent him my next article, 'and this newspaper is not interested in them.'

The port of Gdynia resembled a half-completed building site. Rough wooden scaffolding and mounds of bricks, stones and pipes were everywhere. Streets petered out in sand. Many of the stores and shops were provisional wooden shacks. Buses mingled with horse-drawn cabs. Many naval cadets and garrison officers in four-cornered hats were strolling about. I noticed surprisingly few women.

Before I left for Bydgoszcz, fifty miles to the south, I talked to a ship's chandler who did business with the Anglo-Baltic shipping company. I told him about the ominous growth of German nationalism I had seen among the Nazis. To this he replied, 'The Polish army can look after itself. Moreover, we have a firm friend in France. Indeed, it is French capital that has helped to develop Gdynia.'

'We don't trust the Germans,' he added, 'but we trust the Russians less. If we allowed them to enter Poland as allies they would never leave. Polish policy is to play off one enemy against the other, and to build up a sphere of influence in the Baltic States, Finland and Sweden.'

Bydgoszcz, formerly the West Prussian town of Bromberg, became part of resurrected Poland under the Versailles Treaty. At that time half of its 50,000 inhabitants were Germans. By the time of my visit the German element had fallen to 20,000 and Polish immigrants had moved in, but the town had retained a German flavour. Along the canal were fine timbered warehouses. Faded German signs and lettering still showed on walls next to Polish advertisements. The cobbled streets were uneven and badly lit.

I stayed at a small inn, living cheaply on *Königsberger Klops* (meat balls), sour cheese and poppy-seed cake. It rained every day so I had time to read the German newspapers from Danzig and Poznan and to play billiards with the landlord and waiter. They were bilingual, and both disliked the Nazis. Nazi provocateurs, they said, had begun to stir up the German minority in the Corridor and to start pub brawls. 'The Germans', said the waiter bitterly, 'dismiss everything Polish as inferior. When things go wrong they call it *Polnische Wirtschaft*' (Polish mismanagement).

'Our problem with the Germans', explained the innkeeper, 'is that our temperaments are quite different. The Pole does things with a dash; we are too impetuous. The Germans are perfectionists. Religion has much to do with it. The Protestant Reformation had great success in north and east Germany, but Poland has stayed true to the Roman Church. If a Pole is in trouble he goes to the priest; the German goes to a government office.' I started to memorise a few Polish words. *Swinia* (pig, swine) and *mleko* (milk) were easy, and resembled *Schwein* and *Milch* in German. *Kochac* (to love) and *kielbasa* (sausage) looked strange. 'Girl' in Polish was the euphonic *dziewczynka*. *Bog* was 'God'.

In a side-street I found a bookshop whose owner, a middle-aged Saxon, presented me with an ethnic map of central and eastern Europe and sadly pointed to Germany's lost territories. 'The Germans', he remarked, 'are *Kulturmenschen*. But our old homelands are being swamped by these half-literate "Russians" from Congress Poland.' When I mentioned that I would be crossing the frontier at Schneidemühl (Pila) on my way back to Berlin, he said, 'When you are there, take a walk to the Kuddowerbrücke. You will see a statue of Frederick the Great. It used to stand in the square here in Bromberg,

but the Germans removed it after the war and planted it on German soil.
He is looking back over the fields to West Prussia. It would break old
Fritz's heart if he knew.'

Next day I changed trains at Schneidemühl and had my last look at
Poland. I could see a dusty village, a rutted road, farm carts, flowers and
women wearing kerchiefs. 'No tarmac, no automobiles', remarked the
railway clerk who was with me. 'Nothing but Jews and priests. *Polnische
Wirtschaft*', he sneered. His remark annoyed me. The village and fields,
the haycarts and geese, were a charming, living landscape. There were
flowers and birds. At that moment I resolved to come back to Poland.

Eggersdorf had changed since I was last there two years earlier. The
Nazis had hung their propaganda and flags everywhere and Herr Mark
had lost some of his self-assurance. As a headmaster and local elder he
was respected, but his status in the new Nazified society had diminished.
Kurt, his shopkeeper son, was a senior Party official and ran a car.
Heinz was on a training course. Ernst was still at home. We avoided
the Friedrich der Grosse Gasthaus ('a Nazi drinking club', said Ernst) but
he took me one evening, after dark, to meet a Jewish acquaintance
at his house. He was a grey-haired Russian Jew who had managed a
Russian ballet troupe in Berlin until the Nazis drove him from business. 'Almost overnight', he explained, 'people who were my neighbours and friends – the Bürgermeister was one of them – suddenly found
something detestable about my character. Louts broke my windows,
dragged me out of bed and made me walk in the street in my night-
clothes. I am selling out. I shall get twenty-five per cent of my house's
value, but it won't be enough for me to emigrate. I didn't save enough',
he confessed. 'I never dreamt it would come to this.' His wife no longer
went out of doors ('I do the shopping'). He warned us to tell no one
of our visit.

I spent my last day picking mushrooms with Herr Mark in the wood.
My shoes were worn out and my clothes frayed. Ernst saw me off at
the railway station. He had already taken me into his confidence. 'The
war', he said, 'will start in Poland because only Poles have enough spirit
to stand up and fight against Hitler's territorial demands.' I asked when
he thought that might be. 'In four or five years,' he said bitterly through
his broken palate, 'when the army and air force are fully prepared.'

By now my love affair with Germany was over. Once back in
England, my first attempts to find a job in journalism were disappointing. Harold Stannard, the *Birmingham Post*'s man in London, and Barr-
ington Ward of *The Times*, with whom I had interviews, told me that
I would have to start with a local newspaper (Stannard mentioned the
Wolverhampton Star) and work my way up from the bottom – a lengthy
process that didn't appeal to me. So I asked the Oxford University

Appointments Board to help. They came up with three openings – at Woolworths, Jardine and Mathesons (the Far East shipping line), and Shell Mex. These were 'apprenticeships' at a nominal salary, but with alluring prospects of lucrative promotion in middle age. I took the Shell Mex job and found that my fellow trainee was the Irish rugby international Shaun Wade. Every morning I had to report to a laboratory in Fulham, put on a white overall, and test the malleability of bitumen. I disliked the daily tube journey, the wretched meals of egg and spaghetti in a Lyons Corner House, and the dismal walk back to my digs along the Edgware Road, which was frequented by third-rate whores, some of them elderly and wearing old hats or with a dog in tow. I resigned after a month and bought a Polish dictionary in the Charing Cross Road. Soon after this, to my delight, I saw an advertisement in *The Times* for a post in Gdynia as English editor of a Polish cultural magazine. I met the two previous editors, Dermod O'Donovan and Miss Fenwick, in London. 'Interesting work but poor pay', they told me. Without hesitation, I accepted the job.

Chapter 4

Poland and Romania

I sailed from Hay's Wharf in the Polish cargo ship *Lech* and arrived in Gdynia on a wintry December day. A cab driver wrapped in a rug against the icy wind took me to the offices of the Baltic Institute, on the sea front. Dr Borowik, the Director, gave me a room, a pile of unedited manuscripts and a typewriter, and I was left to get on with the next edition of the quarterly *Baltic and Scandinavian Countries*. I was not used to central heating and threw open my double-glazed window. This alarmed my new colleagues. 'It is forbidden to open the windows in winter', they explained.

Dr Borowik was completely bald and had the face of a toad. He was usually away at conferences. His deputy, Dr Borowy, gave Pani Meznicka most of the work. She was American-educated, charming and clever, and had a husband, a journalist with the *Kurier Baltycki*, who was so fat that he could barely walk.

I stayed at first at the Laguna *pension*, and spent the evenings in a café. There were two. In the Mokka I read the *Daily Express*. In the Baltyk I listened to a string orchestra which played Strauss, Lehar and Moniuszko. My salary, paid in zlotys, was £20 a month, and all my colleagues, even Dr Borowy, had to take an advance (*Vorschuss*) a week before pay-day.

The port area was a place for dock workers and sailors – Swedes, Finns, Lascars and British. Gdynia had no theatre or concert hall, few Jews, and a scarcity of women. 'Gdynia is a sort of Klondyke', Zakrzewski, one of my colleagues, said. 'We are all adventurers here.' The maritime school had a beautiful sailing ship for sea cadets, *Dar Pomorza* (Gift of Pomerania). Osborne, the school's English teacher, organised an Anglo-Polish Society. Ruttledge, the Everest climber, gave us a mountaineering talk, and Robert Byron described his travels in Persia. Byron didn't look like a tough man of action. He was sallow and flabby. At one of the society's meetings I gave a talk on my impressions of Nazi Germany, and was introduced to a smart Polish woman of about thirty who was heavily scented and wore an expensive silver-fox cape. 'You need fattening up', she said to me. 'Come and stay at my house. I will give you as much food as you like, and a room with a terrace'. Her scent, her jewelled fingers and slightly Tartar eyes intrigued me, and I accepted.

My new home was in ul. Lesna on top of a small hill at the edge of a wood. Snow lay on the ground, the sea was frozen for several hundred yards, and to keep warm I used to sprint to the office, which was over a mile away. Wanda Zeeman, my new landlady, was married to a businessman who had been brought up in Russia and was employed in the State bacon export trade. Marisia, the cook, slept in a recess behind the kitchen. On Sundays she was given time off to go to early Mass, when she put on laddered stockings and a freshly ironed head-cloth. For the first time in many months I began to eat well, stuffing myself with borsch drenched with cream, *pirogi*, sweet-cured ham, veal cutlets, pancakes, gherkins and *sauerkraut* while Wanda chain-smoked Russian-type *papierosi* – paper tubes in which the tobacco was inserted from a metal filler.

Mr Zeeman was rarely at home. He would appear suddenly after a journey, unshaven, with a fearful hangover and no money, and go to bed for a couple of days to rest. Wanda had a quick temper and could be a shrew. 'You ruffian (*lajdak*)!' she would shout at her husband. 'Go back to your clap-ridden whores. You have destroyed my life.' Mr Zeeman would listen quietly to her abuse, smile, put on clean clothes and go out on another binge. His favourite haunt was the casino in Zoppot where Müller's bar was papered with worthless German currency notes from the inflation years. Sometimes Wanda asked me to fetch him back from a bar, where I would find him glassy-eyed and penniless among a crowd of workers. The Poles liked him and the police were his friends.

After a time Wanda began to come to my bed. I felt mean, at first. Later I realised (as Zakrzewski put it) that I was 'God's gift to Mr Zeeman', a divinely-sent diversion for his wife's ardour. When Wanda gave a luncheon party it lasted till the early morning hours. Marisia provided a continuous service of food. Polish army officers released on weekend leave from some dismal barracks would come in cloaks and elegant riding boots. Wanda was a provocative dancer. Flushed and unsteady, the officers would pour champagne into her shoe and toast her.

I could rarely afford the Maskot night club where the violinist played tangos and Hungarian schmaltz music, scraping his bow a few inches from the customer's ear. Alas, the hostesses were cunning and heartless. They knew exactly how much one had to spend, and when the zlotys were gone would slip away to another table. Once I uprooted a sapling from the pavement and handed it to the cloakroom woman ('Please take care of my walking-stick'). A few minutes later a policeman appeared. He took possession of the sapling, accepted a drink, and all was well. On another occasion I got caught in a fracas in the port area, where I had gone to a bar with two British merchant seamen. A joke which started as a friendly trial of strength with some Poles flared up into a brawl – even the four-piece band joined in. With two men sitting on my back, another hit me six blows on the head with a bottle – I counted them. This meant a dash to the infirmary and some stitches.

In the summer I swam from a beach lined with sand dunes and coarse grass. The town's marina was little used as the Poles were not fond of swimming. The Institute made no provision for leave, but I spent several weeks travelling daily by train and tram to Danzig to supervise printing of our quarterly magazine. The Polish printers had a small works in the Altschottland district. The typesetting was done on two old Linotype machines and as no one knew English the proofs had to be constantly corrected.

The aim of our publication was to assert Poland's voice in Baltic and Scandinavian affairs and, in face of German counter-claims, to present the Polish case for retaining Upper Silesia and the Polish Corridor with access to the 'historically Polish' Free City of Danzig. Our contributors were mainly Polish academics and professors from the three Baltic States, Sweden and Finland. Much of the material was fascinating: the old Baltic amber and grain trade; the river routes taken across Russia by the Varangians, the 'Red-headed ones' (*Russ*) who gave Russia their name; the customs of the Kashubes, a dying breed of Pomeranian fishermen; the ethnic composition of 'border Silesians'. I helped to produce six of these closely-printed volumes and enjoyed supporting a cause that I sympathised with; for we were barking back at Hitler's propaganda machine, which had opened up a rival institute at Königsberg. Reminding the Germans that Copernicus was a Pole enraged them.

A growing problem was our own safety in Danzig, for we were Poles working for the enemy in a fanatically German town. The Nazis were becoming more and more aggressive. Gangs of youths used to prowl the streets after dark looking for Jewish property to damage. They kept an eye on our printing works and sometimes molested us – after one street fight I returned home with German blood on my shirt. My colleagues refused to be deterred. 'One day we'll drive these German swine (*niemiecki swinia*) into the sea', our compositor would say as three of us sat in an inn celebrating a small victory in tumblers of Danziger *Goldwasser*. Stefan would boast that he would 'screw the German women till they bled' (*Ich werde Ihre Frauen bumsen bis Blut kommt*). A way of getting one's own back was to address Danzig tram conductors in Polish. It infuriated them and the passengers. Another was to sit in a restaurant under a large picture of Hitler and to mimic his voice and gestures. Silly, but it made one feel better.

At the end of the year (1937) it was decided to discontinue printing in Danzig and to produce the magazine in the calmer atmosphere of Bydgoszcz where Poles were in a strong majority. The new printers had Monotype machines, and proof-correcting was easier. I stayed at the Gastronomia. It was a friendly, old-fashioned hotel with huge brass keys and mottled mirrors, and it served substantial meals of greasy duck with rice, *Knödel* (dumplings) and red cabbage with thick gravy. But in Bydgoszcz too Goebbels' propaganda machine had been stirring up the local Germans. One I met in the hotel assured me it was only a matter of time before Hitler took Danzig. My Polish acquaintances jeered at this. 'We have our army and our western friends,' they said; 'in fact, we have more soldiers than Hitler has.' In Bydgoszcz I also found evidence of anti-Jewish feeling. No one liked Jews. A Polish law student told me that Jewish competition at the universities and in the professions kept Poles out of jobs – 'The Jews are not only clever, they have powerful connections.' In a café one evening an artist came in and tried to sell me a pornographic drawing – he had a sheaf of them. My companion pushed him roughly into the street. '*Cholerny Zydek*', he said, spitting on his hands – 'another bloody Jew-boy.'

By the close of 1938, and notwithstanding the Munich agreement, the threat to Poland's future was becoming more apparent as Hitler turned on the heat. Many critics thought that Poland's foreign policy was too reckless. Poland had bitterly offended the Czechs when she took advantage of their weakness to seize the disputed Cziesyn enclave in October 1938. Lithuania had never accepted the loss of Wilno, occupied by Pilsudski in 1920. There had been outbursts of violence among disaffected Polish Ukrainians in south-east Poland. As for the Russians, it was inconceivable that the Poles would allow a Soviet allied army to operate within Polish territory. In the Café Mokka I used to show the waiter the slogan 'There will be no more war' on the front page of Beaverbrook's *Daily Express*, and we would laugh.

My colleagues at the Institute advised me that if I wanted to see Warsaw before it was too late I should go there without delay. So I gave notice to Dr Borowik and waited for my replacement to settle in. Pat Howarth had been to Rugby and Oxford. Like me, he found it fascinating to be in Europe's no man's land at this exciting stage in its history. I introduced him to Wanda ('Not my sort at all') and to the Maskot, and explained that if he were broke by the 20th, he could get a *Vorschuss* from Pani Zofia, the cashier, by being nice to her. In January 1939 I left for Warsaw. It was to be many years before I saw Howarth again; during the war he ran SOE activities with the Poles in Cairo.

To survive in Warsaw I had to have a job, and Egerton Sykes, the British Council's unofficial representative in Warsaw, had recommended the Anglo-Polish school. I had no burning desire to be a teacher. I tended to think of a schoolmaster as a genial failure with a frayed mackintosh and a blackthorn stick sneaking across a field to some rustic pub. The school was run by Mackenzie, a Scotsman. He allotted me classes of mostly married women who were bored, charming, and wanted to impress their friends with their knowledge of Shakespeare's tongue as taught by 'a real Englishman'. At their request we read Oscar Wilde, Bernard Shaw and Dickens. Private lessons, which meant tram rides to dark courtyards with creaking stairs, brought in extra money. Among my private pupils were an ageing Jewess who lived in a musty flat covered in dust-sheets, and a lawyer whose completely bald head, like a shiny egg, matched his name Golab (pigeon). Golab was extremely courteous. He gave me small presents (eau-de-Cologne and cherry brandy) and addressed me as *Panie Profesorze*.

I found a room in ul. Hoza with a grey-haired landlady who had been brought up in Tsarist Russia. My room was cluttered with knick-knacks and faded embroidery. Over my brass bed hung a picture of the Tsar's mounted Cossacks charging a crowd of Polish citizens in Warsaw during the rising of 1863. A rusty iron balcony caught the morning sun. From it I watched droshkies clattering over the cobbles, men pushing barrows, officials with polished leather briefcases, priests, soldiers and Jewish hawkers, drunks and pretty girls with shapely legs. The Saxon Gardens and Lazienki Park were nearby. As it grew warmer, and the rain washed away the last snow and slime from the gutters, I would sit on a bench near the Chopin monument with a book. Chopin's long copper-green hair streamed behind him as though vibrating with music. Warsaw had no good English library and I had to make the most of what I could find – Jack London (a favourite among Poles), Polish history and Pilsudski's memoirs (he had shared his prison cell in Magdeburg Castle with a spider).

My landlady's other lodger owed several weeks' rent and used to lock himself in. Every weekend she hammered at his door shouting 'Pay me, you *bandyta*!' One day he vanished with the key. In the evenings I often went to the Krystal Café. It had a string orchestra and attracted businessmen in suits on the look-out for a typist or a shop girl. The Pod

Bukietem bar provided discreet cubicles. Polish cavalry officers were a nuisance; not only were they unfairly elegant in their four-cornered hats, their cloaks and riding boots – they bagged the best girls. Street-walkers were a special class. They performed in dark doorways and swore obscenely when night porters or doormen tried to move them on. Taking a girl back to one's room involved discretion and a tip to the concierge. For a late snack I went to a night bar for a bowl of stewed mushrooms (*grzyby*), tripe (*flaki*) or sour cabbage (*bigos*) served piping hot. Walking back through the poorly-lit streets to my room I got to know the watchmen. They had staves and caps with ear-flaps. Many were war veterans who had taken part in routing the Red Army in 1922. Their profession had turned them into cynics. The black-out exercises, they thought, meant bad times to come. 'Our leaders make brave speeches, but we don't have the tanks to stop Hitler.'

The black-outs with Polish bombers circling overhead were indeed a reminder of the imminence of war. On 31 March Chamberlain announced Britain's unilateral guarantee of Poland's frontiers. Educated Poles had traditionally preferred the politics and culture of the French, their intellectualism and revolutionary spirit. Now, as the brief Anglo-Polish honeymoon got under way, I became an interesting person. Learning English had become fashionable and the Anglo-Polish school benefited from an influx of new pupils. These were no longer bored housewives but bright young people from offices who wanted a course in commercial English to better their prospects of pay and promotion. About this time I moved from my stuffy digs to a clean, white-painted room near the Plac Trzech Krzyzy. My new landlady was the widow of a well-known Polish theatre artist who had died suddenly during a dental operation. Pani Drabikowa had two other lodgers: Franek, a large, good-natured, idle man who filled the role of lover and 'protector', and Gandhi, a toothless painter with no money. They spent their time eating sardines and playing cards. Soon afterwards all reserve officers were called up and Franek went with them. I was left alone with Gandhi. 'The Germans will attack when the harvest has been brought in', he told me. He asked me about my plans. I had none.

Then I met Dunia. She was small, graceful and dark, with a pale olive skin and large brown eyes. As an actress – she was a regular member of the National Theatre cast, though she did not take major roles – she was sensitive to style. That summer, in her flat straw hat, she looked like a Spanish doll. I began to wait for her at the stage door and escort her home through the flickering street lights and past the cabs and cats. Dunia's mother was a painter and had studied in Paris; her sister worked for Warsaw Radio. Her father, Boleslaw Lesmian, had recently died leaving his family very poor (they lived in two small rooms). Lesmian had been a well known and controversial poet, and through Dunia and her friends I began to learn about him. At that time not many Poles recognised Lesmian's unique merits; for he had Jewish blood (he had added the 'i' to his name to disguise its Jewish origin), and his poetry, with its extraordinary imagination and lyrical language, was said to be erotic and obscure. Dunia told me she had been her father's favourite. He lived with his fantasies, she said, an unworldly poet, small, bird-like, and quite unpractical, fortified by black coffee and cigarettes. His only regular job, as a bookkeeper, had ended in disaster as the result of a colleague's dishonesty.

I used to meet some of Dunia's friends at Pod Wroblem, an artists' café where they drank vodka and cherry brandy in a cloud of tobacco smoke. Lesmian, they said, had genius but was considered 'decadent'; and he had left his family destitute. At one of Egerton Sykes's parties, which I attended with Dunia, Noel Coward, who was visiting Warsaw on a 'cultural' mission, came over to me and asked who my beautiful girl-friend was.

Pani Drabikowa became alarmed when she heard that I was 'following Lesmian's daughter like a goose'. 'A girl like that is not your sort at all. You need someone who will darn your socks. And this is the wrong time,' she added. 'War is coming – and war is the time for *kawalery*, bachelors.'

One of my ambitions was to do some hill-walking in the Ukrainian part of south-east Poland (Galicia). Dunia wouldn't hear of my 'mad scheme' and her mother said, 'Once you are in the Ukraine amongst all those Russians we shall never hear of you again'. So I postponed my plan. Meanwhile Warsaw seemed duller and emptier since the reserve officers had been called up. The Poles by this time were in no doubt that Hitler's continuous threats would end in war. The prospect did not unduly depress them. They were sure that with Allied help they would put up a stout and ultimately successful resistance. Above all, the Poles had had enough of being bullied by Hitler; they wanted an end to the pressures and intimidation that hung over the nation's future.

Dunia and I agreed on a compromise. We would get married and then visit Galicia together. The wedding reception was a small one, held at a farm house in Piekielko, a hamlet a few miles east of Warsaw. Dr Golab was chief guest, and I put a pigeon's egg on his chair, but he didn't take umbrage. We stayed several days at the farmhouse, which was surrounded by a sea of golden corn. Piekielko (an odd name meaning 'Little Hell') was linked to Warsaw by a tiny train of four rickety coaches drawn by a nineteenth-century locomotive with a huge bowl-shaped funnel, known as the *samovarek*. It puffed through the fields along the right bank of the Vistula, scattering goats and cows, and was much used by poor Jews who carried bundles wrapped in newspaper. They sometimes had a fiddler with them. At the farm a gang of hired Ukrainian labourers was getting in the harvest. They slept in a barn, among ikons, and after work sang beautiful songs. I saw one of them kill a cat by swinging it by its tail against a wall. The atmosphere was peaceful – yet eerie. The sun shone from a cloudless August sky, crickets chirped, frogs belched and the stars were brilliant. But everyone remarked that the planet Mars was glowing alarmingly red – an ominous sign; and after dark one heard the ceaseless rattle of army lorries on the road.

When Dunia and I were back in Warsaw and about to take the train to Galicia, Dunia's mother was relieved to see us go. '*Dzieki Bogu*,' she said, 'you will be in a safe part of Poland.' Did she have any inkling that mother and daughter would not meet again for six years? I left my books, papers and clothes behind, including my dinner-jacket (my 'smoking'). I never saw them again. The photographs of my parents and of rugger and cricket teams were probably burned or thrown down a latrine. Perhaps a German soldier flogged my 'smoking' in the flea market. Like my old life, they vanished, taking some of my identity with them.

We travelled through the night and woke up to see a swamp near Lwow crowded with storks. To my regret I found that Dunia was no walker. At Kolomyja, Kuty and Zalesczyki I had to make my trips into the countryside alone. Here was a different world from Warsaw: southern warmth; melons, grapes and sun flowers; thatched and gaily painted cottages, markets with husky Jewish traders (many had red hair), flaking churches with a double-barred Orthodox cross glittering on the dome. This part of the Carpathians was the home of Huculi woodcutters and pastoralists who wore home-made mocassins secured by thongs and spoke their own dialect. At Zalesczyki I bathed in the Dniestr, which formed the boundary with Bukovina (Romania). Giant cockchafers tumbled from the rafters on to our beds at night; cockroaches eyed us from cracked plaster – they exploded disgustingly if one trod on them barefoot in the dark.

From Kuty we went to a guest-house high up in the Carpathian hills some fifteen miles inside the Romanian border. It was a big wooden chalet and the owner, a wealthy country sportsman, stuffed us with venison, cream, honey and red wine. The peasants wore loose linen smocks and straw hats. In the green woodland, their patches of maize, flax and sunflowers glittered like clusters of gold. They had painted their little churches in garish colours. In such surroundings it was tempting to forget the threats of war.

Then suddenly, on the landlord's radio, we heard alarming news. Hitler and Stalin had announced a non-aggression pact and Ribbentrop and Molotov, the blond jackal and the badger, had met to sign it. The unexpected perfidy of this blow shocked everyone. The field was now open for Hitler's panzers to move in. Dunia and I drove straight back across the border to Kuty. On 1 September the town crier thumped his drum in the square. The German army had invaded Poland.

On 3 September I was in Kolomyja, where I had gone to find out the latest news, when a Jew waved to catch my attention and called me over to his shop. A group of men was bending over his radio, and I was just in time to hear Chamberlain's solemn voice: Britain had declared war on Germany. Then the sound of 'God Save the King' filled the little haberdasher's shop with its trays of hair combs, buttons and razors. In those few seconds my status had changed dramatically. People came up and shook my hand. I was no longer a voyeur but a participant in Poland's drama. My first feeling was of relief that England had kept its word to its ally; the next, that Englishmen were going to die in war; and that not only Hitler's armed braggarts but the schoolchildren I had seen in Eisenach six years earlier were now among the enemy.

There was no way of getting back to Warsaw. Public transport had been requisitioned, the post and telegraph services ceased, and buses were ferrying young men to the report centre at Kolomyja. Roused by the news, the Huculi came down from the hills to stare at the mobilisation posters. It was rumoured that the British Navy was steaming into the Baltic and the RAF flying to Poland's help. In village squares the peasants looked up at the sky but there was no sign of aircraft, no smoke trails – though not far away the Luftwaffe was strafing the railway system and roads. Soon the first refugees began to arrive by car from Warsaw, Lodz and Cracow – painters, writers, lawyers, the sort of people with a talent to survive. They had been bombed on the way and had camouflaged their cars with mud.

Shortly before the Russians marched in I was tipped off by a local official that the Red Army was being deployed near the border and it would be unsafe for me to stay ('If the Russians come, you might disappear'). The news alarmed Dunia. She insisted that we leave at once. I carried her fibre suitcase over the wooden footbridge at Zalesczyki and we crossed the Dniestr into Romania. It was a moment of deep humiliation. The Polish frontier policeman who stamped my passport gave me a grim look and said, 'Come back in a bomber'. For me, this was a challenge that had in some way to be honoured. But Czernowitz was not far away. We travelled there by country bus among gypsy women with rank black hair and ribbons and men who smelt of goats, before taking a train to Bucharest.

In Bucharest I went straight to the British Council's Anglo-Romanian Institute. Here, to my delight, I ran into Reggie Smith.

I had known him as a Birmingham University student and he reminded me that I had bowled him for a duck in a Public Schools Trial at Edgbaston. He had recently married Olivia Manning ('Olivia writes'). 'If you want to stay in Bucharest and you like plum brandy,' he told me, 'you can have a job with us. You can also play rugger.' John Amory, the Council's director, immediately offered me a teaching post. But Lord Lloyd, the Chairman, would have to interview me first in London. I could then return to Bucharest as a fully-salaried officer. Dunia, who wanted to stay near to Poland, persuaded me to agree to this. Just before we left, the Romanian prime minister Calinescu was shot dead in the street by Iron Guard Legionaries. The assassins were caught, taken to the scene of the murder, and executed; their bodies were left to lie in the road for thirty hours. Hundreds of people came to gaze at them from behind a police barrier. When a lorry drove up to remove the bodies, I watched the crowd hurry to the bloodstained spot like ghouls, looking for grisly souvenirs.

We travelled by train through Zagreb and Venice. The Italians went out of their way to be kind to Dunia. 'Poland', they said, 'is a Catholic country and it was wrong of Hitler to attack it.' They made jokes about Mussolini ('*Il Luce!*') and someone gave Dunia a huge salami. Crossing through France, we waved at a British Army ambulance train.

When Lord Lloyd called me for interview I found Egerton Sykes waiting in his office to introduce me. Ten minutes later I had the job, and within a few days I was back on the Simplon–Orient Express bound for Bucharest. My brief homecoming, though, had been clouded by sadness. My father was very ill; and another nine years were to pass before I was to see my mother and my old Moseley home again. Before catching the train I had a last drink at a pub near Victoria Station. 'The German army', I said to the landlord, 'is formidable. We are in for a shock.' At this the landlord looked displeased and took me aside. 'We don't want that sort of talk here', he said.

We took over a flat from Crumblecake Thompson, a departed British Council sage. He left us a present. Hidden under his bed in a basket of old clothes was a set of Henry Miller's books and *Lady Chatterley's Lover* in the Albatross continental edition ('not to be imported into Britain'). So Crumblecakes too had his secrets. Amory asked me to lecture on British economic history at the Commercial Academy in Lascar Catargiu and to take evening classes at the Institute. This gave me my first problem: I had to stand in front of an audience as a spokesman for what was called the 'British Way of Life' – to be a *propagandist*. This went somewhat against the grain. Exhibitionism was bad form; and in the Oxford spirit of scepticism I had been taught to pick holes in any

proposition, whatever its merits. Was I to keep silent about unemployment in Britain, the depressed industrial areas, slums and (until recently)
the Jarrow marchers? Or to stress only the glories of the Raj, the Royal
Navy, the thin red line of fighting 'eroes, cricket, and the cool, rich taste
of Flowers Ale?

After the brutal rout of Poland, the Bucharest scene seemed to me
frivolous and unreal. There was no wartime austerity, no black-out. The
British colony – Legation staff, teachers and businessmen – lived well. A
semi-official currency black market supplied us with cheap Romanian
lei. I bought for a song a heavy double-breasted overcoat and several
shirts. Restaurants served caviare and steak, venison and delicious maize
dishes (*mamaliga*) till late at night. *Tuica* (plum brandy) was cheap – to
keep out the winter cold it was swallowed with hot water and a lump
of sugar. In bars and night-clubs gypsy musicians played wild and haunting melodies, the clarinets and strings shrilling like maddened birds
to the rhythm of the cymbalon. Maria Tanassa the gypsy girl was
everyone's favourite. Her passionate singing, harsh, oriental and sensuous (the sound is still with me) kept us up late in a smoke-filled night
bar. The present Sir Robin Hankey (then with the Legation) and Geoffrey Household, a witty man with a bald head who had just written the
best-selling novel *Rogue Male*, listened to her entranced among the wine
bottles.

In the cafés Romanian officers in bright blue uniforms with wide
shoulder-boards tucked into sweet Turkish cakes with their ladies.
Moneyed Jews and their wives in furs and heavy jewellery filled the best
seats at places of entertainment. Yet the officer's batman had holes in
his boots. Away from the royal palace and the boulevards a mass of poor
Jews, gypsies, labourers and street traders lived in cellars and hovels.
In December, the workmen who were building an extension to the
palace in snow and bitter winds wrapped rags round their feet. Outside
brightly lit hotels watchmen shivered over braziers amid the frozen
horse dung. Meanwhile, in camps and hostels destitute Polish refugees
sold their jewellery and waited for transport to the West – soldiers and
airmen had priority. It seemed to me that the Germans were ominously
near at hand. Cinemas showed newsreels of German aircraft machine-
gunning British trawlers and sinking British ships. German newspapers
and magazines were everywhere on sale (*The Times* arrived four days
late). One heard reports of a steady infiltration of German 'experts'.
Yet I sensed no panic among my Jewish students, no dramatic urgency
among those who had applied for visas to America, France or Turkey.
The Jews, through some fatal lack of imagination, seemed unaware of
the storm that was reaching down the Danube to annihilate them.

The British Council carried on as though the war did not exist. My companions lectured on D.H. Lawrence, Shaw and Eliot and I took part in a public debate on 'Woman's Place is in the Home' (the motion was passed). Through the walls of my lecture room at the Commercial Academy I could hear my German colleague bawling out his grammar lessons in a Saxon accent. I pulled his leg about the phoney war, the meaningless communiqués ('Nothing to report') and the killing of a Scottish chicken by a stray Nazi bomb. Yet it was not the Germans – admired for their culture, professionalism and efficiency – whom Romanians regarded as their prime enemy, but Russia, the predatory bear waiting to grab Bessarabia and Bukovina. 'The Russians are barbarians', Romanians told me. 'They have nothing to offer us – no culture and no goods. If we let them into our country, they will come with sacks on their backs and fill them with loot.' German economic strength and commercial blackmail, however, were feared. 'Romania', said the historian Iorga, 'must continue to feed the crocodile, or be eaten by it.'

Among my new colleagues were Hugh Seton-Watson, a linguist and historian who wore a Russian fur hat and mittens and was vaguely connected with the Legation as an 'observer'; Tommy Thomson, a shrewd Scot, who felt he was wasting his time in a Balkan classroom; Bill Allen from Brno, whose English-language text books were used after the war in schools all over the world. Ivor Porter was busy with his university students and I didn't see much of him. He was later parachuted back into Romania and after the war had a distinguished diplomatic career. Reggie Smith I found to be unchanged from his Birmingham University days when he and Walter Allen and other students used to gather in a pub in Edmund Street and argue about the proletariat in literature. Provincial and naïve (as I thought), they were besotted by Lawrence's 'sap and semen' school, Auden and Eliot. Reggie was still large, shambling and untidy, and still a Communist, spouting an ingenuous sort of Marxism. While Communist Russia remained in alliance with Hitler, Britain's cause was not entirely respectable to left-wing intellectuals, and Reggie's support of the Red Army's assault on Mannerheim's 'Fascist' Finland in the winter of 1939–40 distressed many of his friends. Yet despite his views, which were rooted in his working-class background, Reggie's charm outweighed his absurd ideology. Olivia was to hit him off rather well in the character of Guy Pringle, in *The Balkan Trilogy*. She was a pale, skinny girl with a small, oval face, bright button eyes and thin legs. She was not very approachable – she had a sharp tongue – and she was not finding it easy to accept Reggie's gregarious ways and the corrupt atmosphere of a Balkan city. She was already working on her first book, a life of the missionary–explorer David Livingstone, and spent much of her time in a locked bedroom bent over her typewriter while Reggie brought back noisy friends who ransacked the flat for drinks. Olivia thought little of me, classing me as a 'hearty'.

Throughout that winter there were rumours in Bucharest of British plans to sabotage – with the complicity of King Carol's government – the transit of Romanian oil to the Axis. Schemes to sink cement-laden barges in the Danube, to block the Iron Gates with explosives, or to attach limpet mines to railway tanker wagons, came to nothing. A major operation was to be the blowing up of the Ploesti oilfield in the event of German invasion. Major Davidson-Houston, the military attaché, has described in his memoirs (*Armed Pilgrimage*) how he travelled to Galati on the Danube to collect the explosives from a ship specially dispatched from Alexandria. He found some British Army Morris trucks still dust-stained from the Western Desert and their drivers, shivering in cotton dungarees, disguised as deck-hands. The demolition stores must have been packed in a hurry by the field company in Egypt, for he was astounded to find among the boxes a dartboard, an army Bible, some Arabic grammars, a dozen 'filthy pictures' from Port Said, and one Boyes anti-tank rifle. The major was able to instruct thirty British employees of the oilfields how to plant the explosives in the wells, and he then went back to Bucharest to await events.

To counteract the effects of rich Romanian food I went for training runs at night along the boulevard leading to the Arch of Triumph. This brought some embarrassing moments, and set dogs barking. In Britain a policeman might have stepped from the shadow of a privet hedge and inquired, 'Going fishing, sir?' Here in Bucharest anyone running at night was taken for a thief. When the snow thawed I played rugby. Rugby had been introduced to Romania by a wealthy banker, Chrissovoleni, who had learned the game at Cambridge. I played every Sunday in the national league, which could produce a team good enough to play and defeat a French 'A' XV. These were happy moments: a hard ground, frosty air and brilliant sunshine, and 'fans' (including Reggie in a Birmingham University scarf) to cheer us. The Romanian press referred to me as 'an English star'; after the match we would go to Dimitrescu the grocer to drink *tuica* among the hanging bodies of game. Several cavalry officers played for the club; Prince Ghica was on the wing. I have often wondered whether these splendid fellows survived the bloody battles fought by the Romanian army corps that took part in the capture of Odessa and was later smashed in the Russian counter-offensive at Stalingrad. I had an unhappy reminder of them in Odessa in 1945 when I saw Romanian prisoners-of-war clearing up bomb damage in the docks.

Meanwhile Reggie had brought off his masterpiece, a British Council production of *Othello* at the National Theatre. It took weeks to prepare.

Major Davidson-Houston fought a duel as Cassio. Sylvia, the attractive English wife of a Romanian lawyer, took the part of Desdemona. As I had a well-developed torso I was given three lines to say ('What Ho! What Ho! What Ho!') as the bare-chested sailor who announces the approach of the Turkish fleet bearing up on Cyprus. Reggie, of course, was Othello. On the first night, when the nuns and their convent girls were in the audience, he forgot to wear pants under his tights and the glaring footlights turned him into a naked radish; and there was a ludicrous moment when, as he fell dying, his wig came off and slid across the stage. In her trilogy Olivia has changed the play to *Troilus and Cressida*. Olivia helped Dunia with the make-up but she refused to act. In the person of Harriet she speaks slightingly of the performance, 'an amateur production and waste of effort that would be forgotten in a week'. But weren't we all amateurs, with our optimism and naïveté and our belief in the Maginot Line?

A number of Polish refugee artists and writers came to see Dunia to discuss their plans, but no one had news of her mother and sister. When spring came in 1940 I started to feel restless. Although Dunia strongly opposed the idea, I was determined to be a soldier, and Tommy Thomson and I both registered with the British officers' Emergency Reserve at the military attaché's office. My other British Council colleagues showed no zest for joining the armed services. It was considered bad form even to broach the subject; for were we not 'special people', protected by the Foreign Office in a reserved occupation, and had we not been specifically warned by British Council headquarters in London not to break our contracts? Olivia was cruelly outspoken on the subject of 'heroics'. I remember her telling us that she would never allow her husband to throw away his valuable life in some stupid battle. War, according to this view, was for old sweats shipped over from tropical cantonments, for clerks who aspired to authority, for the products of minor public schools, for Durham and Welsh coal miners and for men with handlebar moustaches. Cultural work had priority.

Within a month of this conversation, the Germans had invaded France and the British Army was in retreat. Soon afterwards the military attaché told me to move to Constanza, Romania's Black Sea port, to await transport to Egypt, which would be arranged. I was glad to leave the unreal atmosphere, the gossip and speculation of Bucharest. The detachment of my colleagues from the war made it hard for me to feel loyal to them. In Constanza the local British and German consuls lived in adjacent houses. The German owned a sports car: Mr Kendall had the fatter wife (she was Bulgarian). I played cricket with Mr Kendall in his garden and amused myself hitting the ball into the German's flower beds.

Then one day fifty British oil engineers arrived suddenly from Ploesti, shepherded by the military attaché. Alarmed by the collapse of France, which was followed by Russia's immediate seizure of Bessarabia and Bukovina, King Carol's government had changed its mind about Allied sabotage plans and ordered the British engineers to leave. The ship that was waiting to take us off was a rusty Jewish hulk owned and manned by the Aaronstein family. There was a nerve-racking delay as officials probed the ship for jewellery and money – the crew, who wore cloth caps and greasy suits and looked more like pedlars than sailors, had cunningly sprayed fresh paint everywhere to obstruct the officials in their search (we learned later that they had hidden their treasure in the lifebelts). On the quayside Thomson and I could see the German consul in his white motoring helmet watching us. At last we chugged slowly out to sea, with an escort of porpoises that dived and flashed under the bow like torpedoes. The consul waved goodbye. We were in retreat, a shipload of failures.

We completed the last stage of our journey by train, from Haifa to Cairo, rattling past sand dunes and orange groves, Australian Army camps and the edge of a blue sea to the alfalfa and cotton fields of the Delta. At El Kantara, on the Suez Canal, I had my first glimpse of the British Army. A company of the East Surreys was drawn up on the landing stage. They were wearing pith helmets, khaki shirts and shorts, and ankle puttees. They had the tanned skins and wiry bodies of regular soldiers. They were impressive, and they were compatriots.

In Cairo I went straight to the British Council Institute. To my astonishment I found an old acquaintance, Flux Dundas, grinning at me from the Director's desk. In my last year at school, Dundas had joined the staff as a spare teacher. With his pale, ravaged face, thinning hair, missing teeth and a bad stutter, we had found him pleasant but odd. He told us his health had been undermined during his service as a political officer in the Sudan. It was rumoured that he had played cricket for Oxford, but when he joined us at net practice we discovered that he bowled donkey drops. Later, in my first year at Oxford, Dundas had taken digs in Beaumont Street in order to complete his terms of residence at the university and qualify for a degree. I had thought of him as a delightful nonentity. Now here he was, in a cool tropical suit, occupying a position of great power, the British Council's top man in the Middle East. His advice was that I should on no account quit the Council. 'You will be more useful doing cultural work for the country than soldiering', he said. For a fortnight I gave grammar lessons to a class of Egyptian students. But I wasn't happy. Australian and New Zealand troops crowded the streets – brawny men in shorts and colonial hats. I would have no peace of mind till I was in uniform too.

In the meantime, Major Davidson-Houston must have pulled some strings, for a middle-aged man from the War Office asked me to call on him at the Cecil Hotel. He wanted to know if I was prepared, after training, to be parachuted into Poland. I said I had no objection. But he discontinued the interview when he learned that I had relatives – my wife's mother and sister – in Warsaw ('Too bad – that rules you out'), and I heard nothing more from him. I was sent instead on an infantry training course at Moascar barracks, Ismailia.

The course was designed for volunteer recruits from the British colony in Egypt. Several came from the Egyptian education department (PI), and two of the Ploesti engineers were there. We lived in army huts, with a mess, and were kept busy with weapon training and night exercises. Our instructors were regular soldiers. One member of the course, Christopher Scaife, a leading literary and academic figure in Cairo, used to prowl stark naked through the camp. The local Egyptian staff, who all wore the long cotton *galabya* gown to ward off the sun and dust, thought he was a mad guru. Perhaps he overdid the sun worship, for he was later invalided out of the army with septicaemia.

In our leisure moments we ate mangoes and went swimming in the Bitter Lakes, which was like taking a warm bath. Ismailia, with its hibiscus, date palms and whitewashed villas, was French in style and housed French employees of the Suez Canal company. Some Spanish Legionaries were quartered there; they had a reputation for stabbing people with knives. One avoided the Sweet Water canal that dribbled past Ismailia. Its lush green banks were poisoned by ordure, flies and parasitic snails. Though the canal was heavily infected with bilharzia, this did not worry the fellahin. They came here to wash themselves and their animals, to drink the water and to draw it in clay pots, which the women carried to their huts. It was a place for masturbating and jeering boys. One noticed the Moslem's preoccupation with cleansing his body. At sunrise scores of dark shapes could be seen crouching in the sand outside their villages – men, black-gowned women, and children, like crows at breakfast – all defecating, with a little tin of water for cleaning themselves. This seemed to us a nasty habit. Yet to the Egyptians, the morning exodus to a patch of clean sand was their practical answer to the problem of sanitation. No one wanted to share a place that had been fouled by others. As for using an indoor latrine, the simplest peasant abhors the notion of defecating, as the European does, in his own house. Any other spot will do, especially if running water is handy.

My colleagues at Moascar were decent men torn between hanging on to their comfortable civilian jobs and a desire to serve their country 'at the sharp end'. After completing the course some changed their minds, and did not join up. Others were initially posted to public relations, intelligence, censorship and general duties. Tommy Thomson did not attend the course, and was sent by the British Council to teach in Zagazig. In October I was commissioned as a Second Lieutenant in the General List and sent on a temporary posting as liaison officer with 26 British Military Mission (later changed to 26 British Liaison Unit); my section was attached to General Kopanski's Polish Carpathian Lancers Brigade at Dikheila near Alexandria. I drew my desert kit at Kasr-el-Nil barracks. It included a splendid officer's bed roll, a pith sun helmet (only eccentrics wore them, and I soon lost mine), baggy khaki shorts, a forage cap and a holster without a pistol.

Taking leave of Dunia at Cairo railway station was painful. She feared the worst; and, seeing her tearful face dwindling to a blur on the platform as the train moved out, I felt criminally guilty of causing her grief. This was a disquieting feeling that gnawed at one's morale, and one I never entirely got rid of throughout my army service and my absences from her. It would have been easier if Dunia had been of a more stoical or more sanguine temperament. Yet we were lucky. The wives of regular soldiers were not allowed by army regulations to stay in a theatre of war; they all had to be evacuated, or sent home.

Chapter 5

Egypt

M ost of the Polish soldiers who had escaped after the débâcle of the September 1939 war were routed to France, which they regarded as their natural ally. The Carpathian Lancers Brigade had broken the mould by making its way direct to Egypt via Syria and Palestine. Some of the men had crossed the Tatra mountains on skis. Many had been intercepted in Slovakia and Hungary and temporarily interned. Others had been evacuated to the Middle East by ship from Split. In Syria, under French command, they had been formed into the Carpathian Brigade and supplied with arms and equipment. When France fell the future looked bleak for them. The new Vichy authorities demanded that the Poles should be disarmed and interned. This was asking the impossible of a proud fighting unit. The Poles flatly refused to accept the order; and it was only after bitter wrangling that the French let them go. They were moved to Palestine, where English yeomanry regiments gave them a warm welcome, and then to Egypt, and were now, in the autumn of 1940, manning a sector of concrete bunkers at Dikheila, near the airfield at Mex, as part of the Alexandria harbour defences.

Major Sholto Douglas (Royal Scots), the senior Mission officer, gave me a tent and I was told to familiarise myself with the various units, report on their problems and get to know the officers. The Brigade was poorly equipped. It had salvaged from the French some Citroën trucks and Hotchkiss machine-guns and scrounged some riding horses from Palestine. The horses were the officers' pride. They symbolised the lancer tradition, and the officers exercised them over the neighbouring sandy waste in Polish riding breeches and boots. The Poles were still unused to the idea of wearing khaki shorts. 'We look like a band of Boy Scouts', a *Rotmistrz* (Captain) said to me.

The matters I had to attend to were entirely mundane: dhobi (laundry) bills, labourers' pay, altercations with local contractors, internal security and theft. Not many Poles spoke English. Life among the sun-baked sand-dunes guarding empty concrete pillboxes bored them. The officers found Greek girl-friends and enjoyed themselves in the bars and night-clubs of Alexandria. The nearest enemy, the Italians, though they had advanced some way over the Libyan border into Egypt, were many miles to the west of Matruh. Air protection was provided by a handful of old Gladiator biplanes based at Mex. There were several Italian air raids. The Egyptian anti-aircraft gunners fired back, and shell splinters rattled like hail on the tin roofs of our huts. When it was reported that the Egyptians were failing to fuse their shells, I was ordered to go one night to their command post, with a Polish officer, to complain. Our visit didn't please the Egyptians. I remember that their dug-out smelt of eau-de-Cologne and onions ('Like a brothel', the Pole remarked).

One afternoon the Mission corporal (Warwickshire Yeomanry) persuaded me to go riding with him. I had sat on a horse only once before and had kept it at a gentle trot along a bridle path. This horse, after picking its way through the Polish lines for twenty minutes, got bored. It broke into a gallop and, swerving madly between tents and barbed wire and cheering Poles, it headed back for the stable while I clung to its neck. Just before I would have been decapitated by the lintel over the stable door, I rolled over its rump and hit the ground. Someone picked up my forage cap. After this it was clear to me that I had come to the wrong unit.

That weekend the Poles invited the regimental band of the Royal Welch to show off its glittering instruments and drums, and hosted a football match against some Australian soldiers, which the Poles won. Later I joined a group of Polish and Australian officers in the mess. The Polish campaign of 1939 was being discussed, and when someone asked me for my opinion I said, 'The Poles went to war with flags flying and trumpets blowing. But they had no chance. The Germans were too strong for them and better equipped.' No one seemed to resent my remark. After all, it was the truth. In the morning, to my dismay, I was on the mat. Major Douglas was cold and severe. An Australian officer had reported that I had been spreading gloom in the mess and that I had spoken rudely about the Poles. Major Douglas ordered a court of inquiry.

A Welsh major with pink cheeks and a ginger moustache presided over the inquiry. The complainant and sole witness was Lieutenant Cohen, the Australian detachment's Intelligence officer, a humourless man with a Central European accent. As the Major listened to Lieutenant Cohen's account, he glanced at me with a twinkle in his eyes, as though he thought the whole affair a waste of time. I heard nothing more. But Major Douglas ordered me to stay in my tent until I could be posted away.

I spent a week sitting alone in the sun reading the two books I had brought from Cairo, Dean Stanley's *The Eastern Church* and Thomas Mann's *The Magic Mountain*, and throwing stones at a tin. The boredom was so unbearable that I defied the Major's order twice by walking out of the camp to Mex. At this time British units were being embarked for Greece to try to stem the German advance. Passing an assembly point I ran into Geoffrey Household – now a Captain and OC of a Field Security detachment – draped in webbing, with field glasses and map case, waiting with his men to be taken off. My own posting proved to be to the Western Desert, where I was to join the second battalion of the King's Own Royal Regiment. I was given twenty-four hours' leave and Dunia came from Cairo to see me off. There was an air raid over Alexandria that evening with heavy anti-aircraft guns banging away. Dunia insisted on going down to the air raid shelter, and I realised how highly strung and fragile she was, and yet how resolute in other ways.

On the train to Mersa Matruh, Egyptians were riding on top of the coaches and one-eyed beggars clinging to the footboards. A Coldstream Guards lieutenant was sitting opposite to me, absorbed in a book entitled *Schooldays in Paris*. When he left the compartment for a few minutes, I glanced at it. Some schooldays! The book was a riotous account of brothel adventures and dildos.

The second battalion of the KORR (Lancaster) was dug-in on a stretch of yellow sand flanked by an escarpment. It was a regular battalion and had seen service in the Far East and, during the recent troubles, in Palestine. It was now part of Selby Force and formed a strong-box protected by minefields, anti-tank obstacles, wire and pillboxes (some with old naval guns). We lived in holes linked to weapon pits. There were sporadic Italian air attacks. Lieutenant-Colonel Fitzsimmons, the CO, told me that I was a replacement for one of the battalion's regular officers who had died of a meningitis bug he had picked up in an old Egyptian army post he had been using. At first I shared a dug-out with the company commander, Major Cracker Creedon. Cracker was a big broad-shouldered man with angry eyes, a brown wrinkled face and bristling moustache. He warned me straight away that he was not interested in books, art or politics. In the evening, after his batman had fed us with a warmed-up stew of bully beef and the oil lantern was lit, he would tell me polo stories and discuss wild pig hunting. He didn't smoke. But I had my weekly ration of fifty Spitfire cigarettes; they had an acrid taste, and the saltpetre in them spluttered.

The main problem was to stop the men getting bored. Cracker kept us busy with tactical exercises (ambushing tanks), laying minefields and erecting more wire. I was issued with a .38 revolver and six 'dum-dum' bullets – 'that's all we can spare', said the CQMS. After dark the hot desert air radiated rapidly skyward. The stars were brilliant and the nights bitterly cold (we were still in tropical kit and shorts). Just before dawn, warmed by a mug of tea, I did the round of the sentries. Breakfast was a sausage ('soya turd'), army biscuits and jam. After a fortnight with Cracker Creedon I went to live with my platoon in a hole which I shared with my sergeant. Sergeant Dolling was an excellent, well-spoken man. I practised map reading and the use of a compass with him and he smartened up my saluting. 'The men can hardly wait to get their hands on old Electric Beard' (the general commanding the Italian desert army), he said. 'I remember how our lads used to beat up the macaronis in Shanghai. We bashed them with bits of iron bedstead'.

In the dim light of a candle stump I read my one book (Conrad's *Nigger of the Narcissus*) and some old Western magazines borrowed from soldiers. I was happy lying there in the dark with an empty Canadian beer bottle beside me to pee into. Civvy street and its pecuniary worries – the hand constantly in the pocket paying for a cup of tea or a night's lodging – were far away. I was part of a team. There were no distractions, no women, only a rare issue of beer – and I was in rude health. Cracker's advice to me had been short and simple. 'Keep your men busy. See that they get their meal before you do. Enforce latrine discipline. Trust your NCOs but avoid familiarity. Lead by example. Don't flap.'

The men envied Sergeant Black when he went on leave to Cairo. 'He'll stick a feather in his arse and go round the brothels pretending he's a cockerel', Dolling said. Black promised to call on Dunia and bring back a fruit pudding. Shortly before Christmas, Wavell launched his offensive in the Western Desert and we had orders to move. Alas, we didn't move far. We set up a collecting point for prisoners and were swamped by thousands of Italians. From Sollum and Bardia they were brought back in their own diesel lorries, clamouring for *aqua* (water) and *coperti* (blankets). Among them were wild-looking Senussi tribesmen without boots or proper uniform. The Italian officers stuck together and showed no interest in their men. Some of the NCOs had decorated their pith helmets with a slogan: 'It is nobler to die like a lion than to live like a sheep'. Not everyone behaved well. I shared a tent with a British officer from another unit who tore badges of rank, medal ribbons and buttons off prisoners' uniforms to show off as souvenirs. Daily dust storms added to one's discomfort. Throat, hair and clothes filled with grit and sand; body sweat turned into a brown smear. When the whisky ration arrived, it was half a bottle per officer. One of my jobs was to march columns of prisoners to Matruh railhead. No one tried to escape. Matruh itself had been bombed and shelled and was deserted.

When the battalion moved again it was, to my disgust, in the wrong direction – to Cairo. 'Three cheers for the Dunkirk 'arriers', said Private Newman, a former farm labourer from Somerset. For a few days we lived in tents under the Pyramids. Stripped by looters of their smooth facing, the great blocks of stone were an easy scramble to the top. Nearby, Mena Hotel was crammed with officers, its swimming-pool as hot as a greenhouse. The purple evening sky, the silhouettes of the great tombs, the white patches of our tents, the moving shadows of soldiers, might, to an onlooker, have made a romantic picture. For us, it was simply a matter of making ourselves as comfortable as we could. A week later we took over garrison duties at the Citadel. From the battlements of the old fort we had a magnificent view over Cairo – a shimmering white city in a haze of dust pricked by minarets, with the decaying Tombs of the Dead in the foreground. As the junior officer I mounted the guard and at night inspected the guard posts – they were scattered throughout the city – while my colleagues went off to the night-clubs. An Indian tailor at Kasr-el-Nil barracks made me a service-dress uniform, and to please Dunia I had my photograph taken in it. I played rugby for the battalion, and as an officer was allowed to use the Gezira Club. Once I took my company on a route march through the suburbs. I was in front, and Sergeant Bates said to me with a grin, 'Don't try too 'ard, sir, or you'll be taken for a real soldier.'

The battalion was still under strength, but with the arrival of fresh drafts from England my spell with it ended and I was transferred to the administrative staff of a prisoner-of-war camp at Geneifa, on the Suez Canal. Later that year, the battalion took part in the attack on the Vichy French forces in Syria. I was sorry to leave it, and it was not until 1947, in unusual circumstances, that I met up with its sister battalion in Trieste.

At Geneifa, thousands of Italians captured during the Wavell offensive were being held under canvas in open cages. They were guarded by Indian Army Garwhali troops. Lieutenant-Colonel Duggan, the Camp Commandant, was a pre-war resident of Egypt. His staff included Captain Webster, who was in charge of the disinfestation and bath unit, Lieutenant Harari the interpreter, an RAMC major with a mobile laboratory, and Lieutenant Jones, who stalked about with a hockey stick in place of a swagger cane. The NCOs and other ranks were a mixed bag, some of them crocks. The immediate problem was an outbreak of typhoid. The camp was infested with flies (I also saw lice crawling on tent walls) and the prisoners were under strict orders to get rid of them. Lieutenant Jones used to stride through the prisoners' lines whacking bottoms with his hockey stick whenever he found a fly on a cookhouse table or a blocked grease-trap. Meanwhile, the RAMC major worked night and day for three weeks before he traced the typhoid carriers.

My colleagues were an odd bunch. Lieutenant-Colonel Duggan was a handsome, choleric, white-haired Anglo-Irishman whose Syrian wife and beautiful daughter sometimes dropped into the mess for a Sunday lunch of 'camel steaks' and date pudding. Captain Webster, a veteran of the last war, was a drone. The first time I set eyes on him, at breakfast, he produced a coin, shouted 'Double or quits', and relieved me of ten shillings. He spent most of his time at Cairo racecourse. Lieutenant Harari was so fat that he walked with difficulty, but he was a brilliant linguist and came of a distinguished Levantine family. Lieutenant Jones was a moron; after a time I hid his hockey stick. To brighten up the camp Lieutenant-Colonel Duggan requisitioned bags of cement and got the Italians to erect a colonnade of life-size naked women outside the mess. He used to tap their behinds with his cane. He warned us that the Italians practised buggery on a large scale ('look out for tooth-marks on the backs of their necks'). Many of the Italians were clever with their hands, and to give them something to do they were ordered to make toys out of flattened petrol tins. They produced lewd figures with moving phalluses. Captain Freddy Browne, the England cricketer, a chubby-faced, good natured man, came to our mess to drink whisky. I played football with the NCOs against the Italians. They were rough matches, with much hacking.

Every morning batches of prisoners were paraded outside the bath and disinfestation unit while their clothes were deloused. They stood in the sand like penned sheep, scratching their crotches and calling to each other in high voices, their pale bodies disfigured by patches of dark hair. 'They're not much to look at,' said Lieutenant-Colonel Duggan, 'but by Jesus they're well hung!' Then one day the bath and disinfestation unit was destroyed by fire. Captain Webster was elated. 'I can now go back to Cairo', he said, packing his bedroll.

One of my duties was to confiscate the prisoners' money. Unlike the British soldier, who drew only a small part of his pay while under active service conditions, the Italians were loaded with paper money, which I collected and threw in bundles into empty ammunition boxes. Later, after we had landed in Italy, I sometimes regretted that I had not kept a few notes to exchange for vino and eggs. I heard of no attempts to escape from our camp, though there was much pro-Italian sentiment among the European population. Egyptian labourers who worked inside the camp were regularly searched. At the guard post they were made to lift up their gowns – they wore nothing underneath – while a soldier peered up their anuses.

The second-in-command of the Garwhali troops, a major, used to invite me to his tent. He loved his men. They thought of him as a father and came to him with their family problems. He used to sit on the ground talking to them in Urdu and sharing their chapattis. One of his soldiers acted as my bearer. He washed and starched my clothes and when I was changing for dinner held up my trousers for me to step into like a stork. Once, when I dozed off on a very hot afternoon, I woke to find my bearer fanning me with a magazine. The Garwhali had a shrill band with drums and native bagpipes. Under their puggarees their heads were shaven except for a greased black pigtail which, with their prominent cheekbones, gave them a Mongolian look. On guard duty they stood in sentry towers along the perimeter of the camp. The prisoners used open latrine trenches dug near the wire and some were always squatting there, searching their clothes for vermin. This unpleasant sight must have irritated one of the sentries, for one morning we heard shots. The sentry had fired his rifle at the squatting men. He didn't hit anyone. But two bullets struck the crowded officers' marquee.

Shortly after this we had a visit from the Swiss Red Cross accompanied by Colonel de Salis, a Maltese grandee from GHQ in Cairo. The Italian officers had been complaining about living in open cages; and there was the case of Sergeant Harvey (Highland Light Infantry), normally a patient man, who had kicked an Italian lieutenant so hard that the officer fell down. I was the officer on duty. At the time we thought nothing of the occurrence. No one in those days had heard of 'war crimes'. The Red Cross visit was followed by the arrival of Brigadier Selby, the Area Commander. One of the subjects of his inquiry was Sergeant Harvey's alleged assault on an Italian prisoner-of-war. The RSM, worried about the implications for his own reputation, took me aside to brief me. 'You know nothing, sir. All you know is that the officer tripped over a guy rope.'

The RSM stood behind me as we waited outside the orderly room to be called in by the brigadier. I could feel his breath on my neck. 'You know nothing, sir', he repeated.

Brigadier Selby, a powerfully-built Australian and a stickler for discipline, told me to describe the incident. I was in a quandary. Candour would have meant compromising Sergeant Harvey and the RSM, yet half-truths wouldn't wash. The Brigadier must have been aware of this. 'The Italian Lieutenant', I said, 'was insolent. Sergeant Harvey pushed him away with his foot. The officer lost his balance, tripped over a guy rope and fell. There was no assault, sir.'

The brigadier wasted no words in argument. He gave me a cold look. The euphemism 'pushed' had clearly scuppered me and next day I was sent to the infantry base depot near Fayed. Here I met Lieutenant Annie Aish (Royal Fusiliers) – a small, modest man who had been our college cricket captain and shove ha'penny champion (I heard later that he was killed in action against the Vichy French in Syria; a piece of fratricide that has made me bitter against the French). The depot had a cinema. When, at the end of a performance, the Egyptian national anthem was played, the soldiers jeered and sang their own words to it:

> King Farouk, King Farouk,
> Hang your bollocks on a hook ...

Then I was given a platoon and sent to Qassassin – a huge stretch of empty desert – to put up an emergency camp for several hundred soldiers who were expected after the débâcle on Crete. Sentries had to be vigilant. Local Egyptians had a habit of carrying off tents, which disappeared silently into the night like walking ghosts. They hung them in their feluccas as sails. On a visit to a South African detachment, I came across a lonely, round-shouldered figure with a protruding tooth who was tossing a tent mallet in the air and catching it. I immediately recognised him as 'Tuppy' Owen-Smith. He had been one of our heroes at Oxford. Owen-Smith had played cricket for the Springboks (in 1929 I saw him make a century at Edgbaston, dancing down the pitch like a mad gnome). He had also played rugby for England and won a boxing Blue. He was now MO to a unit of Cape Town Highlanders. They wore kilts, and filled me with beer.

The routed survivors of the Crete battle never arrived. All we got was a forlorn handful – about a dozen – of Palestine Jews in the Pioneer Corps. They were angry and disillusioned, complaining that the navy had evacuated all the English soldiers but left many of the pioneer battalion behind to their fate. If what they said was true, they had cause to grouse. Back at the depot I found a posting order. I was to join the Camp Commandant's staff at GHQ in Cairo.

GHQ MEF was a wired-off enclave of buildings in the Garden City of Cairo. Squeezed into a warren of improvised offices and cubicles that hummed with electric fans, a small army of chair-borne warriors, sticky with sweat, fought the paper war with an afternoon break for recreation (we worked Middle East hours). I shared an office with Captain Brown, a Rhodesian who wore dark glasses to hide the evidence of night revelries, and Captain Cann, a regular officer who read memoranda and stared out of the window. The Camp Commandant, Lieutenant-Colonel Catteral, was unapproachable till late in the morning. By then a dram or two of whisky (he kept a bottle in his lavatory) had prepared him to face another irritating day. Tropical uniform didn't suit him. He had thin white legs and his khaki shorts hung round him like starched bloomers.

GHQ employed a large number of other ranks. I had to take the weekly pay parade, censor the men's letters, and stamp and counter-sign officers' identification cards (including, on one occasion, the Auk's – General Auchinleck's). The men's letters, written on aerograms, gave some vivid glimpses of Cairo life ('the bints are smashing – they've got legs right up to their bums'). The writers signed off with the word SWALK (Sealed With A Loving Kiss). I didn't like reading private mail and managed to get rid of the job. At the pay parade I sat at a small table and at great speed paid out hundreds of soldiers. The cash balance, which I kept in my imprest box, had to be right to the last *mille*. 'If you're found to be a piastre down,' Cann warned me, 'you'll be up for court-martial.'

For some months Dunia had been living in a guest-house at Zamalek near the Gezira Club, and the army paid me a lodging allowance to stay with her. A temporary guest was Lawrence Durrell, who had been teaching in Greece. He was a small tubby man with a big head, a beautiful blonde wife (Nancy) and a small child. He usually carried a book, and kept to his own literary clique. After luncheon (sweet potatoes, egg-plant, rissoles and mangoes) I took Dunia to the Gezira Club to sit under a parasol at the Lido or to watch the cricket.

As office wallahs, we led a sybaritic life. Many of us were ill-suited to desk work and given the opportunity would have jumped at the chance to join a fighting unit. Yet the temptations to stay were many. Parkinson's Law was operative. Staff jobs led to quicker advancement than slogging it out in the field. Indian Army traditions made sure that the sahib lived in comfort. There were two splendid hotels (Shepheard's and the Continental), night-clubs with cabarets, girls and belly-dancers, and Groppi's two cafés for a rendezvous with nubile Greek ladies, who sometimes brought their parents with them.

When the Nile was in summer flood the humidity in Cairo was hard to bear; the papers on one's desk stuck to one's bare arms and sweat stains darkened one's shirt. I walked or took a rattling tram to the office. At dusk, as the sun set in an enormous ball of fire, the slight day breeze dropped, the dazzling white sky turned through red and green to purple and the palm trees stood out against the Nile like black candles. This was the time for the poorer Egyptians to prepare their evening bowls of rice, beans and onions: the pungent smell of cooking wafted out of every alley and doorway. The black-out was only partial. Cafés and eating places stayed open till late and were filled with hawkers, labourers and porters – spitting and smoking hookahs amid a deafening wail of Arabic music. Without exception the British Army looked down on the Egyptians as a lower species – as Wogs; and it is true that wherever soldiers went, they attracted the worst elements of the population. Many Egyptians, moreover, suffered from unattractive diseases or had crude physical blemishes: trachoma and glazed eyes, sores and mutilations, maimed limbs. Men with elephantiasis stretched swollen legs over the pavements. Flies crawled on the eyelids of babies. Donkeys had raw wounds. The women in their black gowns looked like crows. To the young British soldier fresh from some military depot in Lancashire, his stomach already churning with 'gyppy tummy', the lower classes seemed to inhabit a predatory world of deformities and smells.

One evening, out of curiosity, I took a look at Mary's House, the officers' brothel. I slipped in unnoticed and found myself on a dimly-lit landing with several doors. No madame was in sight, no plump whores in crumpled shifts. As I was leaving a door opened and an officer hurried past. I recognised him immediately as a former Oxford rugger Blue and England international. He was wearing suede desert boots; 'brothel creepers' was exactly the right name for them.

By now some of my old colleagues from Romania had been evacuated through Greece to Egypt. Reggie Smith and Olivia were for a time without jobs, and accused the British Council of neglecting them. They had only themselves to blame. Reggie was still spouting a woolly Communism which made him into a joke figure. Olivia was diffident and rude. The Allens, however, being practical people, got down straight away to the business of teaching and were posted to Alexandria.

The great event at this time (July 1941) was Hitler's declaration of war on Russia. I listened to part of Churchill's speech on the radio. The Nazi war machine, he growled, by marching into Russia, had rung its own death knell. This was just what the troops wanted to hear. Meanwhile, Dunia welcomed the fact that I was in a safe job. She didn't want me being dive-bombed by Stukas, now that the Afrika Corps had made its violent foray into the desert. But I was restless, and much relieved when at last I was promoted to Captain and sent as liaison officer to the Polish Officers' Legion at Amiriya, west of Alexandria. The Polish troops who had found their way to Egypt contained a surplus of officers, and the Legion was made up of about two hundred spare reservists, from Lieutenant to Colonel, whom the Carpathian Brigade, now reinforcing the garrison at Tobruk, was unable to absorb. We lived under canvas on a stretch of sandy desert. One of my duties was to instruct the officers in British Army organisation and technical vocabulary, using field manuals. The reserve officers were delightful and witty companions, but the senior men, some quite old, stood much on their dignity, and made the midday meal in the mess a long drawn-out ordeal. Only the Colonel and his cronies (who included the chaplain) were allowed to speak. They bored us with tedious anecdotes about Marshal Pilsudski. The Mess Officer, Lieutenant Barabas, turned out to be an old acquaintance from Gdynia, where he had managed the Maskot night-club. His forte was to prepare 'vodka' from surgical spirit adulterated with fruit juice.

The Poles spent much of their leisure in the honky-tonks of Alexandria. '*Pan Bog wysoko, zona daleko* (The Lord is far away, and so is my missus)', a Lieutenant explained to me in a bar. My British colleague with the unit was Captain Brodie of the Black Watch. The Poles liked him because he wore a kilt without underpants. My driver-batman, Private Whittaker, had been an undersized warehouse boy in Blackburn but was now putting on weight and muscle. 'I 'ardly ever saw the sun or ate decent grub till I came out 'ere', he said.

In February 1942 Stalin informed Cairo that in consequence of the German invasion, which had penetrated deep into the Caucasus, and the shortage of food supplies, he had agreed to release thousands of Polish soldiers and dependents from Soviet internment and to transfer them to British command in the Middle East. This was thrilling news for the Polish forces in the Middle East, as their numbers would now be substantially increased – we were told to expect an initial draft of some 40,000, though not all of them would be fighting men. They were to be assembled at Krassnodar, ferried across the Caspian to Pahlevi, thence transported by road through a chain of transit camps in Persia and Iraq to Palestine. To deal with this contingency, 26 BLU recruited new officers and I was sent to Iraq (part of the PAIFORCE command) to take over a collecting point at Habanya, a few miles from Baghdad. I spent a few days at HQ 10 Indian Division before moving to the Polish camp. HQ was immaculately laid out with oiled roads to keep down the dust and thunder-boxes for officers – one sat on a raised commode screened by hessian while a sweeper with a twig brush waited outside to remove the pot. To counteract heat exhaustion we swallowed an extra dose of salt at meals, and everyone took a siesta, sweating on our Indian string-beds like men with fever. The dried sweat left white patches of salt crystals on one's shirt, and the siesta was such a debilitating ordeal that I gave it up, and indeed never succumbed to the habit throughout my years in the Middle East and in Africa. The moment to look forward to was the sundowner, with a light evening breeze shaking the tent walls under the pressure lamp and a starlit sky that sucked the day's heat from the earth.

There was some panic among the divisional staff when we learned that the first Polish transports would include women. It was decided that they should be segregated and put under special guard. Our fears were of course groundless. The Poles were too hardened to need molly-coddling. The first batch included some girls from an entertainments group, who washed their faces in a bucket and put on a free perfor-mance. Veronica, in crumpled khaki and ammunition boots, stood in the sand and to the astonishment of my Sikh drivers sang like a lark in the headlights of our trucks.

The Poles arrived in open lorries driven by Persians, hungry and dust-covered after a bruising journey over mountain roads. In Teheran they had been paid a little money, and a local contractor whom I per-mitted to set up a canteen (I could hardly refuse him as I had already drunk the 'bribe' – a bottle of whisky he had left in a basket in my tent) made a small fortune selling soap, razor blades, drinks, cakes and water-melons. With the help of a New Zealand transport company the 40,000 Poles were ferried across the Syrian desert to Palestine. At one of the desert staging camps I was knocking in tent pegs when the Divisional Commander General Rees suddenly appeared from nowhere, alone in a staff car. He was so small that I almost failed to identify him. 'What sort of chaps are these Poles?' he asked me. 'Can we make soldiers out of them?' I said they were tough and hungry and took him to the cookhouse where a Pole with a big belly was stirring a pot of 'all-in' Polish stew. General Rees tasted it, poked the cook in the tummy and said, with a twinkle in his eye, 'This chap looks all right'. A few moments later he had driven off in a spray of dust.

The Polish Middle East Army was now concentrated in Palestine and occupied a string of tented camps along the coast. Another 70,000 Poles were due to arrive from Russia in a few weeks, and I spent the interval at a Polish training centre near Askalon. The sea broke against a line of sand-dunes; behind them, a fringe of cactus and wild grapes. A little inland the minarets of Arab villages stuck out above patches of corn and vegetables. The sea had a strong undertow, and several Poles – virtual non-swimmers, who had gone for a bathe – were swept away and drowned. This remote, sea-washed stretch of green-flecked sand, with its braying donkeys and the muezzin's call, had a biblical simplicity and beauty. I liked watching the Arabs bring back their flocks at dusk, stir-ring up a cloud of dust that settled on the old stone walls of Askalon like fine flour. The shepherds with their crooks and fierce, shining eyes, their patched gowns and chequered head-cloths, struck me as entirely in har-mony with their ancient surroundings. The Jewish settlements, by con-trast, scattered along the railway line towards Jaffa and Tel Aviv, seemed to be intruders from Europe. The settlers lived in ugly little con-crete cubes with water-towers and orange groves, sealed off by barbed wire. Tel Aviv was vulgar. It had night-clubs and prostitutes, and was hideously built of concrete blocks facing a hot, humid strand. Many Polish and East European Jews had settled here, an urban colony still bearing marks of the ill-health and poverty they had once suffered in the ghettos of Lublin and Lodz. Yet many of the Jewish youth were in a different mould. They marched about in scouts' uniforms with flags, bawling songs, noisy and bellicose, and they reminded me of Hitler Youth or Mussolini's *Giovanezza*. Whereas Tel Aviv was entirely Jewish, nearby Jaffa was unmistakeably Arab with its tumble-down courtyards and arches, its open-air stalls, the donkeys and wailing music and idle men sitting on stools.

The Poles, as a Catholic people, felt strongly about Jerusalem as a place of shrines and pilgrimage, and every soldier had a duty to visit it. To be closer to me, Dunia moved from Cairo to a hospice in Jerusalem. At weekends I visited her on my motor-cycle (a Norton, maximum speed 60 m.p.h.). Braced by the cool air high above the coastal plain, I tore up the mountain road, swerved round the tortuous bends of the Seven Sisters, passed the cypresses that marked the edge of the Holy City, and thundered into the yard of the hospice with an alarming noise. It was run by German nuns, and a few British officers were allowed to stay there. It was kept immaculate, like a sanatorium, in the customary German way. The nuns had embroidered the pillow-slips with chaste mottoes and angels' wings.

In August I returned to Iraq and was sent to Khanaqin to help prepare a large reception camp for the second draft of 70,000 Poles due to arrive from Russia the following month. Khanaqin was a mud-brick frontier town with open ditches and palm trees on the Iraq–Persian border, overlooked by the foothills of the Pai-Tak Pass. An Indian Pioneer Company under a Madrassi lieutenant had been called in to cover the baking yellow plain with a forest of tents. My six Sikh truck drivers (who refused tobacco but longed for neat whisky) were bemused when I took off my shirt and helped unload and erect tents instead of sitting in the shade with a fly swat. After the sweltering heat of the day, the air cooled rapidly at sunset, the stars seemed to close in and to shine more brilliantly, a faint breeze stirred the tent walls and jackals howled in the wadis. Gloriously content, I sat in a canvas chair with the Madrassi officer and a bottle of Canadian Black Horse beer while his men cooked our chapattis on a charcoal fire. He taught me a few phrases of Urdu which, like my first prep-school Latin, I have never forgotten. I like to baffle the Indian corner-shop owners in Twickenham with them. '*Ham kutta bahut maila hei*, The dog is dirty,' I complain, pointing at some pensioner's mongrel which is sniffing at the vegetables.

The Poles arrived in open trucks with Persian drivers. The latter were lean, scruffy men whom we learned to admire for their skill in steering their battered vehicles over the steep passes of the Persian mountains. The Poles, after their internment in Russia and the long, thirsty odyssey from Kazakstan, were in poor shape. They were suffering from the effects of malaria, typhus (many had shaved their heads as a precaution against lice) or from heat exhaustion. Our MO had advised me to place barrels filled with salt water at the debussing point: 'Every Pole must drink some.' The order caused much embarrassment. Caked in red dust, and parched, the Poles were appalled when they tasted the salty water and they angrily spat it out, thinking that if this was our welcome it was a poor English joke.

An early arrival was General Okulicki. He had a handsome lady with him, and was ashamed of his ill-fitting khaki shorts, wrinkled socks and white legs. I issued him with a brand-new Indian ridge tent and Australian blankets, which pleased him. Exhausted and uprooted, the Poles looked at first more like refugees than soldiers. They had brought a miscellany of camp followers with them: ballet dancers, cabaret artists and musicians, women and children, ageing intellectuals, and Jews. One of them, shuffling through the sand in baggy khaki, was Menachim Begin, the future Zionist terrorist leader and Prime Minister of Israel. Another misfit was the anonymous private who later became notorious in the London underworld as the rent racketeer Rachmann.

With the simultaneous transfer of other Polish army units, including the Carpathian Brigade, from Egypt and Palestine to the Paiforce command, Khanaqin and nearby Qisl Ribat – where headquarters of the new Polish force under General Anders was now set up – seethed with Poles. The first task was to weed out the dependants and the unfit, and evacuate them to Palestine, East Africa, Cape Town and India. The overall plan was to reorganise the able-bodied into a corps of two infantry divisions (two brigades each) and an armoured brigade with supporting arms and services, on British war establishment lines, and to train, equip and prepare them for battle. It was estimated that this would take a year. Many hundreds of drivers, for instance, had to be trained before the corps could become mobile.

I was posted to 5 Kresowa Infantry Division as training and liaison officer, and sewed the divisional sign (a brown bison) on my sleeve. As my Norton was the only motor-bike in the division, it was an object of wonder and admiration until fifty heavy American Harley-Davidson machines appeared and were issued to the military police, who soon wrote several of them off. I shared a tent with Major Macartney, a young journalist from Manchester, and later with Captain Gilbert, a Polish-speaker who had been brought up in Lodz. There were no more eggs and rashers of tinned bacon, or treacle pudding. We ate Polish meals, and 'George', our Polish batman, an illiterate peasant from

Bialystok, brought us dismal breakfasts of bread spread with a mixture of margarine, jam and cheese, and a glass of tea without milk (*herbata*). The Polish cooks used to tip most of the rations into camp kettles and boil everything – meat, rice, vegetables – into an 'all-in' soup. Surplus tea (the Poles found the British tea ration excessive) they flogged to local Kurds for water-melons and hooch.

Every morning at six we were woken by the noise of hundreds of bare-chested men gargling and spitting as they cleared their throats and rinsed their faces in mess-tins of water. It was fascinating to watch an infantry division build itself up from nothing – from the first primitive repair facilities and medical aid posts, cast-off Indian Army Chevrolet trucks, pathetic Boyes anti-tank rifles and old 18-pounder guns, to well-equipped workshops and hospitals, Bren carriers, armoured scout cars, heavy mortars and modern artillery. Mac and I were kept busy attending training programmes and tactical exercises, scooting round the hills with Polish staff officers.

The Kurdish villages in the neighbourhood had been put out of bounds to prevent drunken brawls and indiscipline among the soldiers. Most of the Kurds spent summer on the higher slopes above the valleys, pasturing their flocks among mountain springs and fresh grass. Those who stayed behind lived in thatched huts, with a few crops. The women were unveiled, with tousled raven hair. They wore trailing, colourful skirts, had shrill voices, and looked like witches. One of their jobs was to collect the fresh animal dung with their bare hands and knead it into cakes. When dried, it was burnt as fuel. Men had an easier life. They rode about on horses and carried rifles. When I explored the hills on my motor-bike, armed horsemen in turbans would race me along *wadis*; and when I came to a village, sharp-faced women would duck into their hovels like sand-crabs while a man with a rifle would come out and stare silently at me. Twice I went with Polish officers on a dawn wild-boar shoot. We took cover among swampy reeds, drank brandy, and shot nothing. Despite being warned of the risk of trichina, Poles prepared sausages from the meat.

Maintaining a British liaison presence among the Poles meant drinking with them and joining in their entertainments – football, concerts and parties. Knowing the language was a great advantage ('You're God's gift to the Poles', one of my colleagues said to me sarcastically. When the Poles celebrated with a party, a parade, a religious service or a commemoration, they did so with flair. At one open-air concert in the desert huge trenches were dug in a semi-circle round the stage to seat thousands of officers and men. We ate a lavish meal watching the Krakowiak, Obereczek and Mazurka performed by dancers in traditional costume. At parades the Poles sang their national anthem with moving fervour.

It is a lively, bracing tune, and it was sung here by men who reacted emotionally to its message:

> Jeszcze Polska nie zginela
> Poki my zyjemy
>
> Poland has not perished yet
> So long as we still live.

'*Bog, Honor i Ojczyzna*' – God, Honour and Fatherland – was the soldier's motto. The Kresowa Division's choir with its beautiful Slavonic chants and folk melodies was remarkably professional. It would have thrilled a Welsh (or Irish) audience. Alas, the average British soldier has no musical sense. After a few beers he can bellow like a bull, but he cannot sing. The Poles were proud too of their football team. In Baghdad, it beat the British army Paiforce team, even though the latter fielded the complete half-back line of Bolton Wanderers.

Mac and I became close friends of two lieutenants – Chalupnik (Little Cottager) and Djekan (The Deacon). They kept Palestine brandy and sardines under their bunks. Chalupnik was a schoolmaster and plant specialist: Djekan a minor official – his feet were so flat that he limped; but it was the spirit of a man, not his physical condition, his asthma or murmuring heart, that decided a Polish medical board whether he was fit or not for active service. Chalupnik was making a study of English scatological words. The schoolboy expression for masturbation ('flogging the bishop') delighted him. 'We have the exact equivalent in Polish', he said '*Zastrzepac kapucina*, stroking the Capuchin' (a Capuchin friar too has a hood or *capuca*).

I learned much about Polish morale, and how upset they were by the decision of many Polish soldiers to stay behind in Russia with Colonel (later General) Berling. Berling was assembling a Polish army to fight under Soviet command. My friends considered this to be treachery; Berling and his men were aiding an enemy who had profited from Hitler's invasion of September 1939 to occupy eastern Poland and drag people into captivity. Anti-Russian feeling was particularly strong in the Kresowa Division as most of its soldiers came from the eastern parts of Poland, and they feared that Stalin intended to swallow their homeland.

It was understandable too that the Poles should feel a sense of frustration at being stuck in the military backwater of Iraq far from the victorious campaign being fought in North Africa. They could console themselves initially with the knowledge that, as part of the Paiforce command, they were filling the role of a defensive barrier against a German advance through the Caucasus into the Middle East. But the collapse of Paulus's army at Stalingrad in January 1943 meant the end of this threat. My own feelings were of embarrassment that Britain, despite her guarantee to Poland of 31 March 1939, had been unable to protect her ally during the September campaign. George, my batman, after a drink or two, used to cheer me up. 'Panie Kapitanie, when we return to Poland with flags flying I'll give you a plot of land.'

The Poles were astute bargain-hunters – understandably so in view of their years of privation in Russia. They combed the Teheran and Baghdad bazaars for jewellery and silver filigree work. In Palestine they stocked up with watches, clothes and souvenirs. Our HQ mess officer, an enterprising Jewish Lieutenant, was often away on purchasing errands in Palestine and Egypt. Officers collected Egyptian gold sovereigns. When, four years later, at the end of hostilities, I watched Polish soldiers embark for demobilisation in Poland, loaded with spare blankets and boots, I understood that, for them, these small spoils of war were a vital insurance against a future which might threaten them with beggary. I bought George a watch from Tel Aviv. He never used it, but kept it wrapped up in cotton wool in its little box. The soldiers' habit of hoarding and of saving their pay, however, was unwise, as it encouraged theft.

The lack of women was less of a problem because, if all are celibate, there is no one to envy. The fifty Polish ATS girls who lived in a separate tented enclave, and the hospital nurses, had their calf-eyed courtiers, yet we heard of only one scandal, when an ATS girl (in Kirkuk) shot herself with her boyfriend's revolver. No one thirsted after the Arab girls in Baghdad who were hired out by pimps and wore metal rings that jangled on their arms and ankles. I got my only glimpse of harem life when I slept one night on the flat roof of the Mission hostel in Baghdad. Looking across to the next roof I saw four string-beds on it. In them lay three women shrouded in black gowns. A little later I heard sounds of quarrelling and was fascinated to watch the antics of the husband. He was an old white-bearded fellow in slippers. Every time he sat on one of the beds, the three women pushed him away. Eventually he gave up in disgust and shuffled downstairs to the river bank, where I could hear him urinating into the Tigris.

On Christmas Eve we gathered quietly in the mess, where the second-in-command gave each of us a piece of consecrated wafer. There were prayers, a simple meal, and we went early to bed. After a short, invigorating winter, spring came in with a rush. Within a few days the red-brown earth was sprouting grass and the plain behind our camp turned into a sea of rustling wild flowers. Donkeys brayed and copulated, and the arrival of some birds delighted the Poles. 'They are *polski szpaki* (Polish starlings)', said George. 'They've tracked us down all the way from Poland.' Soon afterwards the Kresowa Division moved eighty miles north-west to Kirkuk to replace 56 London (Black Cat) Division.

Kirkuk has an important oilfield. Night and day it threw off a burning gas flare and filled the air with a stench like rotten eggs. The British liaison section of the Division was now brought together, and Major Quinn's first concern was to build a latrine 'for the use of British officers only'. Hitherto I had used a trench latrine with the rest of the Poles – crouching over it on a windy wintry morning had been a tricky business. Soon, however, we found that Polish other ranks from far and wide were converging on our little screened-off privy. Captain Broughton reported that they 'cleaned their bottoms with bits of wood'. Broughton himself had peculiar habits. He used to get up in the middle of the night and heat a tin of steak and kidney pie on his primus. No wonder he was constipated ('Nothing comes out but bum dust').

Field exercises, manoeuvres and specialist courses kept the Division busy. There were night operations with Indian troops; Polish artillery shoots set fire to Kurdish crops. The liaison section played football matches against the Poles and cricket with a broom handle and tennis ball. Then in April 1943 we heard the shocking news from Berlin of the discovery at Katyn (near Smolensk) of the mass graves of thousands of missing Polish officers. The Germans claimed they had been shot by the Russians. Moscow Radio countered this by accusing the Nazis of the massacre. The Poles dismissed the Russian claim and asked for an immediate International Red Cross inquiry. The result was that Stalin broke off the recently restored diplomatic relations with the Polish government in exile, and concentrated on building up General Berling's Home Army in Russia. In July there was more bad news for the Poles: Sikorski had been killed in a flying accident at Gibralter (only the Czech pilot survived). It was at about this time, with the Poles in a state of gloom, that Brigadier Way sent me on a temporary transfer to Jerusalem. 'You will be able to see your wife again,' he said.

As liaison officer to HQ Palestine Command I had an office opposite the King David Hotel, and a clerk, Corporal Holmes, with shining boots and perfect manners. I had little to do except read the files and help find jobs for Polish Legion officers in the military administration of Abyssinia and other far-away places where there was a demand for 'experienced veterans who could handle men'. I lived at the German hospice with Dunia, sat in its shady garden eating fruit cake, and slept in a bed with a German feather quilt. Captain Rodzianko, the well-known equestrian who had served in the Tsar's cavalry, was a visitor – he was attracted to Dunia. Rodzianko was looking after army remounts left behind at Sarafand by yeomanry regiments who had been mechanised. One day I ran into Reggie Smith. He had been appointed Controller of the English and American programmes of the Palestine Broadcasting Services. The news of his appointment astonished me. In a time of psychological warfare how could a Communist, however genial, be chosen for a top job as propagandist in the Imperial cause?

When 2 Polish Corps was transferred from Iraq to Palestine I rejoined 5 Kresowa Division, which was preparing to move to Egypt for embarkation to Italy. The Corps had turned the coast between Gaza and Ramleh into a Polish enclave. Dunia gave me a small luxury – a sheepskin jacket bought in an Arab bazaar in Jerusalem. I had heard that winter in the snow-covered Italian Alps was grim.

Chapter 6

Campaign in Italy

I sailed from Port Said for Taranto in early January 1944 with an advance party of 5 Kresowa Division in the troopship *Nottingham*, with destroyer escort. The 3rd Carpathian Division had preceded us and had already moved north. Massive desertion by Jewish soldiers had overshadowed the preliminaries to embarkation. The missing men were reported to have gone to ground in the kibbutzim, a total of 3,000, according to Polish sources, of their original number (4,000). Zionist organisations had been actively recruiting among them; but they waited till they had been trained in the use of weapons before deserting. The loss of their special skills – in ordnance and signals, as sappers, artificers and clerical staff – was serious. Yet many Poles said 'good riddance to the bastards!' Moreover, the Jewish soldier's feeling of personal insecurity within the Polish army had to be taken into account. He was never quite accepted, and Polish Jewish officers were rarely promoted above the rank of Lieutenant. It took a little time for us to realise that, for the Jews, as the war unfolded, the enemy had changed. Since Stalingrad Hitler's armies were in retreat, and it was now Britain, the Mandatory power in Palestine, who was the prime obstacle in the way of a Zionist state. It was the British soldier and policeman that Zionist gangs were preparing to ambush and kill.

I had been looking forward to the thrill of setting foot again in Europe after nearly four years' absence, but the first sight of southern Italy was disappointing. It seemed little different from North Africa. Here were the same ragged barefoot children and tousled black-haired women, the same shacks, poverty and donkeys – even a case or two of bubonic plague in Taranto. I pitched my small bivvy tent in a muddy field and took over an abandoned Jeep with no hood or windscreen in which I bumped and swerved through the rutted lanes like a wet rabbit. To safeguard it against thieves I removed the distributor when I parked.

Our first move was in slow convoy to Colle Dell' Arena, a mountain salient near Campobasso, where we relieved the French. On the way the liaison section found billets in villages. The young Italian men had vanished – either called up, captured or hiding in the mountains. Bolder spirits had joined the partisans. The little stone houses were cold and miserable – smoky dens with a tiny fire and a cooking pot on a tripod, and an adjoining room with a large family bed, and onions hanging from the rafters. Many of the villages were perched like cairns on hilltops, turreted and walled, with crooked alleys too narrow for vehicles. We stayed at a priest's house for two days. He had a flush lavatory, and warned us not to block it with paper. There was a basket for used sheets. The priest, a timid, rubicund man, was looked after by a housekeeper who, one assumed, was his mistress.

Our salient was dominated by snow-covered mountains. It was a time of desultory shelling, patrols and fire-fights. There was a 'mad mile' to our forward positions that was under harassing fire and kept drivers alert. Then, towards the end of April, came the exhilarating news that we were moving to Cassino.

Three previous attempts, with bitter fighting and heavy casualties, had already been made by the Allied forces to break through the Cassino defences and thus open the road to Rome. Americans, French, New Zealand, Indian and British troops had tried in vain to dislodge the Germans from their fortified positions among the shattered rocks, the ravines, ridges and mud of a now ruined landscape. The Benedictine Abbey of Monte Cassino, though smashed to rubble by a massive American daylight bombing raid on 15 February, and the adjacent heights running up to Monte Cairo – known as the Gothic Line, with the Hitler Line behind it – still dominated the Rapido and Liri valley approaches from the plain below. To the west, on the sea coast, the Anzio bridgehead continued to be bogged down. The Poles felt honoured to have been asked to play a key role in what was now looked forward to as the fourth and final assault on the stubborn mountain fortress of Cassino.

Advance HQ was set up at the head of the Inferno track. This was a narrow ravine, widened by sappers, leading down to the Rapido valley and the wrecked Monte Villa barracks. Whittaker, my batman, secured my bivvy tent to a cliff wall. Along the crest of the pass behind us, huge camouflage nets had been hung to deny the enemy observation of traffic movement. After weeks of winter rain and mud, spring had brought mild weather and freshened the ragged gorse clinging to the rocky mountain sides. There was no enemy air activity – only one of our own Lysander spotter planes circling overhead – and in our sheltered spot little harassing fire. I took off my shirt and sunbathed.

There were conferences to attend. Kresowa Division was due to relieve 78 (Battle Axe) Division, and at my first meeting with the Irish Brigade's staff officers, in a dug-in bunker, we were stonked. No one took any notice of the interruption. Later, when I rode down the Inferno track on my motor-cycle and turned along the valley road, in full view of the enemy, I felt alarmingly vulnerable, though I was but a pin-point in the dust. The monastery and Monte Cassino seemed to tower over the valley like an all-seeing eye. Their dominating position and artillery observation posts, with Monte Cairo to the north and Monte Maio to the south, gave the enemy an immense moral as well as tactical advantage: we felt exposed, as though being constantly watched. To blind the German observers, smoke canisters laid a screen of smoke along the valley, and daylight movement was strictly controlled. But after dark the Allied front sprang into ant-like activity as supplies, stores and men moved out of their hiding places in caves and gullies to forward outposts. Soon I almost lost my trusty Norton. I had left it at the edge of a supply dump in a bend of the Inferno track, and scrambled up the steep mountainside to visit a New Zealand unit perched on the reverse slope. I was hoping for news of my old Oxford acquaintance Geoffrey Cox, who had distinguished himself as a foreign correspondent and was now one of General Freyberg's intelligence officers. Cox was away. When I descended I found that the dump had been hit and was ablaze with exploding ammunition and flying splinters. Luckily my motor-bike had survived, though the petrol tank was riddled with holes.

The day before the Poles took over from 78 Division I spent with the Inniskilling Fusiliers in their forward positions north of the monastery, making arrangements for the relief. Here a mountain track climbing up a steep and narrow gorge above Villa Maria barracks, known as Cavendish (or Sappers') Road, widened out into an open bowl leading to the German-held Phantom Ridge and Colle Sant' Angelo. It was up this track that the nightly supplies of food and ammunition were delivered by Cypriot pack-mules. The place was under constant fire. The CO of the Inniskilling Fusiliers was sleeping on the floor of a small stone barn, with the chaplain. The battalion, cramped among the rocks and scattered corpses within earshot of the enemy, was weary and looking forward to being relieved.

When the first Poles emerged at the top of the Cavendish track after dark the following night, I was thrilled to recognise my old friends of the 6th Lwowska Brigade. They were sweating under their equipment. Not all of them were young, but they were shaved and smart. As they moved across the open ground to their holes and bunkers we were heavily stonked. No one hurried or looked for cover. I felt happy to be with these silent and determined men.

The Poles spent the following two weeks building up supplies. I was out every night checking and guiding the mule trains and Jeep convoys with trailers carrying stores, water and ammunition up Cavendish Road to the offloading point at the mouth of the gorge. Dead bodies of mules, grossly swollen, littered the lower slopes where they had been tossed over the cliff edge. They gave off the same sickly-sweet smell as decomposing human corpses. The Cypriot muleteers, men of few words, tramped miles every night. They could, however, shield themselves from shell splinters and blast behind the great muscular bodies of their patient animals. Many of the Polish Jeep drivers were inexperienced and it wasn't easy for them, without lights, to pick their way in the black night up the narrow winding gorge. An English Lieutenant sometimes came to see how things were going. During the worst stonks we lay under his Jeep and he told jokes. For the soldiers, cramped and squeezed in their rock shelters and dug-outs within a few hundred yards or less of the enemy, this period of waiting was a trying time. Because it was necessary to conceal their strength from the Germans, the Poles had been forbidden to send out patrols. But the Germans knew that their old Polish enemies were in the battle area. Their artillery fired propaganda pamphlets over our lines. I picked one up. It had a grinning death's-head, was written in Polish, and called on the Poles to desert. The Poles, it said, were being tricked into shedding their blood for the western Allies when their real enemy, the Russian Bolsheviks, perpetrators of the Katyn massacre of Polish officers, was already threatening the Polish homeland. Meanwhile there was a steady drain of casualties, and the dead of several nations, blackened and ghastly, lay unburied among the rocks and jagged stumps and gorse.

Towards the mouth of the gorge, on a reverse slope, there was a Polish mortar position. The officer was a wiry, thin-faced Lieutenant with gold and metal teeth. He would give me a hot drink when I crawled into the cairn of stones which his men had fashioned into a bunker. Like other Poles his wartime memories were of the Russians, not of Germans. He repeated the old story about the Russian camp guards being so thick that some prisoners had 'strapped painted onions to their wrists and sold them as watches'. Through the entrance to his little shelter we sat listening to the howl of *Nebelwerfer* rockets and watched them burst in gouts of flame and red-hot splinters. The rockets, electrically fired from trucks with multi-barrelled launching platforms, had perforated fins that made them scream in flight like banshees. The Poles called them 'Stalin's organs'. They were not only spectacular – they were dangerous because the salvoes had an unpredictable spread.

I saw little of my British colleagues at this time. Divisional HQ was over a mile to the rear. People there were going about their normal business – eating regular meals, with batmen-drivers to wash their shirts. Shelling there was sporadic, the sky almost empty of enemy planes. One was struck by the unfairness of war: the gulf between those who slept in comparative safety in their bunks or bed rolls and those, less than two thousand yards away, who could scarcely move without being shelled, mortared or shot at, let alone carry off their dead.

On the eve of the assault, an operations section of Advance Division HQ moved into a cave towards the top of the Cavendish gorge. Captains Zebrowski and Lysek were in charge. Both were bright young staff officers who had been posted from England to fill gaps in Anders's staff. Lysek, as the result of a wound, had an artificial hand in a leather glove. The battle plan was that the Eighth Army would break into the Liri valley, deal with Cassino, and push on towards Rome along Route 6. On the left, the Fifth Army would advance towards Rome astride the other main road, Route 7, and through the mountains that made up the left wall of the Liri valley. The task of the Polish Corps, operating from the mountain salient north of Monte Cassino, was to drive the parachutists from the Cassino massif, and pushing down the slopes to cut Route 6, where they would link up with 13 Corps on its left. This meant that the Carpathian Division was to take Point 593 (Snakeshead Ridge) and Albaneta and attack the monastery by way of Points 569 and 476. Kresowa Division was to take Phantom Ridge and Colle Sant' Angelo.

At 11 p.m. on 12 May the jagged mountain skyline was lit up by a sheet of flame as over 1,600 Allied guns opened up with a thunderous roar along the whole of the 8th and 5th Army fronts. The tremendous barrage lasted for an hour. I was lying on a rocky slope with one of the reserve battalions near its start line. Despite the racket, I remember a nightingale calling among the burnt gorse and shattered tree stumps. When it was light I went to see Colonel Rudnicki of 6 Lwowska Brigade at his command post in a small stone farm building. The area was being shelled from Passo Corno. The news was not good, and the colonel was looking grave. The Poles had been beaten back from their objectives and obliged to withdraw. Casualties were heavy and the wounded were being brought down the mountain (one of the ambulance vehicles I saw in the Liri Valley was manned by some splendid American Quakers). A farm building where I took cover was hit and soldiers were wounded. For the Poles it had been a disappointing day.

My recollections of the following days are fragmentary and I am no longer certain of the exact sequence of events. Often it is the irrelevant that I remember most clearly: a Maori soldier holding a bottle of beer and wearing a top hat in a Jeep loaded with cheering New Zealanders; a Polish general's white bottom as he stopped to crouch behind a rock; the mortar officer's steel front teeth; a capsized field gun and a soldier rolling down a steep bank; and bodies – the carcass of a mule with its stiffened legs stuck up like a praying mantis; the greenish faces and staring blue eyes of dead Poles. After the failure of the first attack, the Poles regrouped, sent out patrols, and got ready to try again in two or three days' time. I was sent with an English gunner officer to look for an OP from which counter-battery fire could be directed on enemy positions that were harassing the Poles from the slopes of Monte Cairo, at Passo Corno. I remember an unpleasant moment – and the smell – when we found a suitable spot and I put my hand on a German helmet. It had the maggoty remains of a human head inside it. Coming back, I was asked to escort a German prisoner to the first aid post. He was a young Panzer grenadier with a round grimy face and was wounded in the arm and shoulder. I gave him my arm to lean on. He was relieved to see that I was English. *Polacken*, he said, had a reputation for shooting their prisoners.

Then there was a comic incident when two or three Polish tanks that had managed to drive up Cavendish Road were being viciously stonked at the edge of open ground. Colonel Bobinski, the regimental commander, was strolling about with a stick as though on a Sunday walk. Some of the crew jumped into a hole dug underneath one of the tanks and I joined them. I was the last man in. Alas, my bottom was sticking out and I felt a sudden sharp stab from a splinter. A 'buttock' wound! Colonel Bobinski laughed. I think it was on this day that a Polish signal informed me that Dunia had given birth to our daughter Gillian in Cairo.

The Poles attacked again on the night of 16–17 May, with Kresowa Division concentrating, as before, on Phantom Ridge and Colle Sant' Angelo. By midnight they had taken Phantom Ridge. But they were held up at Colle Sant' Angelo and driven back. They were now critically short of ammunition. As I knew the exact location of the dump, I was told to take a party of some twenty men – hastily gathered together from cooks and drivers – to fill sandbags with ammunition and see that they were delivered to the forward companies. I was glad to be of real use, and the job was done. In the morning I found the battalion commander (Colonel Damien) and some of his men standing on the captured ridge among corpses. We were still under fire, and the enemy was hammering away from Passo Corno. But the Poles had moved down the southern slope, isolating the monastery, which a patrol of the

Carpathian Podolski Lancers entered later that morning. By then the Germans had withdrawn from the monastery ruins, leaving behind a few wounded and some Italian civilians.

The first thing I saw as I walked towards the great pile of debris was an Allied tank with its crew lying dead on the ground. The tank had been part of a mixed armoured force sent weeks earlier, on 17 March, during the third Cassino battle, to attack the monastery from the rear. The operation was badly managed. The tanks had been halted near Albaneta Farm and the Germans had used the pause to destroy most of them. The tank with its spread-eagled crew had got closer to the monastery than any of the others, but its gesture had been in vain.

The monastery had been smashed into an enormous pile of blackened rubble. Only the western wall was still standing. A few ragged civilians were moving like ghosts among the debris. The Polish flag was flying from a mound of broken masonry. There had been a brief ceremony when it was hoisted, with a Polish bugler sounding the Cracow *hejnal*; a Union Jack was added later. My feelings as I stood there were mixed. The savage results of the bombing were awe-inspiring. It might have been said that this calculated act of aerial destruction was vandalism and blasphemy. Yet pulverising the Abbey into smoke and dust had significantly boosted Allied morale. Everyone had hated that all-seeing eye gazing down into the valley, watching and dominating our movements. Nevertheless, there were those who thought that the bombing of Cassino and the Abbey may have been a tactical mistake. It resulted in a barrier of craters and rubble that was a death-trap to attacking soldiers and that the Germans found easily defensible. The Poles felt especially bad about the wrecking of this great religious building. 'We are Catholics,' they said, 'and the Polish nation is not at war with the Italians. We are here to fight Germans.' The captain of a pack-mule company whose bunker (lined with empty beer crates) was at the foot of the Inferno track told me he had watched the bombing with trepidation. 'The bombing wasn't very accurate. Stray bombs fell among my men and mules and there were casualties.' General Freyberg, however, the man on the spot, had concluded that the bombing was tactically and psychologically necessary, and Alexander had accepted his judgment.

As I came back, picking my way through charred stumps and stones, I passed some Polish soldiers burying the German dead in a shallow common grave. The field-grey bodies lay crumpled and distorted among the boulders. The rocks and ridges hid other corpses – those of Allied soldiers who had been lying unburied for weeks, the flesh mummified, faces shredded into bony masks, their boots, polished by rain, unexpectedly black and shiny. Rough mounds, some with a helmet placed on a stone or a piece of wood with a name, showed where

Moroccan *goums* and Americans had been buried. I saw my old batman, George, with a stretcher-party. They were bringing back Polish dead, wrapped in blankets, and adding them to the rows piled alongside the advanced dressing station in a swarm of flies. When I got back to the cave where I had left Zebrowski and the Operations section, I found that my motor-bike, which I had propped in a hollow in the cliff, had been squashed in the night by a tank and thrown over the edge to join the dead mules.

Isolated Germans on Points 575 and 505 continued to hold out until the following day, and I recall watching a Polish officer interrogate a captured prisoner from an Alpine Jaeger regiment. I felt embarrassed, as the officer was threatening the man with his pistol. The young prisoner stood there, looking dumb. On the 20th the Poles moved on to attack Piedimonte, the strongly-fortified pivot of the Hitler Line which ran behind the Gustav Line from the slopes of Monte Cairo through Aquino and Pontecorvo. Piedimonte was protected by a screen of dug-in Tiger tanks. When it fell to the Poles on 25 May the little town was wrecked: a single church tower, its top crumbling, was still standing. With Zebrowski I went into some of the German bunkers. They were dry and solidly built. Discarded weapons, equipment, clothes and cooking gear were lying about. I took a Mauser rifle and a leather belt with *Gott Mit Uns* stamped on the clasp, but I soon gave them away.

My last memory of Cassino was a magnificent view from the top of Monte Cairo. It took me well over an hour to climb there, and I had to look out for mines. The Germans had left behind signals equipment, ammunition, tinned food and scattered letters. The neatly wrapped packets of dark rye bread brought back memories of my camping trips in Germany in the early 1930s. The summit of Monte Cairo was a superb observation point. The mountains, range after range, cut by ravines and passes, winding tracks and stream beds, lay below like a wild jigsaw puzzle. To the south the road to Rome through Aquino shimmered in sunshine. Cassino itself, in its pall of dust, looked as though it had been gutted, chopped and lacerated by giant claws.

After the battle the Poles moved out of the line to rest, replace casualties and re-equip. We were billeted in a village. Every morning I walked with a book to a field and watched the farmer plough it with two big white oxen. I envied him. He had survived the bombing and the war, he had not been taken prisoner and made to squat on his heels with a tin mug and spoon and lice in his shirt. He was not hiding in the mountains, or cowering with partisans in a ditch. He had been up since dawn; and at midday he took a siesta under a tree. The fields were sprinkled with poppies, the air free of the sickly smell of death. In the last few weeks I felt I was getting to know a little more about myself:

the element of danger was not unattractive and I had steady nerves. As for the Poles, they had won back some of their trampled honour; and among them I had found people I could admire and identify with.

Encouraged by the capture of Rome, the army now had high hopes of sweeping the Germans from Italy and marching on Vienna. From our rest area the division moved on east across the mountains to the Adriatic coast, then turned north through Ortona and Pescara to Castel Borodino, following the battle-scarred route opened up by the Canadian Corps. Ortona was badly damaged. It would have been too much to expect its few shabby citizens to raise their hands in welcome as we rattled past the broken shops and bomb craters. Again I had the uncomfortable feeling that a soldier is not only a 'liberator': he is a destroyer. The dust on the churned-up road was so thick that the Sikhs had covered their mouths and beards with strips of cloth that made them look like mummies. Cool, blue and empty, the sea slid away on our right but there was no stopping to bathe. From Castel Borodino we turned inland into the foothills, and now the business of hunting the retreating Germans began. It was exhilarating to have them on the run. The terrain, however, was intersected by rivers and streams flowing down from the mountains to the sea, and the *Todt* organisation had prepared the German defences well. The approaches to river crossings were mined and covered by enemy strong points, bridges were blown, and every crossing cost time and casualties. A cloud of smoke followed by a rumble a mile or two ahead meant that the German sappers had demolished another bridge or culvert almost under our noses.

I had been issued with another motor-cycle (an Ariel) and bowled through the foothills and rolling fields and vineyards as though on a picnic. It was a joy to be alone. Farmers came out of their cottages to wave and offer me wine and raw eggs, which I sucked through a hole in the shell. I remember well the dark, creased faces of the farmers and their wives, their black, friendly eyes and thick brown fingers and the greetings we exchanged in my broken Italian – 'Dove il ponte?' 'Il ponte e rotto.' 'Dove i Tedeschi?' 'Niente – Tedeschi finito, sono andati via – hanno tutto rubato . . .' 'The Germans have gone – they've stolen everything – not a chicken left.' At one village I was given a civic welcome. The mayor and his cronies, a few wild-looking partisans with firearms, a donkey and a blind man were waiting outside the *prefectura*. They gave me pasta and wine. The mayor made a speech, and I grinned like a moron. I knew I was bogus: an interloper being treated like a royal messenger. Yet the villagers' joy was touching. For them the bombing, the razing of homes and the maiming of cattle by gun-fire were over. The battle zone, like a forest conflagration, had moved on, and they had survived.

'Liberating' the Italian countryside was not always a picnic. As we entered one village with a ford we were greeted by salvoes of shells. The partisans who had come out to cheer us vanished with their weapons, tiles fell off the *taverna*, and we had to take cover behind a wall while the road erupted into craters. Near Filitrano, next day, the Germans put up stiff resistance. We had casualties – at the ford a young soldier was hit and fell, staring back at us with sightless eyes, another was severed through the waist into two bloody pieces of flesh like butcher's meat. I attached myself to a company that was held up in a maize-field by machine-gun fire. Reinforcements quickly arrived by Bren carrier. The men were shaved and clean, and immediately came under fire – it seemed they were loath to take cover. This was something I had learned about the Poles – they didn't like digging-in, or scraping out holes. I think their 'carefree' attitude, often described as 'recklessness' – the Poles were notably aggressive in attack – was bound up with their old cavalry traditions and their code of *honor*. At midday I was stuck for over an hour in a farm building with two soldiers while we were heavily mortared. Pieces of roof fell in and holes appeared in the walls. It was one of those situations where one had time to reflect on one's attitude to being killed or wounded. I think it can be agreed that in battle one accepts the risks and maybe is exhilarated by them; given luck (or is it faith?), a certain degree of natural caution (the survival instinct), and the comradeship of his mates, a soldier has no grounds to complain.

During a pause I joined Major Florkowski, CO of 18 Battalion, whose troops were attacking a white palazzo screened by trees. A unit of the Italian Liberation Army was in support. Some were in shorts, without helmets. They lay on the ground with their bare legs looking like hairy caterpillars among the brambles. Major Florkowski was young and agile, with a sense of humour. I was lying a few yards from him when a mortar bomb pitched right in front of me. It didn't explode. '*Job tvoyoo mat!*' I said to the major, using an obscenity. He smiled as we both crawled behind a small mound. How comforting is the ground as the soldier hugs its every protuberance like a dung-beetle. When the Poles took the villa in the afternoon, it was wrecked. Furniture, bedding and books were piled on the floor. Among the books I spotted an illustrated copy of *Pinocchio* and put it in my pocket. Later that evening the Germans opened up with self-propelled guns, but there was no counter-attack, and I slept in a farmyard. A wounded Pole was brought in on a stretcher. He was dying, and talking to himself. '*Polska ... Boze Matka ...*' The words were like a prayer, and indescribably desperate. Even this dying peasant was a romantic dreamer, talking his strange tongue in a foreign land.

From the fighting round Filitrano and Jesi, during the Poles' advance on Ancona, I have a vivid memory of an anti-tank gun blasting an Italian farmstead, and the shelling of some white cottages on the breast of a hill where the Germans had a machine-gun post. The armour-piercing shells went straight through the walls of the farm and wrecked it. Two elderly Italians and a small girl crawled out into the yard, shell-shocked and caked in dust. Their three magnificent white oxen, huge, docile animals, lay dead in a field. The German machine-gunners had vanished from the hill, leaving their familiar smell – leather and sweat – behind them. I wondered at the Italian family's obstinate courage in trusting to the protection of their flimsy walls instead of fleeing from the battle zone. They were not the only ones who had stayed behind. Those who did were generally old people with a granddaughter and the small farmer's indomitable desire to safeguard his property. They cursed the Germans ('They stole everything') and feared that they might counter-attack and come back. The Poles had a special feeling for the Italians as fellow Catholics and dealt kindly with them. The soldiers didn't loot much. How in any case could they cart the stuff away? Some took bicycles and mattresses, but soon abandoned them. The Italians, once they were convinced that they were safe, quickly showed their true nature, and began to haggle. 'No eggs, no wine, no chickens,' they would say, 'the *Tedeschi* have taken the lot.' Meanwhile you could hear a hen clucking in a cupboard, or would find a drawer full of eggs.

From Loreto I was recalled to my BLU section, which was some way to the rear. I was sad to leave Major Florkowski and to miss the capture of Ancona; and I suspected trouble, for I should have reported back earlier to Major Potter at Divisional HQ. ('Once you're out in the field,' colleagues used to tell me, 'you simply vanish'.) It was as I feared. I was switched to a quiet section attached to Polish Corps HQ and joined the drones and office clerks. This was for me a punishment station. We were camping in tents near the sea (at Recanati, I think). Our senior officer was a colonel with a hatchet-face and huge dentures who, before breakfast, sat naked on his bed-roll on the beach doing his yoga exercises. The G II, a major, suffered from piles but was a tireless womaniser ('I never let a week go by without dipping my wick'). The presence of two Italian women with brooms whom we employed to look after the mess and laundry had driven the two officers into a state of sexual frenzy. One afternoon the major drove one of the women to the beach. But his love-making was rudely interrupted by a bathing party of naked English soldiers who ran up and down in front of the couple, waving their private parts.

A welcome diversion – for senior officers only – was calling on Italian contessas marooned by the war in their country villas. The major and a colonel from an armoured regiment asked me to accompany them on a visit to one lady who 'is pining away with a useless husband who looks like a hairdresser'. We took gifts of bully beef and whisky in a haversack, and the contessa, who was thin and seemingly highly strung, received us in a silk pyjama suit. After whisky and egg-brandies our hostess suddenly turned a cartwheel on the floor. Her husband, who was preparing smoked ham and figs, came out of the kitchen to quieten her. Our visit was an absurd parody of lust and snobbery. The other ranks' philanderings were more forthright. They whistled and gestured at the barefoot farm girls with swarthy legs as they walked to the pump for water. Staff Sergeant Fenwick explained to me the 'raper's mate' technique. 'You call at a farm with a mate. He distracts granny's attention while you entice her granddaughter away for a quick scuffle. No harm done, and you leave 'em a couple of tins of bully – and sugar if you've got it.' The British soldier regarded all Italians as Wops. The country girls were hairy and thick-limbed; they screeched when they sang. It was said that the men carried knives. Families slept behind bolted windows in a fug of sweat, smoke and drying vegetables. And there was their dreadful 'messy food'. Nevertheless, once hostilities were over, many soldiers married Italian girls, and according to reports have not regretted it.

Allied prisoners of war who had escaped from Italian captivity were sometimes reported to be in hiding with Italian families. I was sent to look for two of them. I traced one man to a hospital where the nuns had been passing him off as a bed-ridden Italian. The other man was a New Zealander living comfortably on a farm. Neither wanted to give up his cushy life and rejoin an army unit with the risk of being thrown into battle again at the sharp end. Eventually a tracing unit was set up to collect footloose British ex-prisoners.

It was about this time, near Fermo, that I began to feel seedy and my urine darkened to the colour of horse-piss. The MO diagnosed jaundice and I was taken by hospital train, among a crowd of wounded and groaning men, to a hospital in the south whose whereabouts I have forgotten. Here I was put to bed in an officers' ward with twenty other sufferers whose skins had turned weird shades of yellow. Hospital discipline was strict. Before the doctor's round we lay swaddled and motionless in our blankets ('lying at attention'). There was a good deal of flatulence. I was advised to hide my wedding ring ('the nurses are nicer to bachelors'). The cure was rest, fruit juice and a fat-free diet. No one knew exactly the source of the disease, and of our ghastly yellow skins and swollen livers. 'It's an officer's complaint,' the orderlies said with a smirk, 'brought on by too much vino.' Others said that jaundice was spread through nose droplets in crowded quarters, or through sharing mess utensils, or that it was carried, as in Flanders, by rats. The punishment for catching jaundice came after being discharged from hospital: a warning to keep off alcohol for three months ('Your livers', warned the MO, 'will be as soft as sponges'). One officer in my ward died; he had been prostrate for weeks.

When I rejoined my BLU unit the Apennine winter was setting in. The Poles had consolidated their positions along the Santerno facing German-held Imola. The final offensive to capture Bologna was planned for the spring. The battle front was quiet except for the usual patrols, fire fights and enemy harassing fire. It was a Brueghel landscape of snow-streaked fields and ditches and leafless trees where shells burst in unexpected places and pockets of Germans were lying-up in bunkers and farm buildings. The Poles had found comfortable winter quarters in farms, sleeping in big peasant beds under strings of onions, eating lumps of sausage with penknives and drinking *grappa* they had distilled from grapes. Their old *élan* had diminished since the failure of the Warsaw rising (General Bor capitulated on 2 October) and the Red Army's relentless march through the Polish homeland. Still feeling a little groggy about the knees, I visited old friends with forward units and joined a night patrol. The guns on both sides kept up the ritual of war: there was gun-fire on Christmas Day. My last memory of the Poles was at an observation post from which fire was being directed at some farm houses. The white walls crumbled as though smashed by a fist. It was soon after this that I was transferred to a reinforcements centre to await further posting. This was a miserable place. I slept with six other officers on a cold stone floor. We ate tinned beans, spam and soya turds. I took some Italian lessons with a local schoolteacher, a prim woman who lived in a freezing room, wrapped in a blanket; I attended a concert – the musicians played with their overcoats on; and I read Scott and Thackeray in the Everyman edition, which I found in a small Forces library at Faenza. The books had been provided by the kind people of Kent and were a Godsend. Heroes, villains, chivalry and treachery – what escapist dreams those Victorian story-tellers wove.

I was in Naples when I heard from the Poles the disastrous results of the Yalta conference of February 1945. They were heartbroken; many of Anders's soldiers came from eastern regions that were to be incorporated in the USSR under Communist dictatorship. If they returned to their homes they would lose their Polish identity and become Soviet citizens. 'The Allies have betrayed us', the Poles told me. 'We have been shedding our blood in vain.' There was talk of the Polish army refusing to continue to fight. During this unhappy period, I was told to report as interpreter and liaison officer to deal with a Soviet Military Mission at Taranto. By what seemed to the Poles to be an act of apostasy, I had gone over to the enemy.

In retrospect this may have been the right moment for me to leave the Poles. Their immediate future, alas, was overshadowed by bickering, disappointment and the fear of permanent exile. They went on to capture Bologna in April, but by then it had become for them a useless battle trophy. The Poles were splendid soldiers and good companions. Yet their historical grievances, their long tradition of revolt and their political world were too complex for most of us in the field to comprehend. The British soldier was lucky. His home, family and friends were waiting for him. The fact that the Red Army had been allowed, even encouraged, to entrench itself in the heart of Europe, the problem of millions of refugees, of devastated towns and starvation, were not his concern. The whistle had blown; but for Poles it was only for half-time.

In February 1945 I started my new post as administrative officer to a camp of Turkomans held in a prisoner-of-war enclave at Taranto. My first impression was of a mass of figures with dark, cropped heads milling about behind wire fences, like sheep in a crowded pen. These 8,000 men of 162 Turkoman Infantry Divison had been rounded up in the Ravenna area while fighting with the *Wehrmacht*. The rest of the Taranto enclave was overflowing with German prisoners, most of them *belastet* (implicated), that is, members of Nazi units with no hope of speedy release. The Turkomans enjoyed special privileges. Immediately after capture, in accordance with the Yalta agreement, they had been elevated to the status of Free Soviet Citizens (*swobodni sovietski grazhdanie*) and exchanged their German uniforms for British Army battledress. Now, under the administration of a Soviet repatriation mission from Moscow, they were awaiting transport to take them back to the USSR. In line with their new status these 'renegades' (as we considered them) were being fed like fighting cocks. They were issued with NAAFI stores, overpaid according to the dubious Red Army ranks the Soviet mission had claimed for them, and posted their own guards, who carried staves. Major Gromasov and a small Russian staff were in charge. The British authorities were represented by a camp staff of about twenty under Lieutenant-Colonel Thornhill. Both our interpreters were Palestinian Jews, one of them born in Odessa.

Whereas the German cages were crammed with gaunt and ragged Nazi soldiers staring silently through the wire, the Turkoman camp buzzed with stocky, swarthy men who had decorated their tent lines with flags and posters of Stalin and with green sprigs torn off trees. Apart from a small number of non-Turkoman Russians, who tended to keep to themselves, they were all Muslims – Kalmucks, Khirgizes, Uzbeks, Tatars and Kabardines – and their nominal rolls were a chaotic jumble of Muslim names. They were a docile, illiterate and cheerful lot. Major Gromasov kept them busy drilling, marching about the compound in snake columns, singing, cheering and organising concerts. Our

main problem was to stop them roaming through the Italian countryside, where they got drunk and stripped farm buildings – a company of
men would be let out like a column of worker-ants and come back
carrying bricks to build their Russian-type field kitchens with (they
stewed everything in great soup cauldrons). When admitted as patients
to the British General Hospital in Taranto, they would discharge themselves, look for drink, and go missing until picked up by the military
police.

As I had little to do I kept fit by exercising with a heavy stone behind
my tent: and I read Gogol in an edition with beautiful woodcuts that
I found in the camp library. The absurd fantasy of Gogol's *Nos*, the story
of a *kolejeski assessor*, a civil servant of respectable grade, who woke up
one morning to discover that his nose was missing (his drunken barber
was to find it, embedded in his breakfast roll), seemed to fit in with
my own bizarre situation as a British officer entangled with a band of
strange Oriental misfits who were being fattened up – though none
of us suspected this at the time – for a Siberian sacrifice. The Russian
junior camp staff invited me to several parties. They were rough, drunken affairs with thick potato soup and pickled gherkins, toasts, speeches,
Red Army songs that shook the tin walls of the hut and soldier musicians who were pulled out of bed at midnight with two or three Russian
girls and accordions. Red-faced and maudlin, we swopped confidences
over the spilled potato soup and mugs of brandy, slapped each other on
the back, and embraced the quartermaster, who sang the old gypsy
and Volga songs with a voice like a bull and presented me with Red
Army buttons which he tore off his tunic. Then, escorted by orderlies
with lanterns, we would stumble back to our bunks while our 8,000
Turkomans lay under the stars in their new British underwear.

The Turkomans had been told that their repatriation to Russia was
imminent. The prospect didn't seem to depress them. Perhaps they were
fatalists; and their initial sufferings in German captivity where they had
endured starvation and, some of them, cannibalism, may have dulled
any spirit of initiative they might once have had. It seemed that they
believed, or wanted to believe, in Stalin's amnesty promise – which was
backed by Major Gromasov's assurances – that they would return safely
to their homes and help rebuild their shattered villages. Despite what
the Poles had told me about Russian brutality I was inclined to accept
the logic behind the amnesty assurances. After all, in view of the USSR's
terrible war losses, Stalin would be anxious to harness every scrap of
manpower he could lay hands on rather than liquidate it. Meanwhile the
Turkomans organised concerts with native instruments and costumes
and had improvised a stage where they put on sketches. A crafty Armenian merchant with a hooked nose was the favourite comic character.

When our small British staff challenged Russia's Free Soviet Citizens to a football match the whole camp turned out to cheer. We lost by two goals. Their players had short square bodies and legs and a low centre of gravity like Gurkhas, and were difficult to knock off the ball. One day I was astonished to see a gang of them, with poles, lift a large and unwieldy Nissen hut and move it to another site.

I liked the Turkomans best when they sang. With twinkling legs they marched about in close order like millipedes, bellowing their patriotic songs. A tenor vocalist marched in front. His high pure notes, floating through the air like birdsong, would be taken up by the rest in a mighty roar. The German prisoners watching from their wired cages must have felt bitter when their former comrades-in-arms strutted past them in British uniforms singing *Katushka* and *Rossiya Moya* and other stirring Soviet songs, one of which – extolling the *svobodny vozduch* (free air) of Communist Russia – must have brought bile to the throats of these anti-Stalin renegades.

Major Gromasov and his colleagues, among them Major Fedorov and Lieutenant Lydia Zhar, the mission's interpreter, a rosy-faced girl with flaxen hair and a splendid bosom, offended Lieutenant-Colonel Thornhill by their extravagance. At a luncheon party to which Gromasov invited several British officers we found a bottle of whisky standing in front of each guest ('A year's ration', he grumbled). The colonel had always set an example of thrift, advising mess members to mark the level of whisky or gin on their personal bottles after each sundowner. But he soon lost face with the Muscovites. The colonel was built like a stork and wore bleached baggy shorts which hung round his thin thighs like bloomers. One morning, when presiding at a conference, he sat in his canvas chair in such a way that he unwittingly exposed his scrotum (two pink globes covered with ginger hair), and the more he fidgeted the more he revealed of this unattractive sight. The Russians were at first horrified, then amused, and Lydia began to giggle. The meeting broke up with nothing achieved. Major Federov, whenever we met later, used to greet me with a smirk and a scatalogical gesture.

When the time came to repatriate the first draft of 1,651 Turkomans they flocked quietly on board the New Zealand refrigerated meat ship, the *Arawa*, that was to carry them from Taranto to Odessa. They were still docile and cheerful and no threats or violence had to be used. Smokey Joe was taking them back into the fold. Even had they resisted, the Turkomans did not, in the British soldier's eyes, deserve much sympathy. They were, after all, turncoats, men who had fought alongside the German enemy while their own Red Army and the Allies were losing lives in a bloody struggle against Hitler. Not many of us seriously bothered – or had the necessary knowledge – to analyse the motives that must have led these men to throw in their lot with the Nazis: not only were the Turkomans members of an ethnic group persecuted by Stalin, but after they had been captured by the Germans on the eastern front they were forced to choose between starving to death or fighting as *Wehrmacht* auxiliaries against their natural enemy, the Bolsheviks. And there was another consideration. The Turkomans were Asians, not 'white' Europeans. This made it more difficult for us to identify with them.

I accompanied the draft as escort officer. The voyage to Odessa took several days. The atmosphere at first was relaxed. We ate huge helpings of mutton, crowded the rails when we passed the rocky humps of Greek islands, and in the evenings the Turkomans put on their oriental costumes and embroidered caps and entertained us with songs and dances. The ship's captain gave a party at which Major Gromasov startled everyone by calling for a bottle of Jugoslav brandy. 'I will show you how we Russians drink', he said, as he tipped up the bottle and drained it. We were meant to be impressed, but all he earned from the ship's captain was a disapproving look. The effects of the draught gave Gromasov a troubled night, for I could hear him in his cabin muttering and singing to himself.

We passed through the Dardanelles and lay off the Golden Horn for a day. It was at about this time that some of our Russian – not Turkoman – passengers came and spoke to me privately. There had been rumours and they were worried. Would Stalin honour his amnesty? Would they really see their home villages, or would they be packed straight off to some wilderness as convict labour? Several showed me certificates claiming that they had fought on the Allied side as partisans in France or Italy. As I watched the Istanbul ferry-boats and the clouds skimming over the domes and minarets I wondered why no one tried – if their fears were real – to jump overboard. There was no doubt that a shadow had fallen over the ship, and there were no more entertainments. When we passed through the Bosphorus and were met in the Black Sea by a Soviet gunboat, more anxious prisoners came to see me. 'You should have spoken up before', was all I could say. 'Now it is too late.'

At Odessa we tied up in a dank sea-mist at a quayside blocked with piles of oil pipes, rusting machinery and damaged crates. For two days no one was allowed to leave the ship. Our sole visitor was a Russian quarantine officer. An armed sentry stood with fixed bayonet at the foot of the gangway, and when some of the British crew threw him cigarettes he kicked the packets into the water without a word. When at last the Turkomans trooped off the ship on to their native soil, a ragged military band came to the quayside to greet them with a few tunes. Well fed, shaved, in clean British battledress, with full packs and polished boots, the Turkomans looked smart and healthy. The bandsmen, by contrast, had the thin sickly faces of privation.

We were unwelcome. We had succoured and cosseted a shipload of treacherous Muslim trash. I persuaded the Russians to give me a landing permit (*propusk*) and followed the route taken by the Turkomans. I found a batch of them paraded in a square in front of a huge picture of Stalin. They had been stripped of their British Army greatcoats and packs and were being harangued by a Soviet officer. Looking dejected and cowed, they were then marched off under armed guard. I asked some onlookers what would happen to them. 'Twenty years' penal servitude,' they said, 'if they survive.' One man took a handful of coarse *mahorka* (tobacco dust) from his pocket and asked me for a scrap of newspaper to roll cigarettes in. Another man asked me for a shirt.

I walked slowly back through the town centre. There were many damaged buildings, and nothing in the shops that I could see except exercise books and pamphlets and dummy goods made out of wood. I called at the hotel where, I had been told, an Allied liaison representative had an office, but he was away. I didn't use the toilet. Perhaps, if you flushed it, scalding hot water would gush out. My last glimpse of Odessa next day was of women with their feet wrapped in rags sweeping the streets with twig brooms. In the docks I watched working-parties of Romanian and German prisoners-of-war clearing up bomb damage. They towed a small cart with a tub of green liquid – their soup – and were guarded by Russian women with rifles.

Before he left the ship Major Gromasov wrote us a letter of thanks (which I had to translate) 'on behalf of the 1,651 Soviet citizens who would remember', he said, 'the voyage home to their Soviet mother country as one of the happiest memories of their lives.' The figure he gave should have been 1,652. When we sailed away, we found that Gromasov's interpreter, a White Russian *émigré* doctor with Italian citizenship who had volunteered for the trip, was missing. We heard later that he had been seized with the Turkomans. For me, the cat was now out of the bag. Stalin's amnesty promise was a manifest falsehood. I would use this knowledge in any future dealings with Russian repatriation.

In exchange for our Turkomans we embarked about a hundred French men and women and six Warsaw Jews (one of them a girl). The Jews spoke no French but had managed to smuggle themselves into the draft. The French had been arrested by the Germans while working for the Resistance and when their gaolers fled had made their way to Odessa via Lublin. Such was the exchange ratio: one that was, like the Yalta bargain as a whole, in point of the numbers involved, grossly in Moscow's favour.

We took our French passengers to Marseilles. The women were exemplary. They came on board haggard and tousled, went straight to the purser's shop for cosmetics and soap, and within two or three days had recovered much of their charm. The Jews kept to themselves. They made no attempt to be friendly, and lay about the deck in grimy vests looking suspicious and morose – it seemed that their struggle to survive had taught them to trust no one. The girl, who was seventeen, had a strikingly handsome face. It was from her that I learned at first hand of the huge number of deaths in Hitler's camps. She told me that a Polish family had saved her life by hiding her from the Germans. She was to stay with relations in Paris, and gave me her address (which I lost).

The Marseilles authorities gave our passengers a heroes' welcome. Red Cross workers with stretchers scrambled on board. A military band struck up with a fanfare, and a white-bearded French general embraced everyone. The crew was given shore leave and within ninety minutes I saw the first four seamen brought back dead drunk in a taxi. Before we left we took on board a fresh draft of Soviet repatriates. The *Arawa* was to return to Odessa with them. They were Russians, and as they had their own British escort officer and gave no trouble, I kept away from them. In my report, which I wrote in Taranto, I stressed the falsity of Stalin's amnesty promises. Also in Taranto, I was just in time to hear the announcement of Germany's surrender.

The news didn't particularly thrill me. Hitler's defeat had been a certainty for months. The Red Army was taking the place of the *Wehrmacht* as a threat, and Britain was still at war with Japan. But I was bitterly disappointed to have missed the 8th Army's final thrust across the Po. For me, the war had virtually ended when I left the Poles. I took a bottle of vermouth from the mess to share with the two German soldiers we employed in our cookhouse. This was my final act of apostasy. Instead of celebrating with my friends of the Kresowa Division in a Bologna tavern, I was hob-nobbing with Germans and Russians. The bulk of the British army had its eyes fixed on the calendar and was thinking in terms of demobilisation. But I had already decided to defer my own release. In the chaotic state of Europe, with the Red Army on the West's doorstep and an incalculable number of rootless and wandering people to administer, there was plenty of work to be done.

Chapter 7

Prisoners and Repatriation

I was now sent to join a small British staff responsible for holding about eighty Russian men and women in a casually-guarded camp on the Via Appia just outside Rome. The Russians were a mixed bag, with some Don Cossacks and Georgians, and a number of rootless women who did the chores. On my first visit, to everyone's amusement one of them, a coarse, wild-eyed blonde, tried to drag me into her tent. They all had an implacable hatred for the Bolsheviks and were in a state of anxiety, for they had heard of the harsh reception given to returned Turkomans in the USSR and, more recently, of the British Army's surrender of thousands of Cossacks to the Red Army in Carinthia, which had ended in bloodshed. They had refused attempts to repatriate them, and though their number was small their refusal to go had turned them into a headache for the British military authorities.

First, I had to get to know them. A veteran Georgian opera singer became a regular visitor at breakfast and in return for toast and marmalade he sang Mussorgsky's 'Blacha' (The Flea), with its mad chuckling accompaniment, 'Ochi Chornie' (Black Eyes) and 'Volga, Volga, Mat Rodnaya' (Volga, Native Mother). Another visitor was a young Orthodox priest with a pointed beard from *Russikom*, the Russian department within the Vatican. But it was the frequent visits of Lieutenant-Colonel Jakovliev of the Moscow Mission in Rome that perturbed everyone. He was threatening the refugees with dire consequences if they persisted in refusing to be repatriated. Jakovliev was a hard man to deal with. Two Russian girls in the camp who claimed they had married Frenchmen and pleaded for permission to go with their husbands to France, as French subjects by marriage, had their request

treated with contempt. To refuse to return to the USSR and to choose
to live abroad was an act of treachery.

The solution I adopted was to register the inmates as displaced
civilians – which was not strictly true: there were former officers and
nurses among them – and to encourage them (unofficially) to disperse.
This I did with the help of the young priest, who set up a temporary refuge for them in a building in Rome. The few who stayed
behind under British military control preferred their army rations to the
poor fare provided by *Russikom*. When I told the CO at Rome HQ of
my arrangements he didn't discourage me, but he preferred to know
nothing officially about them. The significance of this episode was that
it marked a stage where the British in Italy, faced with the possibility
of having to repatriate Russians by force, declined to do so. But an
ultimate decision on the principle of forcible repatriation had still to be
taken.

Rome at this time was convalescing in the sunshine. Lieutenant
Megzamen, a Pole from Lwow who was employed at the Town Major's
office, was my guide. In starched khaki drill we prowled through
the city, along the Corso and into the bars. 'The girls call you Sieg-
fried', he said to me jokingly. Yes, we were conquerors then. Many
years later, when I met Megzamen again in Johannesburg, where
he had become a successful white-haired barrister living in a fine villa
full of chiming clocks, he reminded me of an occasion when I couldn't
pay the wine bill. 'You said to the waiter, "Never mind the liras –
I'll give you a ride on my back instead".' The Roman women were handsome, sensual and shapely, with rich black hair hanging to their
shoulders and splendid teeth. During the war and despite the shortage
of Italian men they had kept homes going, and now that the fighting
was over they managed suddenly to look attractive in faded cotton
dresses. Megzamen introduced his girlfriends to me. All they wanted
was a satisfying meal and small gifts of NAAFI sugar. Fate, however, was to deal Megzamen a cruel blow. One night his black house-
boy stabbed him to death with the knife he kept under his pillow for
protection.

I played cricket on a matting wicket at the Mussolini stadium. There
were some good players: Wellard (Somerset and England), Hill (Hampshire) and Rhodes (Derbyshire). Wellard, tall and strong, specialised in
driving the ball for six – he once scored a century for Somerset in 55
minutes. One weekend I drove the Orthodox priest from the camp
and the prettiest of the Russian girls to the beach at Ostia, where the
priest took off his robe and got painfully sunburnt. The Moscow mission
invited me to luncheon at the Soviet Embassy. Lieutenant-Colonel
Jakovliev and Lydia Zhar were present. It was obvious that the Russians

regarded me as an intelligence agent ('a spy') and were weighing me up. 'The Russians who are refusing to be repatriated', they said, 'are Fascists and fools. The West doesn't want them, and they will starve and perish.' Talking of Russian music, they said that 'Ochi Chornie' and other old tunes that the West was familiar with were degenerate stuff. 'We have our own Soviet tunes, and they are better.'

At about this time I got news from Polish Corps that Dunia's mother and sister Luisia had arrived from Austria by Red Cross transport and were at a camp in Porto San Giorgio, on the Adriatic. This was exhilarating news. I went to see them straight away, and found them destitute but healthy. Mrs Lesmian and Luisia told me they had been transported from Warsaw to a forced-labour factory in Murnau, and had lost all their Warsaw possessions. The Polish Red Cross had undertaken to send them to London as dependants of 2 Polish Corps, but they would have to wait months before this could be arranged. As Dunia was still in Cairo, an early meeting was impossible: it took place the following year in unexpectedly sad circumstances.

In July 1945 Allied forces HQ Caserta sent me to Bellaria, a few miles north of Riccione on the Adriatic coast, to report on the 10,000 soldiers of the Ukrainian Galicia Division who were being held there as SEP (Surrendered Enemy Personnel) after giving themselves up to the British in Carinthia. My instructions were to assess, in terms of the Yalta agreement, whether these men, or a proportion of them (they were vaguely thought of as some sort of 'border Poles'), were liable to be returned, if necessary by force, to the USSR. The Ukrainian *tabor* (camp) and the much larger Rimini airfield enclave were under the administration of 218 Sub-Area HQ in Riccione. I was briefed by Major Cronin. The British view of the Yalta clauses, he explained, was that citizens who had been domiciled within the pre-War (September 1939) eastern boundaries of Poland should be regarded as Polish nationals and were not to be repatriated without their consent. The Soviet authorities, on the other hand, were being difficult. They were still insisting that all citizens who originated from the territory lying east of the old Curzon line (including Polish Galicia and Lwow) were Soviet citizens and should be returned. The British military authorities, however, had become increasingly opposed to the use of force. The forcible surrender of the Cossacks and their dependants to the Red Army in May and June had left an unpleasant taste, and a similar attempt to hand over thousands of Ukrainians would be a degrading and messy business involving bloodshed and damaging publicity. My immediate task was to establish the identity of the Ukrainians. Were they to be listed as 'Polish' or 'Russian' Ukrainians, or even, some of them, as true Poles? – though General Anders's army in Italy would have nothing to do with them, and Polish friends had told me that they despised the Galicia Division as 'Fascist bandits'. The imminent arrival of a Soviet repatriation mission meant that their moment of crisis was at hand.

The Ukrainian camp at Bellaria was guarded by 55 Light Anti Aircraft Regiment. A number of prisoners were let out each day on working parties. I got on well with Major Jaskewycz, the camp commandant, and his adjutant. The Halychyna (Galicia) Division had been formed in May 1943 in the Lwow area as part of a Ukrainian National Army on condition that it was to be used only against the Russians. It had been trained in Silesia, incorporated into the *Wehrmacht* in June 1944, and in July sent into action against the Red Army at Brody, near Lwow. The battle was a disaster, with 3,000 survivors out of 16,000. The division had regrouped in Silesia, moved to Slovakia, and in January 1945 started to withdraw westward in the direction of Vienna and into Carinthia to escape the Red Army. After its capitulation at Klagenfurt the division had been transferred to Italy via Udine at the end of May.

My preliminary findings revealed a cartographer's nightmare. There was a number of genuine Soviet citizens in the division but, with so little time and without facilities, proper screening was impossible, and any attempt, for instance, to winkle out 'war criminals' (which was in any case not my concern) would have been a farce. I recommended therefore that the Ukrainian formation should be treated as a cohesive whole; and that all should be given the benefit of the doubt and classified as Polish citizens from Polish Galicia. Just before the Soviet repatriation mission arrived I warned the Ukrainian camp leaders and Major Jaskewycz to be absolutely firm with the Moscow officers: they were not to fear them and they would not be under duress. I would be present to see fair play.

When the Soviet team, under General Basilov and Colonel Jakovliev, entered the cage the whole Ukrainian division, paraded for inspection, watched them in silence. Major Fedorov sneered at the flimsy bivouac tents where thousands of thin, sun-tanned men slept in threadbare uniforms on the ground, and at the British-style cookhouses and rations. General Basilov was given a ladle of soup to taste and he asked if there were any complaints. There were none. Indeed, the uncanny silence of the assembled men struck me as unusual and significant. This was a tussle of wills: the Soviet war-machine was facing not merely a few thousand unarmed yet determined men, but a test of its reputation and integrity in the eyes of the Allies.

The Soviet officers spent many days interrogating the Ukrainians. They worked relentlessly, without meal breaks, loosening their collars, in a tent pitched inside the cage. I was present at every interview.

The men were grilled individually. Asked why they had taken up arms against the USSR they answered – with vehemence as they gained cofidence – that they 'hated the Bolsheviks for having murdered and persecuted them and their families'. Each prisoner, standing to attention before the trestle tables where the Soviet officers sat, kept his eyes on me at this critical moment as though my uniform were a lifebelt. General Basilov's mission failed. Only a handful of Ukrainians volunteered to return home (they were immediately segregated). The General himself, a tired, courteous man who took medicine poured for him by his female interpreter, left after a few days in disgust. It must have been humiliating for him to endure the increasing rebuffs and rudeness of the prisoners. The remaining Soviet officers began to shout at them. A colonel freshly arrived from Moscow to ginger things up was permitted to address the men by companies. 'You are the grey mass (*tiomnaya massa*)', he cried to the wooden faces gazing at him. 'You have nothing to offer but your hands. The world doesn't want you. For them, you are rubbish. Be warned. Sooner or later the Soviet Union will have you.'

The colonel went back to Rome and a little later Brigadier Block, the Area Commander, took me with him into the cage to address the senior officers. It was a dramatic moment, for the fate of the whole division depended on what he was going to say. The Brigadier spoke briefly and to the point. 'You are safe now', he told them. 'The mission from Moscow will not bother you any more. You must continue to trust us, and we will not let you down.' He complimented the soldiers on their good behaviour and asked them not to relax their discipline. While I was interpreting I looked straight at Jaskewycz. His hard, sergeant-major's face was shining with relief.

A major factor leading to the reprieve of the Galician Division was its tenacious morale. The real strength of the Ukrainians lay in their cohesion, their relative literacy, and an extreme national consciousness. They had their own language, ranks and uniform, their own religion with its Uniate cross and marvellous chants, a superb orchestra with fifty balalaika players, their own history. They prided themselves on being part of the Ukrainian freedom army and had been using Germany as an ally in their fight against Bolshevism. Without the most intimate knowledge, no outsider was entitled to sit in judgment on their loyalties and actions during the war. But they had no friends. Even the Poles had a historic grudge against them.

When Tom Bower interviewed me in December 1989 for a BBC television programme on war criminals, he argued that the British authorities had been culpably negligent in reprieving the Galicia Division without first screening them for the presence of war criminals. I told him that we had no facilities for proper screening, that no reliable evidence concerning war crimes was produced, and that Moscow's assertions of such crimes were ignored by us as propaganda. The interview with Tom Bower was rather long (almost an hour); the script was cut to a bare three minutes. It did not include the crux of my remarks, that my immediate British colleagues and I, despite Soviet pressure, were not interested in witch-hunting, but in ensuring that the prisoners were humanely and justly treated and in due course released to civilian life, where they could make their contribution as workers and family men instead of perishing behind barbed wire.

At the end of September I was sent to Udine to report on a camp of Russians and to help arrange the evacuation of a Russian hospital. Captain Marcus, a delightful person but not a Russian linguist, came with me to the camp. At Area HQ we learned that a train was waiting to transport repatriates to the Soviet zone in Austria. Out responsibility was to supervise screening operations and make sure that no one was returned against his will. The Russians in the camp were a mixed bag of men and women. They were claiming refugee status but the two Soviet officers in charge were intimidating and putting pressure on them to return to the USSR. Marcus, who kept a diary, wrote a letter to me not long ago describing our meeting with the Russians.

We arrived at the camp to find our entry blocked by a little squirt of a Russian lieutenant at a trestle table in the foyer. His only reply to your eloquence was a series of 'niets'. No doubt profiting from previous experience and knowledge of the Russian mentality, you pressured me into donating my recently drawn whiskey ration, which you plonked on the table before him. A hurried withdrawal, a smiling return, and we were ushered into the inner sanctum to be greeted effusively by the senior Russian. With his other officers we were invited to sit round a table with them. Our offering was poured into glasses up to the brim. Then a series of toasts. You had already briefed me, by a kick under the table, that there were no heel-taps. By this time our bottle had been replaced by an inexhaustible supply of replacements, followed in due course by a large platter of some kind of meatballs, which went down very well. After a few rousing choruses of 'Kalinka' and 'Black Eyes' we then staggered out into the courtyard where, to our astonishment, chairs had been lined up against the walls and an orchestra of sorts with balalaikas and accordions was waiting. We were given seats of honour and made to dance. The dances were extremely fast. When dancing with some of our male hosts I was whirled round with feet hardly touching the ground and feeling quite dizzy. Later, at our hotel, we dined with two Georgian officers (one of them a glass-eater) who were going to defect from the camp, and two Dutch nurses. I can't remember much more, but I do recall that on mounting the rather grand marble stairway to our room, you remarked that the two miniature palm-trees in fancy urns flanking the stairs were wasted there, and would look much better arrayed at our bedsides. We were quite startled to see them there next morning.

I had already made it clear to the refugees that it was up to them entirely whether they chose to be repatriated or not. Two Soviet officers were present when the Russians were brought in for screening next day. A few Turkomans who were sick or crippled said they would return to the USSR. The others refused. 'I remember vividly a Turkoman with no legs being brought in before us on "piggy-back" – whatever could the future hold for him?' Marcus noted. Despite our assurances, according to Marcus 'we were mobbed on leaving by despairing people begging us to save them somehow from repatriation, when they would be branded as traitors and would perish.' I told them again that they had nothing to fear. They were safe as long as they did not fall foul of the *carabinieri*, who were themselves under Soviet pressure; if they were arrested they would be handed over to Soviet officers representing the Moscow Embassy.

Marcus left, and I toured the former German hospital to interview the patients. They were mostly Turkomans. Many were severe amputation cases, some were dying of tuberculosis. The small hospital staff were Russians. The wards smelt of pus. As I walked round the beds I made it clear to every man that he was free to stay or to be repatriated. No one volunteered to stay. The Russian doctor and his female assistant also said they would go. The Turkomans, as I had expected, thought and acted like an extended family. Clearly the patients preferred suffering and dying among their own folk to facing the loneliness of exile. Yet they must have known that to Moscow they were not only useless mouths, but traitors, and that their hope of survival in the USSR was very small. 'There are no artificial limbs in Russia', the doctor told me.

At the final conference between Area HQ and the Soviet officers, the latter seemed to have forgotten the toasts and the drunken promises of goodwill. In their official capacity, whatever the state of their livers, they showed themselves as unrelenting as ever. They demanded at first that we should hand over the whole of the hospital equipment, surgical instruments and medical stores (we compromised on this), in addition to the patients. About eighty boarded the German ambulance train (boxcars, with a German Red Cross staff) that was to take them to the Hungarian frontier. I travelled as OC train and escort officer. I had a batman-cook, Gunner Skinner, an iron stove, rations and a comfortable bunk bolted to the floor. We jogged quietly over the Alps and in the early morning stopped at the Soviet zone border at the Semmering Pass.

To my alarm, when I looked out I saw two Red Army soldiers with brushes and buckets of whitewash painting the hammer and sickle and a serial number on every boxcar and on our splendid American locomotive. Losing a train would be an expensive fiasco – I had already heard stories of British train escort parties being left stranded in the Soviet zone. So I hurried into the small town. The square was crowded with light wooden carts, drawn by two ponies with the driver sitting on a pile of straw. I found the commandant in his braces, shaving. He was a big red-faced man and was probably a bully, but I had caught him off guard. He poured schnapps into a beer glass and said, 'Because you speak our language, you may keep your train.'

We arrived at our destination – Bruck-an-der-Leitha, on the Hungarian border – on the fifth day. For twenty-four hours nothing happened. The boxcars stayed shut and the German medical staff was careful not to show itself. Walking along the platform, I could hear the Russian doctor and his female assistant quarrelling. When at length a Soviet major appeared with a thick-set female lieutenant in jackboots, he handed me a piece of typed paper and said 'Read and sign this, and we will evacuate the patients.' 'The British military authorities', I read among other accusations that included theft of hospital equipment, 'have transported dangerously ill Soviet citizens in inhuman conditions.' The effrontery of the claims made me laugh in the major's face. 'It is your own delay', I said, 'that is endangering the patients.' I signed the piece of paper immediately. My admission would, I knew, be added to Vishinski's file, one more trumped-up piece of evidence in his attacks on the Allies for misconduct and bad faith towards the USSR. Such propaganda rubbish meant nothing to me, stuck on a deserted platform with a train-load of groaning men.

I watched our patients being dumped roughly on the floor of open horse-drawn carts. It was raining. Their bundles were thrown on top of them. Legless men rode on the shoulders of comrades. The carts jolted off along a track to a large red building on a hill. The callousness of it was inevitable. Men who couldn't work were not wanted in the USSR; and men who had fought against their comrades in the Red Army were better off dead. There were scattered farms in the neighbourhood (no cattle) and I went into several of them. They were bare and poor, with empty kitchens and scarcely any furniture. 'The first wave of

Russians was not too bad', the farmers told me. 'They were fighting men and in a hurry. It was those that followed who stole everything.' A train packed with returning Hungarian soldiers halted in the station. The officers' uniforms were clean and they were spreading *real* butter on their rye bread (I had been living on tinned margarine for years). In a siding there was a Russian loot train crammed with a chaotic mass of objects – furniture, radios and sewing mechines, bicycles, perambulators and mattresses, even door-locks. The Red Army soldiers who had pillaged and humped this treasure-trove for their own use would not see it again.

On the way back, at Vienna, I slid open the door of my boxcar and let in two Austrian women who were trying to escape from the Soviet zone to Salzburg. They were nurses. Gunner Skinner was taken aback. But they proved their worth by showing him how to fry marmalade pancakes; and one of them, who wore an old-fashioned hat, taught me the words of that beautiful soldier's song by Uhland which begins 'Ich hatt' einen Kamaraden, Einen bessern findst du nit'.

At Wiener Neustadt, Red Army soldiers were scavenging among wrecked buildings. A train-load of aircraft engines, bombed by the RAF, was spattered over a siding. At the Semmering border halt I told the two nurses to keep out of sight. But there was no search, and no one tried to steal the train.

When I got out at Murz-zu-Schlag, my driver was waiting for me with a 15-cwt truck, and the opportunity for a swan to Bavaria before returning to Italy was too good to miss. The road to Munich had been blown in several places. We passed fields crammed with brand-new American bombers. Munich was a desperate sight. Whole streets had been smashed into piles of rubble. Mounds of bricks had been stacked to form shelters with tiny entrances, where the surviving occupants lived like troglodytes. It seemed to me that this aerial punishment of the enemy by remote skymen was excessive and indiscriminate. Like a crazed *soldateska* we had decided to kill the German soldier's wife and family at their fireside.

At Innsbruck, occupied by the French, I found Vieider's mother and elder sister (with whom I had stayed in August 1935) at home, ageing, a little worn. I wished I had something to offer them – a roast goose, or a huge chocolate cake – but I had nothing but bully beef and cigarettes. They were sitting in their damaged flat wearing their overcoats to keep warm; and when we talked about the past it was like resuming an interrupted conversation. Neither showed any hostility towards me, despite the heavy bombing that had wrecked many of Innsbruck's beautiful buildings. Vieider, having served as a staff interpreter with the SS, had been put into the *belastet* category of men who on capture had to answer for their political record and could not expect early release. He was in hiding somewhere in Bavaria.

Riccione, in the summer, had been a delightful place for soldiers. The army took over the beaches and the best hotels, organised Italian dance bands, and a troop of girls came from Bologna to flirt and look for husbands among the soldiers – the few Italian men were chivvied away. The officers of the North Irish Horse were the most obstreperous. They were dashing fellows who swarmed up the marquee poles like apes to bombard the dancers with spaghetti, and they bagged the prettiest nurses. Winter, though, was unbearably cold. There was no heating and we lay on our beds with our greatcoats on. I whiled away the time reading Surtees and Thackeray. I enjoyed most my daily run along the beach to Cattolica, a headland that stuck into the sea a few miles to the south-east. Unobserved, unmilitary, I jogged past the concrete bunkers and washed-up mines till the sun set over the jagged cliffs and walls of San Marino, which glowed like a great red sail.

But soon, through a combination of my own bloody-mindedness and the demon vino, I was awaiting a new posting. It happened like this. I had been invited to a Polish Corps artillery party at the Grand Hotel, Riccione, and on impulse took Major Fedorov and Lydia as my guests. The war was over. Why shouldn't the Russians and the Poles get together over a few drinks? Lydia, with her blonde good looks and stunning bosom, would surely go down like a bomb among the Polish subalterns. Brigadier Block was pleased to see us. But the Poles, alas, took umbrage. I saw that I had deeply offended them. When the party was breaking up, in a moment of pique I lifted the bar counter (a heavy marble slab) and tipped it onto the floor with its load of bottles. There was a disgusting crash. I was court-martialled 'for conduct unbecoming to an officer and a gentleman'. The board consisted of officers who knew me and I was let off with a mild reprimand. But I had to wait until the New Year for my next posting.

I was attached to GHQ British Troops in Austria (liaison section) in Vienna and was told to 'put myself in the picture' by reading the office files. They dealt with minutes of conferences held between the four occupying powers whose troops were garrisoning the capital, reports on the food and fuel situation, and military discipline. Vienna in winter, surrounded by Soviet-occupied territory and suffering the punishment of the defeated, was a dismal city – cold, wet and hungry. Buildings were unheated, many windows had no glass and were sealed by sheets of plywood or cardboard. St Stefan's Cathedral was a shattered wreck with rain pouring through gaps in its roof. Along the splendid Rotenthurmstrasse Russian artillery had left a trail of ruin. Red Army soldiers were

1. Captain of Cricket, King Edward's School, Birmingham, 1932

2. A night-club in Gdynia, Poland, 1937

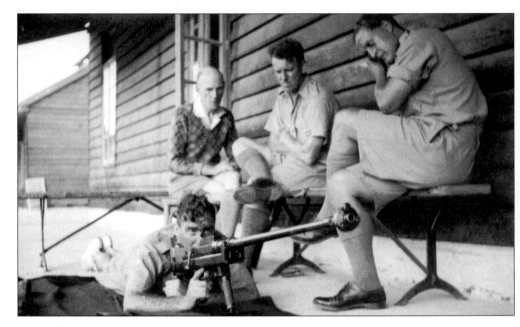

3. Reduced to sleep by a lecture on 'the pathetic Boyes anti-tank rifle', Moascar, Egypt, 1940

4. Dunia in Cairo

5. DH in Cairo, 1941

6. Generals Sulik and Szysko-Bohusz at a Polish banquet with the 5th Kresowa Infantry Division at Khanaqin on the Iraq–Iran border, 1942. 'Tables and chairs' created by digging a ditch

7. With Eva, the 'Displaced Person' from Russian Georgia, at Riccione in Italy, in 1947. DH engineered her escape from an internment camp in 1948

8. DH at Mittelberg in the Klein Walsertal, where he started his skiing journeys in the early 1950s

9. At the top of Mount Ararat: DH on left, Muzaffer centre holding the summit book in which climbers record their names, and Dr Bozkurt

10. Muzaffer, DH's Turkish climbing companion, a young army sergeant

11. Ingrid in Kampala, 1971

12. Mount Demavend in Iran, climbed in 1957

13. David Winfield, restorer of Byzantine churches, with DH in front; behind, Ingrid with the *muhtar* of the Pontic mountain village of Yusufeli and his family

14. A highland Laz near the Kackar massif in north-eastern Turkey

15. In the first Georgian hamlet on the Asian side of the Kackar massif

16. Haho, one of the ancient Georgian churches in north-eastern Turkey explored by DH in 1962–3

17. Climbing the dome of St Sofia in Istanbul, 1963

18. Reuben, DH's guide among the volcanoes of Western Uganda, on the Congo border

19. and 20. Teuso or Ik porters (*left*) and a Teuso with his son (*right*) from the Turkana/Uganda border

21. A corpse, one of Amin's victims dumped by the lake near Entebbe

22. A still from the film, *The Rise and Fall of Idi Amin*, made in Nairobi in 1979. DH plays himself

everywhere – trundling about in open lorries and staring up at the buildings like village tourists, or roaming the streets with broken suitcases and sacks for carrying loot or black-market goods. It was a common sight to see them, in their greasy forage caps and muddy boots, entering buildings like ferrets in search of something to carry away. They were never without their weapons, unlike the British soldiers, who were issued with arms only when on duty. The files contained numerous reports of incidents involving Red Army soldiers. Some had held up trams and robbed the passengers at gunpoint, another had emptied his magazine into a crowded dance-hall. Russian security men were busy hunting for war criminals – one file described how in their search for a 'Herr Schmidt' several Schmidts had been arrested and taken away. During these trying days the Viennese preferred to stay indoors in their cold rooms, eking out their ration of lentils and beans among the family photographs and knick-knacks. There was a huge black market. All soldiers were tempted to flog rations and stores. Penicillin, pilfered from hospitals and army stores, was in great demand (venereal disease was rife). Red Army officers, conspicuous in their wide shoulder-boards, had joined the scrounging racket. The few Russian wives of officers were recognisable by their fur wraps and pointed shoes.

My unit was billeted in Richard Strauss's villa. Gloomy and cold, we munched our spam, baked beans and soya turds among the splendid furniture. On the landing a massive, rubicund Flemish blonde in a frame greeted one on the way to the lavatory. I found time to search for my old friends, the Jewish Weiss family, with whom I had stayed in 1933 in Clusiusgasse, near Franz-Josef railway station. The house porter told me that Jews in the neighbourhood had disappeared or been taken away under the Nazis. 'The Weiss parents were in any case old.' He recalled that Fräulein Weiss had married a Jewish doctor who specialised in lung diseases.

Except on official occasions, which tended to be dull and drunken, the Red Army was not encouraged to fraternise with Allied soldiers. One evening I spoke to a Red Army lieutenant in the street and asked him to join me in a drink. We had just sat down in a bar when a military Jeep pulled up outside. Three Red Army military police got out. Without a word to me they ordered the Russian to leave and bundled him into their vehicle. I felt guilty about this and wondered what sort of punishment the lieutenant would receive for 'communicating with an enemy agent'. It was clear that our relations with the Russians had turned sour. They seemed to resent our presence. It was, after all, their own Red Army that had stormed Vienna and driven the Germans westward through Lower Austria and Styria to Carinthia. We British had arrived in Vienna when the party was over. We had taken over Schönbrunn

Palace and the Park Hotel. We enjoyed better rations, more comfortable accommodation and plentiful transport. But we were intruders, and we were spoiled. In the eyes of the Russian *strelok* (rifleman) we looked in summer, with our bare knees and khaki shorts, more like scouts than a victorious army. My stay in Vienna, however, was to be brief. After a few weeks I was posted back to Italy, where the future role of General Anders's army was shortly to be resolved, and it was thought that I would be more useful at AFHQ, Caserta.

Caserta palace was an enormous building. The lower floors were used as offices. We slept on the top floor amidst our kit, with German batmen to bring early morning tea and make our beds. The rooms were bare cells, and climbing some 200 steps to get to them was an ordeal. Some people never left the building for weeks at a time; or, like insects entering a termite mound, they entered it and were never seen again. With no exercise and plenty of booze we must have been one of the unfittest body of soldiers in the army. My room-mate was a middle-aged Pay Corps captain who had just been flown out from England. He was drunk every night, urinated against the wall, walked about naked except for a dingy hernia strap, and snored like a beast. I tried at first to wake him by throwing my army boots and a jug of cold water at him. 'Swine!' I shouted in his ear. None of this had any effect. After several disturbed nights I dragged him and his bed into the corridor, where he lay naked except for the strap round his groin.

At first I had little to do: a few translations of Russian and Polish texts, visits to the San Carlo opera house in Naples, dinner at the officers' honky-tonk with Marcus and two Polish nurses, and rugger. Then on 20 March I was hastily summoned to a locked room with a desk, pen, ink pot and paper, and in conditions of absolute secrecy told to translate Bevin's statement to the House of Commons on the future of the Polish army which was to be transmitted by signal. The gist of this was that once plans had been made for an orderly demobilisation, the Polish army under British command was to be disbanded, though no pressure would be put on the soldiers to return to Poland against their wishes. This was a bad time for the Poles. Their hopes of a triumphant return to Poland had already been dashed by the intransigence of the Warsaw government. They had now become a bargaining counter in the diplomatic exchanges between a British government that no longer needed their services and the vindictive Warsaw clique installed by the USSR. Had I still been attached to the Poles, the shame and disappointment of this denouement would have been hard for me to bear. It wasn't until the British government issued its plans for a resettlement corps that Polish morale began to recover.

About this time I was promoted to major, and early in April

I was sent on a special mission to La Spezia. According to AFHQ, an 'inflammable situation' had developed there. An illegal shipload of Polish–Jewish refugees had been seized in the act of setting sail for Palestine, in defiance of the British naval blockade and the quota restrictions on the number of Jewish settlers allowed in. The Jews were about to go on hunger strike and it was rumoured that their leaders had threatened to blow themselves up with the ship if they were not permitted to sail. I was to look at the situation and send a report on it. Since we were dealing with law-breakers, a military police lieutenant came with me. He wasn't happy about the job. He told me of British navy boarding parties that had intercepted Jewish blockade runners being 'driven off with clubs'.

The SS *Fede* was a small 1,000-ton hulk berthed at a quayside sealed off by *carabinieri*; 1,200 refugees had been crammed into it. It had been roughly fitted out with plank platforms to carry human cargo, and stocked with water, army rations and fuel for the passage to Palestine. The deck was crowded with thin shabby people. They had just started their hunger strike and I was advised not to go on board – 'they're in an ugly mood and will whack you over the head.' However, I immediately went on board – alone, and of course unarmed (by 1946 British officers had long ceased to carry pistols) – and greeted everyone in Polish. Some women spat at me and one cried 'sadist!' and tried to claw my face. I then introduced myself to the leaders. Knowing Polish was an advantage – we had common ground – and when we went to the captain's tiny cabin and began to talk, they became less suspicious and hostile. I advised them to call off their hunger strike while the British authorities considered the next step. The British, I said, would not show much sympathy under duress; desperate public gestures such as arson or staged suicides would only make things worse. I made it clear to the leaders – one of them a strong, determined youngish man – that I sympathised with them and would do everything I could to help them get away.

This was the solution I had decided on as soon as I set eyes on the refugees. These ravaged-looking people in crumpled old clothes bore the marks of long privation. They were thin and ill, the women ugly with suffering. What they needed were not guards, barbed wire or military policemen but homes, care and affection.

The hunger strike continued next day. My military police colleague, realising that I intended to exceed my brief ('politics', he said, 'are not in my line') went back to Caserta. Meanwhile, some Jewish Agency officials and a number of pressmen whom I recognised as Jews had arrived, and began to row round the *Fede* in small boats. An unwelcome scandal was already brewing. Because of the fast the ship had gone strangely quiet, though the young leader told me that milk was still being issued to mothers and children.

I tried to sort out my own feelings. At bottom – though perhaps not emotionally – I am an old-fashioned English snob. As immigrants to the British Empire 'these chaps' didn't look at all like the right sort of material. They were ghetto-birds from poor Polish townships. The Arab with his fat-tailed flocks and maize-fields and village minaret fitted naturally into his ochre and green landscape. These Jews would simply swell the cellar population of Tel Aviv. Besides, their compatriots had not only deserted in shoals from Anders's Polish army: many had retained their weapons and in Palestine were now shooting British soldiers as they slept unsuspecting in their tents. And yet – these people had suffered and were suffering. They had escaped death by a miracle. Conscience demanded that they should be helped.

At this point I got a signal from AFHQ informing me that Professor Harold Laski, the London University academic and Labour politician, who was on a lecture-tour in Italy, would be allowed to come to La Spezia to talk with the refugees. I was to escort him on board the *Fede* and keep an eye on him. So I again asked the Jewish leaders to defer any drastic acts they had in mind, and to see Laski first. I promised them that I would then go immediately to Area HQ Genoa and put their case before Caserta.

Professor Laski arrived with his wife – a small, neat man, looking tired and on edge. To me he was rather offhand, treating me as another dim army officer – I resisted the temptation to tell him that at Oxford I had found his essays on political science both turgid and difficult to follow. I took him on board the *Fede* to address the Jewish representatives. About a dozen of us squeezed into the small cabin, where we sat by candlelight. Laski spoke at length. To his credit, he praised Britain's humanitarian record and asked the Jews to respect it. He begged them to call off their hunger strike. Threats and violent demonstrations, he said, would only harden the British Government's attitude. 'Bevin and Attlee are my friends', he concluded. He promised that as soon as he returned to England he would speak with them on the refugees' behalf. Meanwhile, they should co-operate.

While the professor was speaking I looked at his audience. The candlelight and the shadows had deepened the lines on their faces; they were grim and haggard and expressed implacable determination. Professor Laski was doing his best, but he was an academic. He had not suffered in the flesh. He was unscarred, spruce and shaved, uncommitted. The audience was not convinced.

With Laski and his wife out of the way, I hurried to Area HQ Genoa to send my report and recommendation to AFHQ Caserta. In my signal

I advised that the *Fede* be permitted to sail forthwith, both for reasons of humanity and to prevent further damage and discredit to the reputation of the British Army. The staff captain who handled my signal grunted when he read it and remarked, with black humour, 'The best thing would be to tow the boat out to sea and drown the buggers.' But the authorities must have moved quickly (I could not, of course, assess the total weight of pressure being brought to bear on them), for when I arrived back at La Spezia the hunger strike had been called off and I watched about thirty athletic young Jews (the hard core of the operation) celebrate with a victory parade under the Star of David flag. They had been lying low among the shabby crowd of refugees. These were the 'activists': men professionally dedicated to planting Zionism in Palestine.

Militarily, my decision to help the Jews was wrong. But army regulations do not provide for every situation. I had wanted to extinguish a small glow of hatred before it grew into a flame. When I returned to Caserta a military police major questioned me closely on my part in the affair, taking down my statement in the ponderous jargon of all policemen. He was particularly concerned to know what undertakings I had given to the refugees, and what Professor Laski had said. Clearly my advice to let the Jews go was mistaken – after all, they had broken every rule in the book (false papers, theft of fuel and rations, illegal use of military vehicles) and their compatriots in Palestine were ambushing British soldiers. Nevertheless, two or three weeks later I heard that the *Fede* had sailed and that its human cargo, crammed like sardines on plank beds, had been admitted to Palestine. The Jews had won this battle of wills.

I haven't regretted my decision, though my colleagues thought I had exceeded my brief ('a jumped-up major telling GHQ that the *Fede* should sail'), and they laughed about it.

Later I heard an entirely different version of this episode. In 1975 I planned to visit Israel, and wrote to the Israeli Embassy in London explaining that I had been involved in the *Fede* affair and asking for news of the *Fede*'s passengers as I wanted to meet some of them. An embassy counsellor agreed to help me, but made these remarks in his reply. 'The *Fede* incident is a part of Israeli folklore. It was written up twenty years ago in a book called *The Secret Roads* by Jon and David Kimche. Leon Uris used it in his book *Exodus*, transposing the setting to Cyprus and changing the passengers to children. I suspect you are the Major Hill referred to. If you are, you may feel the authors present your role rather unflatteringly, but please take into account that this is a highly journalistic account by journalists and not, in any sense, an official record.' The counsellor enclosed the chapter containing the relevant passage.

The Major Hill referred to by the Kimche brothers is certainly not I. In their bizarre version the major, despite being 'supported by troops and armour', was forced to withdraw in ignominy. Thus journalism is promoted to mythology, and propaganda turns into folklore. The Kimches' book is relentlessly hostile to the British. It is a sad commentary on those days when we and the Jews fought Nazism together as allies, that they should be perpetuated in Israeli legend as ending in perfidy, with Bevin – as quoted by a character in Amos Oz's novel *A Perfect Peace* – joining Chmielnicki, Petliura, Hitler and Nasser as the leading villains.

At the end of April I was posted to a repatriation camp set up at Cervinara, near Naples, for the relatively small number of Poles who had opted to return to the now Communist-dominated Poland rather than settle down in Britain or the Commonwealth and build a new life in exile. The total strength of General Anders's 2nd Polish Corps before repatriation began was 112,000. Of these only 7 officers and 14,200 men had applied for repatriation, and of this number 8,700 had joined the Corps after the end of hostilities. A mere 310 were men who had come with the Corps from Russia. I found the atmosphere in the camp unpleasant, the soldiers politicised, suspicious and confused by divided loyalties. A communist colonel from Warsaw who wore a magnificent peaked cap was responsible for the Polish side of the evacuation. He thought the British were impeding his arrangements, and he was making difficulties. I had been sent from AFHQ to help sort them out.

This was a bad time for Polish morale. The British government's abrupt decision to disband Anders's army had come as a bitter disappointment. Battle-hardened soldiers, at the peak of their form, were to be decanted back to foggy England with a free suit per man, a set of underwear, a trilby hat and a small gratuity. The trouble was that the Poles refused to believe the war was really over. How could it be, with Russians in occupation of their country and a lickspittle Communist government in Warsaw? Soviet propaganda meanwhile continued to brand Anders and his army as Fascists. On 8 June the Victory Parade in London was held without a Polish contingent because it would have been 'politically inexpedient' to have them present. The twenty-five Polish airmen from the Battle of Britain who were invited to attend declined to do so in sympathy with their comrades in the Polish Army and Navy who had been excluded.

The volunteers for repatriation from Cervinara were a mixed lot. Many of them were men whom Anders had recently recruited – Poles of 'uncertain' background from the German border provinces (Silesians, or '*Wasserpolacken*', for instance) whence they had been initially conscripted into the *Wehrmacht*. Others who opted to return included brave and disciplined soliders, but very few officers. The NKVD was also watching the camp. I recognised Colonel Jakovliev of the Moscow Mission snooping about – among his camp contacts was a Zionist Jew. I got the British Camp Commandant, Colonel Charnock, to eject them, and to unlock the camp gaol. Just before the last draft left by ship from Naples a medical inspection found about fifteen cases of VD, including syphilis. They were put in a truck to be driven to the general hospital, but jumped out and disappeared.

I was at the quayside when the last draft of Poles climbed up the gangway of the American Liberty ship that was to take them from Naples to Poland. They were heavily laden with kit, with spare blankets and new boots tied to their packs and a tin mug hanging from a strap. They knew that anything extra they could take with them – a good knife, a watch and woollen socks – would help them to survive the difficult days that lay ahead.

In the meantime, in addition to army duties, I had been tackling an urgent personal problem. Dunia's mother and sister were being well looked after by the Polish Red Cross, but news had come from Cairo that Dunia had fallen ill and was in a Greek nursing home. The army was immediately helpful and I was flown to see her. She had pulmonary tuberculosis – both lungs were affected – and when I took our daughter Gillian for a medical check I learned to my dismay that she had developed a glandular form of the disease. The Greek doctor warned me that to save Dunia's life I must get her away immediately to a cooler climate. This double blow filled me with despair. Dunia had always suffered from delicate lungs, but for Gillian to be struck down too was cruel. From that moment I hated Cairo, which seemed to have cast an evil eye on two fragile lives.

The army medical services were splendid. They evacuated Dunia and Gillian by hospital ship to Naples, where I visited them with Dunia's mother and sister, who had been moved to a families camp in Benevento awaiting a ship to England. It was now up to me to make further arrangements. Switzerland seemed the best choice for Dunia. I resolved to send her with Gillian to Davos because of its international reputation for tuberculosis treatment. The problem of how to pay the sanatorium fees scarcely entered my mind. Again the medical authorities at AFHQ behaved splendidly. They hitched a special Red Cross carriage with a British nurse on to the train for the journey to the Swiss border and we were able to travel together. Dr Wolff, head of the Waldsanatorium, was waiting for us in Davos – it was the same sanatorium Thomas Mann used as the scene of his disturbing novel *Der Zauberberg* (*The Magic Mountain*). Dunia was put under surgery, and a lung was collapsed. Gillian was placed in a children's nursing home run by nuns. Because of the risk of cross-infection the two were not to see each other for some time. Before I left, Dr Wolff insisted on X-raying my chest – 'just in case'. It was perfectly healthy.

The paradox of Davos was that it was full of sunburnt, clear-eyed people who looked the picture of health – cafés were crowded with people wolfing down rich cakes and spiced ham – yet many of them were consumptives: some were incurable, and some stayed in the sanatoria for years. The fees were stiff – I found that the monthly bill for Dunia and Gillian would take 80 per cent of my major's pay – and Dunia remained in Davos for another two years before she was well enough to rejoin me in Vienna (1948). Her exile was to change both our lives. I was disgustingly healthy. Dunia had become an invalid, part of a reclusive community obsessed with its health. By contrast I had my army life – a life that was extrovert, cheerful and unpredictable. To reconcile two such worlds and to accept them both required from me an act of mental adjustment that was no simple matter.

In August 1946 I was posted back to Riccione to take part in Operation Keelhaul. This was to be a preliminary to the final solution of the Russian repatriation problem in Italy. It involved separating the Russians into two categories – sheep and goats. The goats were to be repatriated to the USSR, if necessary by force. The sheep would be given Displaced Person status and remain in the West. Under Keelhaul, 498 Russians were rounded up and sent from Bagnoli camp to Riccione (a smaller number, 432, was concurrently sent by the American authorities from Aversa to Pisa). When the Riccione draft arrived I put the goats and the sheep into separate cages, as indicated on the nominal rolls which had been prepared by Major Simcock in Bagnoli. Among them were women and children. No one protested at the segregation, though the mood was serious. My orders were to rescreen everyone and to prepare the final nominal rolls that would decide their fate. My first task – it took me many weeks – was to draw up a maximum list of condemned Russians without exciting their suspicions. The leader of this group, Major Ivanov, a tall man and a strong disciplinarian, was co-operative. He believed, and I was not in a position to disabuse him, that if he and his men behaved themselves they would earn our commendation and eventually be given the status of political refugees. Through *naïveté* or honesty most of those who had served in the Red Army and/or German armed forces readily told me so. Others who at first tried to hide a military record were identified during the screening process through informers or careless gossip. At one time I thought, quite wrongly, that Major Ivanov himself might have been a Soviet 'plant'.

When I had completed my condemned list I started to execute my real, long-term intention, which was to reduce the list to a bare minimum. Under the currently enforced terms of the McNarney–Clark Directive, of which I had been given a copy, the three categories of Soviet citizens to be repatriated were (1) those captured in German uniform, (2) former members of the Soviet armed forces, (3) persons who had voluntarily rendered aid and comfort to the enemy. Category (2) I took little notice of unless combined with (1). The third category I ignored. But I qualified and to a large extent nullified the first category with a new one of my own invention: a non-repatriable category of 'para-military' personnel who, I informed AFHQ, had served only on guard duties along lines of communication or in base areas; as pioneer labour or Organisation Todt workers; as grooms, cooks, batmen and hospital orderlies. The German army had in fact employed a considerable number of such camp followers. AFHQ accepted the new 'para-military' classification. It was elastic and enabled me, by gradual elimination, to make a very large hole in my original condemned list. But it took time, for I had to submit each individual case for reprieve to AFHQ for approval.

I invented one other non-repatriable category – the 'ex-partisan'. But this I had to use sparingly. Certain other persons I eliminated from the list by telling them privately to escape, or by giving them certificates as Stateless Persons. Shortly before repatriation was due (Operation Eastwind) I took the long-calculated risk of striking the whole of the Kabardine group – 101 men – off the list. The Kabardines were a band of dour, illiterate Muslims. They stuck together like leeches and acted and spoke only through their leader, a former schoolmaster whose utopian wish was to emigrate with his flock to Syria. I persuaded AFHQ that these men had served with the *Wehrmacht* only on guard duties, armed with rifles (they and the Turkomans had in fact a reputation as looters).

Having got these men off the hook, I could do no more. By patient wangling, like a shopkeeper cooking his books, I had more than halved the original list of sacrificial goats (from 500 to 180). Senior officers at AFHQ would be growing uneasy at the continual erosion of names and Moscow, expecting to receive several hundred repatriates (its Soviet Mission had copies of the original Keelhaul nominal rolls prepared by Major Simcock), was going to be very angry. Indeed, the fact that I was deceiving my own authorities by doctoring the lists gave me an unpleasant feeling. But the two or three colleagues at 218 Sub-Area HQ, Riccione in whom I had confided gave me their full co-operation.

What struck me among the Russian soldiers and refugees was their lack of initiative, their apathy and fatalism. Two young Russian soldiers who escaped from their cage one day, instead of going to ground, got immediately drunk and were picked up and put back behind the wire. Major Ivanov actually punished them for escaping! Where women were present in camps there was a lot of denouncing. Even Germans, when captured, despite their soldierly qualities, lacked spirit. Their major concern was food. For an extra ration they would salute a corporal. The mixed 'German–Poles' were more troublesome; they never ceased complaining.

As the war receded, Riccione slowly came back to life. I had a German batman to bring me a sandwich lunch on the beach; another used to blow up my rugby ball. For these duties they were registered as working prisoners and so were allowed to draw extra rations. When news came in late autumn that the wives of British servicemen would be coming out to join their husbands, there was panic as well as joy. Married officers with Italian girl-friends had to dismiss them or hope and pray that they would keep out of sight. A major from AFHQ came down to Riccione to meet his wife off the train. Going to bed drunk, he was woken up, he told me, by a woman standing over his bed. He panicked. 'Go away, you whore!' he shouted. 'Denis,' he said, looking at me over his gin with a foolish smile, 'it was my wife.' From a Christmas party attended by several London Irish officers in the Officers' Hotel I retain an unforgettable picture of the regimental chaplain, an Irishman, lying on the dance floor with a whiskey glass in one hand, tripping people up by their ankles.

A surprise arrival at Riccione was a Romanian fugitive, Mihail Farcasanu, a newspaper editor, his wife Pia, and a pilot who had made a daring escape from near Timisoara in an old repaired bomber, and landed at Bari. Under strict security arrangements they were sent to Riccione and ordered to be kept out of sight – Soviet officers were still in the neighbourhood and would have made a great row had they been discovered. We put them up in the loft of the Officers' Hotel and I used to drink vino with them by candlelight.

I visited Dunia again after Christmas 1946, and during the ten days I stayed in the sanatorium its strange, hallucinatory atmosphere haunted me. Dunia had to rest most of the time. The lung that had not been permanently collapsed was slowly recovering. Gillian was expected to leave the nuns' hospice later in 1947. In the patients' struggle to get well, it was the temperature chart that obsessed them, the X-ray plate and state of the pneumothorax, the jar of expectorated phlegm, body weight and bowel movements. The cure was based on strict rules. Wrapped in blankets and furs on winter days, the patients lay like mummies on their balconies breathing the pure, expensive air of conifers and snow mountain.

In Riccione, winter had brought snow and slush and grey seas that smashed on to the shore. The officers' wives, having nothing to do, bickered and had family quarrels round smoky stoves. Out of boredom (it seemed fun at the time) I poured sand from a fire bucket into a Free French officer's bed. The huge Rimini enclave still held thousands of German prisoners awaiting release and transport home – former SS troops, i.e., recalcitrants, were at the end of the queue. There were also small groups of mixed or doubtful nationality – Czechs of the SS Prinz Eugen division, Bosnians of the SS Handzar division, border Poles, Croats, *Volksdeutsche* from the Banat conscripted into the German Field Police, Balts and Volga Germans. They were being screened by visiting missions from Prague, Warsaw and London, and the Croatian Ustashi especially were sifted for war criminals.

The Czech mission consisted of three officials who looked staid but had a repertoire of anti-Stalin jokes, and a chestnut-haired woman who was an outrageous flirt. Her apartment in Rome (which I visited) had been fitted out as a sumptuous love-nest paid for, she said, by a rich Italian. In her Rome-tailored uniform she looked quite out of place chatting with black-bearded Bosnians with faces like Barbary pirates from the SS Handzar division, several of whom were registered as syphilitics. I questioned some *Feldpolizei* soldiers from the Banat. They were elderly men, dragged into the war at the very end 'to keep law and order'. They struck me as harmless, but they belonged to a service with a record of atrocities and their chances of a speedy release were nil. The tin eagle in the cap badges worn by the Poles of the Warsaw mission had lost its crown. They were torn between grudging respect for the fighting record of General Anders's Poles and official disapproval of their 'Fascist' politics.

Brigadier Fitzroy Maclean's Refugee Commission from London was not concerned with Ukrainians or Russians. Its brief was to screen and sort out the confused political and ethnic affiliations of the Yugoslav prisoners and to look for war criminals. As an unmilitary group of young Englishmen they were not the type the army was used to and I described them (uncharitably) in a letter home as long-haired and spoilt – 'they slop about in carpet slippers and complain when there is no hot water or the lights fail . . . They think we are stupid. We probably are. We must seem a dull lot.'

One night in April I was sent with an escort of armed soldiers from the Royal Sussex Regiment to arrest some alleged Yugoslav war criminals at a refugee centre some miles to the south. Stephen Clissold of Brigadier

Maclean's mission came with me. We entered the camp dormitories at dawn, and seized the men without fuss. It seemed cruel for armed soldiers in helmets to burst into the sleeping quarters of these miserable families – the women wide-eyed and aghast, the frightened children peeping out from under the sheets. Clissold reassured me. 'The men are bad hats', he said. 'Now we have winkled them out, the other refugees will be left alone.'

As the date for the Allied withdrawal from Italy drew near, so did the day of reckoning for the Russians held in British and American custody: and when, at last, the eviction order was given, it was all over within a few hours. On 8 May 1947, under Operation Eastwind, the 180 British-held Russians were rounded up and, with the exception of nine married men, brought to Riccione railhead to be put on a sealed train for surrender to the Soviet authorities at St Valentin, on the zonal border in Austria. I went to the station to see them. They were orderly, and rather dazed. Though they realised what was going to happen to them as soon as razor blades and knives were removed from their kit, they showed no open resentment; but they had the strained faces of men about to go into action.

Major Ivanov, looking haggard but calm and in control of his men, broke away and came over to me. This was the Judas moment I had feared. I must go through with it.

'So you are sending us to our death after all', he said. 'I believed in you. Democracy has let us down.'

'You are the sacrifice', I answered. 'The others will now be safe.'

Ja znayu kak eto bilo trudno dla vas', he said. 'I know it has been difficult for you.'

So in his chivalry he was making it easier for me. He shook my hand and I gave him my cigarettes.

'This is a rotten job,' the officer in charge of the escort party of the Royal Sussex said to me, 'not really a job for soldiers at all.'

The nine married prisoners and their wives had been segregated. Since AFHQ had no wish to use force on women, we had given the wives the choice between accompanying their husbands to Russia or staying. On 9 May the nine couples were brought to a small building where, with Captain Bruce (a colleague) present, I interviewed them and posed the cruel alternative for the last time. One or two of the women could have been persuaded, or were willing, to accompany their menfolk into captivity. But none of the men would allow this – and we ourselves would have prevented them, in their own interests, from going. There was lamentation. Banderovicz, a young Cossack with a rosy face, and his wife were looking at me in such a way that I had to turn my back. On impulse I picked up the telephone and told Major Condron at AFHQ that I had discovered a last-minute error – Banderovicz had been a 'partisan' and I ought not to have put him on the list. I heard Major Condron swear. There was a pause till his voice came back. 'The Brigadier is furious,' he said, 'but it's all right.' The women were taken away, some of them struggling and wailing.

This incident illustrates the quandary in which the politicians who signed the Yalta repatriation terms had landed the British soldiers responsible for carrying them out, and the absurd power of a whim to decide a man's fate. One had a duty to be equally just, and therefore equally harsh. Why had I spared Banderovicz and not Grigorenko? Partiality was in itself an act of injustice. Why, for instance, during the earlier screening process, had I favoured a Caucasian lieutenant and his beautiful Armenian 'wife'. Because they were young, and deserved to be happy? (I certified her as a 'Stateless Person' and told him in confidence to escape.) Why, on the other hand, did I expose Colonel Lobisevicz, who had been lying low as a civilian? Because he had grown fat, hiding among the 'sheep' with a woman in his bed? Or because he had been a Cossack commanding officer and ought therefore to suffer with his men?

Why did I allow and encourage Major Ivanov to remain leader of those earmarked for sacrifice in Cage 7? Because, despite the omens, *he wanted* to be deceived? (A dozen other prisoners with a sharper instinct for survival, including the shrewd Georgian officer Matarashvilli, had taken alarm and escaped soon after arriving in the Rimini enclave.) Because of his unwitting efficiency as an agent of the repatriation plan? Because – and this was for me a compelling reason – I thought he was tough enough to take his punishment and to help others to do so? Why, indeed, had I done the job at all?

That was the cardinal question. I had brooded over and discussed it with two close colleagues (Captains Gorringe and Bruce), and I was sure of my answer. I had the authority and was in a better position than others to contrive a minimum sacrifice. The responsibility for the condemned would be mine, but that – and the embarrassment of having to bend the rules – was inherent in the calculation.

With Eastwind over, the remaining Russians wasted no tears on their departed comrades. In this they showed a rather ugly trait; but they were realists. They did not reproach me for the part I had played. They drank wine, celebrated, packed their bundles, and were dispersed as civilian refugees to Displaced Persons camps. The bearded Ukrainian priest whom I had allowed to live in one of the Russian cages gave me as a memento a heavy brass crucifix, and went back to Rome. Then came the truly happy ending. With the last-minute token sacrifice of the 170 scapegoats the authorities calculated that they had done enough to appease Moscow. Moscow's final demand for the surrender of the Ukrainian Division was bluntly refused and the whole formation was sent to England to be resettled in civilian life. Many later emigrated to Canada and Australia.

Even the move to England had its farcical incidents. War Office orders were that only those female dependants with nursing experience and without 'encumbrances' (children or elderly parents) could accompany the Ukrainian draft. This meant that a number of Ukrainian 'wives' did not qualify. Again the nominal rolls had to be doctored to find place for them and other unattached women (I classified them all as Red Cross workers). The three nurses from whom I had taken Russian lessons in the women's cage gave me a cushion they had embroidered in a traditional Ukrainian pattern. When the draft arrived at Southampton one of the unmarried women was seen by the reception committee to be heavily pregnant. London sent us an angry signal reprimanding us for including her in the draft.

When repatriation first started from Italy in 1944, there was little or no sympathy for the Russians bundled back to the USSR. In the British soldier's view they were, technically, deserters and traitors. Two years later, however, his mood had changed. Among the vineyards and the friendly Italian people soldiers were forgetting their wartime enmities. The Eastwind operation aroused various complaints. The Vatican protested against its inhumanity, and the matter was taken up by the British MP Richard Stokes in the House of Commons (21 May 1947). Moscow radio and press, on the other hand, accused the British – specifically naming me, 'Major Gills, a Fascist officer of the British Army' – of having 'spread Fascist propaganda among Soviet citizens and prevented them, against their wishes, from returning home.' For months before Eastwind I had been pressing AFHQ for an early decision that would put an end to the anxiety of people 'rotting in their cages'. When Eastwind was over I sent a final report to AFHQ on the whole episode. A little later I was asked to make an abridged version of this report for the War Office, who wished to be briefed for questions in the House. Let me look ahead for a moment to follow the later history of that report.

In 1974, while I was living in Kampala, I read Nicholas Bethell's book, The Last Secret, in which he described the forcible repatriation of Russians by the Allies in 1944–47. I wrote to him that I was the 'anonymous Captain A' (I was in fact a major) whom he had mentioned in his account of Operation Eastwind. Bethell's reply never reached me as in the meantime I was packed off to Amin's gaol;

and it was not until my release and return to England in July
1975 that I learned of the outcry stirred up through the media by
Bethell's revelations and by Solzhenitsyn's *Gulag Archipelago*, which
had appeared some months earlier. Bethell asked me to see him in
London, and I also met Nikolai Tolstoy who was researching his *Victims of Yalta* and wanted my testimony. It turned out that my AFHQ
report had been leaked to an American newspaper and had caught
Solzhenitsyn's eye in Russia while he was compiling the material for his
Gulag.

Solzhenitsyn's comment was as follows:

It is surprising that in the West, where political secrets cannot be
kept for long, since they inevitably come out in print or are disclosed,
the secret of *this* particular act of betrayal has been very well and
carefully kept by the British and American governments. This is truly
the last secret, or one of the last, of the Second World War.

Having encountered these people in camps, I was unable to believe
for a whole quarter-century that the public in the West knew *nothing*
of this action of the Western governments, this massive handing
over of ordinary Russian people to retribution and death. Not until
1973 – in the *Sunday Oklahaman* of January 21 – was an article by
Julius Epstein published. And I am here going to be so bold as to
express gratitude on behalf of the mass of those who perished and
those few left alive. One random little document was published from
the many volumes of the hitherto concealed case history of forced
repatriation to the Soviet Union.

Solzhenitsyn then quotes some of the words that I used in my
'random' – and for him revealing – 'little document'. 'After having
remained unmolested in British hands for two years,' I had reported,
'they [the Russians] had allowed themselves to be lulled into a false sense
of security and they were therefore taken completely by surprise . . . They
did not realise they were being repatriated . . . They were mainly simple
peasants with bitter personal grievances against the Bolsheviks . . .' They
were given, I concluded, the 'treatment reserved in the case of every other
nation for war criminals alone: that of being handed over against their
will to captors who, incidentally, are not expected to give them a fair
trial.' Solzhenitsyn commented, 'they were all sent to destruction on the
Archipelago'.

I had concluded my AFHQ report by saying: 'The decision to
repatriate one category (military personnel) and not the other (civilians)
was essentially an arbitrary one, based on the principle that an adequate number of bodies should be handed over to the Soviet authorities

in order to appease them ... Now that the damage has been done, it is essential that constructive measures be taken immediately to release and rehabilitate the surviving Russians in this enclave. Our prestige is at stake.'

In a broadcast in London in April 1976, after his eviction from the USSR, Solzhenitsyn repeated his charge of brutality against the British for their surrender of Russian men, women and children to Moscow – 'treacherously disarmed,' he says, 'bound, and handed over to the Communists to be killed, or sent to the labour camps in the Urals where they mined uranium for the atom bomb to be used against you yourselves.' What Solzhenitsyn had particularly in mind here was the forcible surrender of the thousands of Cossacks and their families whom the British army had rounded up in Austria when fighting ceased in May 1945. These men, confirmed 'anti-Bolsheviks', had enlisted in their own formations within the *Wehrmacht* during the war. Some of them were White Russian *émigrés* of long standing. 'You did not shrink', says Solzhenitsyn, 'from using the butts of your rifles on seventy-year-olds, those very men who had been Britain's allies in the First World War and who were now being hastily handed over to be murdered.' But Solzhenitsyn does not mention, and Bethell does not dwell on, the other side to the repatriation operations, for not all the facts were known to them, such as the calculated reprieve of the Galician Division, and the rejection, under Eastwind, of Moscow's demand for its expected tally of victims.

Bethell has rightly stressed the inhumanity of the Allies' forced repatriation policy. Underlying the original Yalta repatriation agreement was fear that Moscow would use the relatively few Allied prisoners-of-war it held in its territory as hostages against the surrender of the (infinitely larger number of) Soviet citizens who were in Allied hands. But even in this cynical sense, Eastwind was neither necessary nor relevant.

The British media have been conducting for years a *post mortem* on these events, and Nikolai Tolstoy's attempts to pin the blame on public figures have not only failed, but have cost him enormous libel damages. To many of us who were on the spot, however, the Russian men and women, the refugees, prisoners and deserters we had to handle, were not mere names on a nominal roll, or War Crimes statistics. They were human beings, sometimes our batmen, cooks, orderlies and mechanics. This is what the higher authorities, who never set eyes on the men whose fates they were controlling from far away offices, ignored or did not sufficiently recognise.

In early 1976 I shared a BBC television interview with Zoe Polanka-Palmer to coincide with the paperback publication of Bethell's *The Last*

Secret. Zoe, a young girl from Odessa, had survived with a badly gashed leg the violent scenes in the Drau valley in June 1945 when British soldiers, using their rifles as clubs, had been ordered by their senior officers to hand over thousands of Cossacks and their families to Red Army soldiers in the Soviet zone. As she sat in the studio relating this horrifying experience her voice did not falter, but I could see tears dropping slowly from her eyes. It was 'the cruelty of the British' – astonishing because so unexpected – that had appalled her ('The British would not do such things'). I said little.

The Keelhaul operation at Riccione reappeared like a ghost in 1978 when I was in Gwelo, Rhodesia. *The Times* of 20 February carried a front-page article, 'British Army officer tried to save Russian war refugees'. The article explained that documents had been declassified and published in Washington from AFHQ files on Operation Keelhaul disclosing my early attempts to whittle down the list of Russians liable for forced repatriation. These, I read, had incurred the displeasure of higher authority. 'Major Hills's action in releasing Soviet citizens was incorrect ... All Soviet citizens will be retained in military custody.' As I read the article, people I had forgotten about for years suddenly came to mind: the old Russian who had lost a leg, the peasant with metal teeth and a sack of potatoes ('my iron-ration for Siberia'), the ex-Polish Corps soldier who had lost his way.

The Times rang me up in Gwelo and, according to its reporter, I made these comments (21 February) on British repatriation policy: 'The British Army was tired. We wanted to go home. Then we were faced with this enormous problem of refugees. People could not be bothered. They had become callous through their experience in battle. They wanted to get rid of these people as quickly as possible and close the files. If we had had a few officers who had read a few books we could have done a better job. They were good soldiers, but they knew nothing of Russians or Poles. It was not a question of inhumanity.' In the words of *The Times* reporter, 'The lesson Mr Hills draws from the forcible repatriations of 1945–47 is the need to give serving officers more scope in such difficult circumstances. "In a military organisation one was not in a position to be humane, particularly at the highest levels, where orders were taken from the War Office." '

When the reporter asked me if I had been court-martialled for bending the repatriation rules, I said no. But I admitted that I had been court-martialled shortly afterwards for another offence. 'It was for doing gymnastics in the square at Trieste. I was rather drunk at the time.' *The Times* seemed to think this was the right note on which to end the interview.

One reminder of those old times is a farewell letter sent to me by Major Jaskewycz, typed in Ukrainian with English translation:

Ukrainian Camp Leader
Rimini, Italy   28 April 47

To Major Hills

Dear Major,

Leaving Italy I would never find peace on the hospitable English land if I would not express to you, dear Major, the sincere gratitude on behalf of the whole Ukrainian Camp Rimini as well as my personal gratitude for your highly humane work you have done in connexion with the special situation of this camp, defending the principles in the name of which the second world war has been started.

Your name, dear Major, has passed into the history of our camp as a symbol of truth, and not only into our camp life, but into the history of the struggle for independence of the whole Ukrainian nation which strives for the realisation of all the liberties granted by the Atlantic Charter of the well known four freedoms.

I realise that when the gates of the British Empire are now open to us, so this is, in the first rank, your merit. We shall never forget this as well as the wide circle of Ukrainian people will remember your work for our benefit.

Once more I thank you for all this, and I wish you much happiness in your private life.

Sincerely yours,

Jaskewycz
Major and Camp Leader

Here is another echo from the past. In an article ('You are the Grey Mass') that I wrote for *The Spectator* in December 1989, I described the Soviet military mission's visit to the Galician Division in the summer of 1945 (pp. 109–14 above). Svyatoslav Wasylko of the Federation of Ukrainians, Nottingham Branch, sent me this comment:

We could clearly see that the NKVD was poised to take 'that grey mass', only this time we were unarmed. Only the presence of British officers, their calm and uncommitted attitude, gave us some hope that nothing definite was decided on your part. Oh, yes, Mr Hills, or if we are not mistaken, Major Hills, you cannot even imagine how intently we were watching you and other officers in British uniforms. Having now read *Stalin's Secret War* and *Victims of Yalta* we can finally realise how lucky we were then. Everybody was tired of war, everybody wanted to go home – politicians, military personnel – and here were 'unknown Ukrainians – German collaborators – to bother about'. A single stroke of a pen, one tired attitude of a military commandant, could have sealed our fate for ever. And ever present was the NKVD team, like Lucifer's given gift, who were willing, oh so desperately willing, to take this burden off your hands. After so many years we still shudder and wonder, how on earth were you able to resist such temptations?

Thank you for being there at that time.

By now AFHQ had been broken up and the British element had moved via Padua to Venice where Danieli's had been requisitioned as an officers' hotel, the *vaporetti* didn't charge, and we, the latest spearhead of Italy's many invaders, sat in our starched khaki shorts in the cafés watching the pigeons foul St Mark's Square. In Riccione there were still a few loose ends to attend to. We heard, for instance, that the Italian *carabinieri* were holding, at the request of the Soviet Embassy, several Georgian officers on Lipari island. I obtained their release and sent them to join other Russians in a Displaced Persons camp. I learned too that once the British Army was out of the way and the Italian theatre closed down, the Soviet Embassy planned to put pressure on the Italians to rearrest and intern a number of Russians whom we had already released to refugee status. Some of the Russians who had survived Eastwind were now living as Displaced Persons in Riccione and had started little black-market businesses, in American cigarettes rerolled from stub ends and in pickled eels. Eva, a handsome woman who had caught my eye on the day of her arrival among the Keelhaul sheep and goats, was one of those who stayed behind. In the following weeks I got to know her well. She had had enough of the bickering and squalor, the petty thieving and betrayals, that spoil the lives of people locked up together like rats in a wired cage. Eva taught me Georgian songs (one of them haunts me still) and she was a good swimmer. We used to row out from the shore for a mile or more and take it in turns to swim back. When the coast had vanished into a blur and the shining salty waves scoured my body, I felt I had left the war behind.

Soon afterwards I was posted to Trieste, where at Duino Castle, perched above a turquoise bay, the adjutant was a Guards major. He had read my report on Eastwind and remarked, 'It's going to be difficult to find a niche for you.' I knew what he meant. I had shown myself as vaguely unreliable; I bent the rules. I was then told to see the senior Field Security officer in Trieste ('he may have something for you'). But I didn't want to become a bogus policeman. After a late night and much to drink, it was dawn when I walked back to the town square to find transport to Duino. The workmen's cafés were just opening and I had another vermouth. When I came to Trieste square – a huge colonnaded space paved with marble – it was deserted except for a single *carabiniere* leaning on his rifle. I gave him a cigarette and said, 'I'll race you round the square.' The *carabiniere* looked sheepish and shook his head. 'How about a few handsprings?' Alas, I had just begun to give him a demonstration when an army Jeep appeared bursting with regimental police. They were Cameronians, a unit notorious when on foray for thwacking Italians with their belts, and they must have been overjoyed at their catch. My 'unbecoming conduct' meant another court martial. But while I was waiting for the court to convene I noticed one morning that my urine had turned a horrid colour. The jaundice bug had got me again. I spent the next month in hospital.

At the court martial, where I pleaded guilty, my escort officer, known as the 'prisoner's friend', said a few extenuating words on my behalf. 'The defendant has been under stress through his recent involvement in Russian repatriation operations' – a form of excuse I would not have offered myself, for to my mind 'stress' is something of a cant word. The *carabiniere* gave evidence in court. He grinned at me and seemed to think the proceedings were a joke. I was given a reprimand and, minus a rank (I was demoted to substantive captain), I was sent on home leave to await another posting. I had no wish to be demobilised. Dunia's cure in Davos would take another year, and I needed my army pay to foot Dr Wolff's bills.

After seven years' absence it was a shock to come home – bombed houses standing among dock-weeds, unsmiling faces. I was still wearing battledress and felt out of place. My father had died soon after his retirement. My mother, a little greyer and slower, was still running the family home. My middle sister had died in childbirth in a Welsh clergyman's manse – I used to visit her in the thirties, when the valleys were full of unemployed men in caps and mufflers sitting round a tea-pot in leaking kitchens. A *Volltreffer* (direct hit) had demolished my brother's house in Moseley while he was at his air warden's post, but his wife and two small children were sitting in their Anderson shelter and emerged from the rubble unhurt. Moseley had become poor and shabby. Nothing had been painted for years. My pitifully small weekly food ration was just enough to stuff into my fore-and-aft cap. The old tradesmen were still at their posts – the butcher, baker, fishmonger and grocer, the chimney-sweep and the window-cleaner with their brushes and cleaning rags, their cheeks thinner and their faces more windchapped. But Mr Williams, a property-owning neighbour, had keeled over from a heart attack when two of his houses were smashed by German bombs.

There was some good news, too. Gillian was now well enough to leave Davos and she joined me at my mother's house. The nuns had taught her '*Schweizerdeutsch*'. I chopped wood, went for runs after dark, trotting past the wet privet hedges into the open fields where the winter mist lay in patches, and sat over a bright log fire till late at night. It seemed unfair that Britain should be suffering under such austerity, as though the Labour government were punishing us for having won the war. When I went into The Trafalgar Arms for cigarettes a toothless man in the ill-lit bar said to me, 'Still in the army, you poor bugger?' I met a few old school-friends. They had returned to their professions, and one or two were monstrously fat.

Soon after Christmas 1947 I received a new posting order from the War Office. I was to report to a War Criminals camp at Wolfsberg in Carinthia, Austria. At the same time I got a disturbing letter from Rome which confirmed my worst fears. The writer was an elderly White Russian officer whom I had helped to elude the Soviet trap. He used to wear a cap badge with the Tsar's emblem on it and had compromised himself by serving with the anti-Tito partisan Kazachy (Cossack) Corps. He wrote that some of the Displaced Persons I had released in Italy had been seized and sent to an internment camp. Among them was Eva. He asked me urgently to help her. I wasn't keen on bending the rules again, but I decided immediately to try to release her. On arriving at Wolfsberg I asked for a week's leave, borrowed a civilian jacket and trousers – I could not wear uniform in Italy as the theatre had closed down – and took the train to Rome. At Rome I persuaded the United Nations Refugee Relief Association office to type me a release document, which I dictated, ordering the Italian Camp Commandant to hand over the prisoner to me on authority of GHQ Vienna.

The journey by slow train to the camp took over an hour. When I got out at a small station I could see an open wired cage in the valley below me, dotted with huts and tiny, smoking chimneys. As I walked down the hill a few thoughts troubled me. Here I was, a bogus military document in my hand, about to deceive the Commandant, who might be a decent, friendly man. Yet I felt an overwhelming sense of loyalty to the old Tsarist officer who had taken my help for granted. Eva, I knew, was tough. But once the Russians got hold of her and threw her into a filthy, freezing cattle-truck it would be the end of her.

The Italian Commandant was a civilised man. He must have sniffed a little conspiracy when he saw Eva and some other women inmates wave to me over their laundry buckets. Within half an hour Eva had packed her bundle, the gate was opened, and we were out in the *campagna* standing amid rough grass, as free as the singing birds. I could do nothing for the others. At Rome we went to the office of *Russikom*; the priest recognised us both. I knew from Eva and other sources that *Russikom* had ways and means of smuggling Russian refugees to Spain and thence to Latin America. The priest was reassuring. 'We will look after the lady,' he said. Indeed, when I next had news from Eva, she had arrived safely in Rio de Janeiro, where she later married a fellow-Russian. Over twenty-five years later, on my release from Amin's execution cell at Bombo barracks, one of my most pleasant surprises was a telegram handed to me by the Foreign Office. It was a message from Eva and her husband Jerzy Orzeszko which had been forwarded from the British Consulate in São Paulo (30 June 1975). 'Old friends from Italy, residing in São Paulo, Brazil, wish you a prompt return to normal life and express their firm conviction that God Almighty shall help you, as you helped to save the lives of so many people during the post-war years in Europe.'

Chapter 8

Austria, Germany and England

It was midwinter. The War Criminals' camp at Wolfsberg with its eighty inmates and British staff was on the old Packstrasse pass not far from the border with Styria. It lay in an icy bowl ringed by snow-covered mountain peaks near the small town of Wolfsberg which was dominated by a castle, the seat of the Count von Donnersmark and his lively, flirtatious wife. The camp was a collection of closely guarded army huts embedded in frozen slush. The prisoners shuffled about in clogs on half-rations, wearing threadbare greatcoats and caps with ear flaps – they looked like those familiar pictures of men captured on the Russian front. They were given senselessly destructive jobs to do, such as dismantling unused army huts with crow bars. Colonel Cubitt, our CO, was a small rotund man with a fiery complexion and white Father Christmas moustache. He spent the afternoons learning to ski on the nursery slopes behind the mess with a Jewish captain who spoke German. Cubitt had a high, whinnying laugh which increased to a mad bray as he slipped and staggered in the snow. We messed in a villa in the town outskirts. As we sat round the great tiled *Kachelofen* (stove) reading paperbacks we were waited on by one of Cubitt's discoveries – a strapping wench of mixed Austrian and Slovenian blood with Junoesque thighs and bottom in a skirt so skimpy that every time she bent over a flush of frustrated lust inflamed the officers' faces and Cubitt squealed like a child. Our two young subalterns, Courage and Smith, referred to our unit as 'Cubitt's Follies'.

The Jewish officer was in charge of the prisoners' files. As soon as I took over I looked through them. They were almost empty except for a few personal details. They were, in fact, worthless. One was left to deduce that more detailed case records were kept at GHQ in Vienna: our own job was simply to ensure that no one ran away. Yet the administrative establishment in Vienna made no signs of coming to a decision about the prisoners. It was top-heavy with staff who didn't want to lose their jobs. I amused myself by interviewing the prisoners, who were Germans, Austrians and Yugoslavs. All I could do for them was to allow a few family visits on 'urgent compassionate grounds'. One man was a locally-born doctor whose wife lived nearby; another was a confused and tongue-tied veteran from an SS-Totenkopf unit – he may have been a villain, or senile (towards the end of the war the *Wehrmacht* was scraping the barrel for burned-out old men, and youths). My impression was that after 'a due lapse of time' the prisoners would be released *en bloc*, and their uncompleted files tucked away in an archive. As for ourselves, we had cushy jobs, a warm tiled stove, our drinks, and the monumental serving maid to excite our fantasies.

Sometimes important war criminals passed through the camp, among them an SS general and a Yugoslav Ustashi colonel. I had to escort the colonel with an armed guard to the Yugoslav border at Lavamünd where I handed him over to Tito's soldiers. He was calm and quiet during the journey and we didn't converse. Stephen Clissold would have called him 'one of the bad eggs'. Then there was General Wilhelm Schmalz, former commander of the Hermann Goering Division in Italy and one of the permanent prisoners. The general wore clogs and a threadbare greatcoat and was tall and haggard. We used to talk together. He told me he had ridden in Olympic events before the war and liked the English. At Cassino his fighting troops were among Germany's élite. He asked me to send his regards to the *Gräfin* in her huge unheated castle. The *Gräfin* invited me to her weekend parties there. The guests were Austrians with no money and plenty of charm. They thought it wrong that General Schmalz, a brave fighting soldier, should be treated like a common criminal.

As far as I could ascertain, the General was being held in Wolfsberg because troops under his command had carried out reprisals against Italian partisans. He struck me as an excellent and modest man. One afternoon I took him out for a walk. The sun was shining out of a blue sky on white fields of glittering snow dominated by jagged mountain peaks. After a time we stopped at a small *Gasthaus* and stayed drinking while the General chatted to local villagers who wanted to talk about the war. We walked back through the still, icy night singing, and the general slipped back into his cage like a lamb. I slept on the floor of the orderly room. In the morning I was on a charge – I had annoyed the duty sergeant by upsetting the files, which I used as a pillow, and – as

I was told later – my last words as I went to sleep were 'The colonel is a silly old c..t.'

For the next two weeks I was confined to my room with intervals for exercise. My escort officer was a former Lysander pilot. His first action on waking up in the morning was to reach for the gin bottle. While he lay in bed the two subalterns took me out for exercise. We soon discovered an inn that sold cheap and very sour *Most* (cider) which gave us diarrhoea. By now my own interest in the army had reached a low point. In fact, I tried my hand at writing verse in the style of Tennyson's *In Memoriam*. Courage and Smith thought some of my lines quite impressive ('. . . in a Styrian mountain bowl, Where icy giants look down on men in clogs'). The daily arrival of *Pravda* in a coarse brown wrapper also perplexed Colonel Cubitt. I had taken out a cheap subscription to the paper to extend my knowledge of Soviet affairs – it was the period when Ilya Ehrenburg, the journalist turncoat, was writing feature articles and the USSR had cynically switched its support from the Zionist Jews in Palestine to the Arab League. My colleagues considered my subscription a piece of bravado: and *Pravda* was dreadfully dull reading, with its interminable production figures and notes on Heroes of Labour.

It was in the inn where Courage, Smith and I stopped for *Most* that we met a dark, good looking girl, a former art student from Graz, who had a room in a farmer's cottage. I arranged to visit her after midnight, tiptoeing past the sleeping pilot, floundering through the snow and icy blackness and stealing into her room. The two subalterns were right to envy me. From the bleak world of army boots, gaiters and spam, and the ragged men with pinched faces who haunted the guarded huts, I had found a momentary escape. I visited her again in the frosty black nights. The picaresque side of the adventure added spice to it. No commitment, no broken promises were involved.

At the court martial General Schmalz denied that we were drunk. 'Why were you singing?' 'To keep warm – it was a cold night.' 'What did you drink?' 'Coffee, mineral water – a little wine.' I got away with a reprimand and the sergeant who had shopped me gave me a friendly smile. One member of the court told me later that, when the court was informed after the sentence that this was my third reprimand, 'their eyes popped out like organ-stops.'

Before I left, General Schmalz gave me his address in Germany and said wryly, 'I would like to have had you as one of my officers.' I have learned since, from his son (*Fregattenkapitän* Hubertus Schmalz), that the General was eventually brought to trial in Florence in 1950, accused of executing Italian partisans during the last days of the German retreat. He was acquitted on all counts, and retired to his family home in Laimbach, where he died in 1982. General Schmalz devoted his retirement to organising relief funds and assistance for old war comrades who were in distress. He spoke little about his years in captivity as a prisoner-of-war; but he developed a form of claustrophobia and couldn't bear being in closed places (*in kleinen Räumen könnte er sich nicht lange aufhalten*). The general is honoured among Germans as a war hero, a sportsman and a true gentleman. He was married to a niece of the Kaiser.

From this frozen hole I was sent to Bruck-an-der-Mur in Styria and attached to a liaison and security section. Captain Knight was in charge. He had picked up a crotch fungus and a medical orderly had shaved his private parts and painted them with gentian violet. He was so proud of the surreal effect ('I look like a baboon') that he unbuttoned himself and made me inspect the horror. I was billeted at the *Gasthof zum Schwarzen Adler*. It was a fine old coaching-inn next to a cobbled archway, with a clock tower on the hill above it, and was a favourite venue of anglers who came to catch trout in the mountain streams. We lived well – trout, veal, bilberries and wild strawberries, Viennese pastries – and were served by a ponderous old waiter who wore a frock coat and looked like Jeeves. The receptionist was a plump, nubile girl. She attracted the mating calls of officers. One billet-doux which she found on her pillow was from a well-known general ('Expect me at 23.00 hours').

My job was to interview a number of selected Austrians who had recently returned from prisoner-of-war camps in the USSR, and during their captivity and employment in labour gangs or in skilled trades were deemed to have picked up information of military value to the Allies. Some of the survivors were in good health: others looked battered and ill, or were suffering from the after-effects of oedema. The information, which they gave voluntarily, varied in value. But it complemented information collected through air reconnaissance, agents and informers and from other sources, and was collated by the War Office. I talked to these men for hours on end and they gave me an unforgettable picture of their life in Russia: the disease and deaths, the callousness of the MGB and guards, the treachery of agents planted by the camp authorities, the virtual impossibility of escape, the grinding poverty of the Russian factory- and farm-workers.

I liked Bruck. I had a BSA motor-cycle to tour the valleys and visit ex-prisoners in their homes. The steep *Almen* were dotted with barns and small farms. There were clear streams, flour mills, agile black and white cows, men in *Loden* and leather breeches and women in embroidered blouses. The inns with their big sloping roofs and wide eaves smelt of sour wine and woodsmoke. Every hamlet had its small Baroque church. Like extravagant toys, they glittered with gilt and painted Madonnas.

From Bruck I was transferred to Vienna, where I stayed at Schönbrunn in the requisitioned Park Hotel. I was allotted a few selected senior Austrian officers to interrogate. Apart from one divisional commander (*Hoch- und Deutschmeister* Division), a small, irate man, they were extremely co-operative and prepared lengthy written reports on their wartime experiences. Among them were the general commanding the German flak defences at Ploesti oilfields ('Your bombing raids were a nuisance but they never stopped the oil flow – we had brilliantly-organised repair teams'), an engineer colonel who had been close to Field Marshal von Paulus after the surrender at Stalingrad, and an infantry colonel with unusual theories. He believed Hitler should have launched his main offensive on Russia from the south and, taking advantage of the river system and the more favourable climate (an early start), he would easily have reached Moscow before the onset of winter.

I visited the officers in their homes. They lived in poorly-furnished apartments with faithful wives who scrimped and saved to make both ends meet. They would have liked to offer me hospitality but had nothing to spare; we drank my NAAFI cognac instead.

In July I had a shock. I was ordered to report to GHQ Vienna, where a solemn-faced colonel was waiting for me in his office. 'Did you write this?' he asked, showing me the document I had given to the Italian commandant some months earlier when I took Eva out of the internment camp near Rome. I said yes. 'Explain the circumstances.' He looked at me severely for a few moments, then said in a friendlier tone, 'Don't do this sort of thing again.' I gave him a cracking salute and walked back across the parade ground as though floating on air. The Colonel must have been a nice men. Later he used to stop me and ask about the Austrian officers' reports. 'They read like a novel,' he said.

About this time Dunia was at last allowed to leave the sanatorium at Davos and join me in the Park Hotel (Gillian was still with my mother in England). She was very frail, and mentally on edge. A fistula that showed no signs of healing added to her low spirits. She spent most of her time resting. I soon found that she didn't care for my officer colleagues, and that she detested the restrictions imposed on one's personal life by the military machine. The fact is, we had both changed. It was going to be very difficult for me to look after an invalid wife as long as I stayed in the army, and it was for this reason that I decided not to defer my release. Soon after Christmas we left Vienna for Liverpool Street by troop train (I was put in charge of twenty men). I had just been presented with a goose by a jolly publican. I put it in the bath tub and gave it next day to my staff-sergeant.

I collected my civilian clothes from an army depot – a suit that didn't fit with an arrow-head pattern, which I later swopped in Germany for some cognac, a trilby (or was it a pork-pie?) hat which I soon lost, and a modest gratuity, based on nine years' overseas service, to tide me over a fresh start in civvy street. Dunia and I stayed at my mother's in Moseley. Our reunion with Gillian was under the austere conditions of rationing and utility goods. With relief I accepted a post with the Allied Control Commission, Germany, and in April 1949, with a new suit-case instead of my old tin ammunition box, left for Bad Driburg in Westphalia. Dunia and Gillian were to follow me later. As the train skimmed through north Germany it passed some youths playing football in a field. The Allied Control Commission official sitting next to me grunted with disgust. 'Look at those bloody Nazis playing football,' he said. 'One would think that it was we who had lost the war.'

The unit at Bad Driburg was working as an interrogation team for the Joint Intelligence Bureau in London, with a branch at Herford. There were about eight of us, all German linguists; three were serving RAF officers. I was already familiar with what was required from my previous posts in Bruck and Vienna. Specially chosen ex-POWs recently released from the USSR were brought to Bad Driburg, fed and comfor-tably lodged for a few days, and questioned on what they had learned of intelligence value to the Allies during their captivity. The range of JIB interests was wide, covering economic, industrial and technical intelligence. Towards the end I was asked to concentrate on the work of German engineers who had been involved in Soviet rocket develop-ment, based on the V2, notably in Krassnogorsk. A team of German specialists and draughtsmen worked with us – without them, the qua-lity and detail of our reports would have been immeasurably poorer. My own German assistant was Dr Plessner, an expert on jet propulsion from Peenemünde.

Bad Driburg was a small Westphalian spa town. The arrival of the British, who had requisitioned the spa facilities and fenced them in with wire under a security guard, had killed it as a resort. Graf von Oeynhausen, the local count, deprived of access to his property, was living with his family outside the perimeter fence like a poor relation. We used the Graf's tennis courts, sat in the sun amid his flower beds, swam in the local open-air pool and were splendidly waited on by a German staff. The Graf was a dark, rather vain man. He chose me as his doubles partner in tennis, and hated losing. The Gräfin had poor health and rarely appeared.

The Graf had managed to retain a powerful turbo-charged Mercedes Benz in which he sometimes roared through the town. His daughter spent her time riding – there was British Army show jumping at Hameln, where I met my old Jerusalem acquaintance Captain Rod-zianko hobbling about in riding boots. The Graf's house was always full of refugee families and relations from East Prussia. They were destitute and charming, the girls athletic, bored and flirtatious. One of the von Borcke family, a ravishing blonde known as '*das blaue Wunder*' (her picture was used to advertise the spa's curative powers), used to climb over the barbed-wire security fence into our compound. We sometimes supplied the *Graf* with drink, but our unit was not officially encouraged to fraternise with him and his circle; and from his point of view we were intruders. We had plonked ourselves down in his spa with our rude Tyneside accents, our Marmite, sauce bottles and cognac, were sleeping in the guests' bedrooms, and five years after hostilities had ceased we were still denying him his home and his business.

I stayed in Bad Driburg – later in Herford, working with the JIB supervisor Dr Stern – for over a year. By then the flow of prisoners from the USSR had virtually dried up, Stalin claiming – what was not true – that the only Germans left behind in Soviet captivity were being detained as war criminals. When I returned to England with Dunia and Gillian, Dunia found a room in a Polish boarding-house near Notting Hill Gate. Dunia didn't like Germans, and she was relieved to come back to her own Polish people. Most of them had no money. My neighbour at table was a simple man who spoke little English and was on night-shift in a biscuit factory – his perks were a bag of broken biscuits which he brought home from work every day.

Our boarding-house was in a decayed Georgian crescent with flaking stucco, and we lived in a small room with a primus. Everything creaked – the stairs, the floorboards, the ceiling and the doors. I felt I was in a cage. I missed my army friendships, the privileges of rank in an insulated society and the self-assurance they had given me. I had become a nullo in civvy street, a nothing, among people whom in my former arrogance I had looked down on as leading dull, money-grubbing lives. I found it annoying to have to pay cash for everything – for a pair of socks, a bus ticket, even for a roof over one's head. For years I had slept under the stars, under canvas or in billets. Living in sunny climates had spoiled me. London was grey: grey skies, grey people, grey buildings. Worse, England was in the grip of a Socialist government. I had always been opposed to Socialism. Since my undergraduate days I had associated it with church-burning in Spain, with the *New Statesman*, with woolly pacifism and naïve adulation for Stalin's Russia. It was the Socialists who had got rid of Churchill in his moment of victory.

As I had no intention of settling in England, I looked round for an overseas post and called in turn on a Jewish businessman (recommended by an army friend) who had trading connections with Poland, Robin Hankey (now head of the Northern Department of the Foreign Office), the British Council, and the Oxford University Appointments Board.

I traced the Jewish merchant to a dirty little office in Surrey Docks – he took one look at me and told me to go away. Hankey told me that my role in the handling of Russian repatriation operations in Italy would be held against me ('You are certainly on Russia's black list'). The British Council official in Hanover Street informed me, in a squeaky voice, that the Council was reducing not increasing its establishment of teachers. 'In any case, you owe us a month's salary for breaking your contract when you joined the army.' The Appointments secretary at Oxford offered me a job as a public relations officer for some charity or other. This, however, was not a wasted journey. I rode to Oxford on an uncle's bicycle, slept behind a haystack where I woke to a beautiful sunny morning, and called on Chambers, head porter at my old college in The Turl. As I was talking to him outside the lodge, two undergraduates staggered past holding up a third, who was being sick. I was astonished to see how young they looked – and how tiny the college buildings seemed.

As a temporary escape from London, I made several long trips through the south of England and the Midlands on my uncle's bicycle, an old Raleigh model of 1922 with a heavy green and black frame. I slept out at night, in woods and fields, wrapped in a thin blanket and spare pullover, with my raincoat as groundsheet. I was woken by birds singing madly in landscapes wet with dew and the sun breaking through the early mist. In Alton I remember – and will never forget – the pure, tireless notes of a nightingale calling to its mate through the shadows. In a wood near Marlowe I was woken by a man who started back when I opened my eyes. 'I thought you was dead, sir.' I dozed on Chobham Common in a bed of grass and brambles. The ruined arches of Malmesbury Abbey made it look as if it had been ravaged by Scythians. These maverick escapades into the countryside were my act of defiance against the rules. The hum of my Dunlop tyres on the tarmac, the rush of wind in my face, the mug of cool dark beer at a small inn, gave me a sensuous thrill.

When my money ran out I called at Paddington Labour Exchange. They offered me a job as a night watchman at Whiteley's big store in Queensway, then changed their minds and sent me instead to the Festival of Britain organisation, which had its headquarters in Savoy Court and was working feverishly to prepare the South Bank site. Here I became a filing-clerk, with other misfits, at £5 a week. We were allowed to smoke and chat and read the paper. One of my colleagues was a former Tank Corps major. He sometimes carried away a parcel of office stationery which he flogged in a pub for drinks. At 5 p.m. when everyone else had gone home we would sit for an extra hour over the gas fire, clocking in overtime. Our boss was a lovable First War veteran, a Scot who had won a VC with the Black Watch in Flanders. One day he said to me, 'You're wasting your time here. There's a vacancy in the public relations department for an executive officer. Put in for it.' I did so and was accepted, at a glorious salary of £80 a month.

The Festival of Britain's aim (in its own words) was 'to portray the British way of life in a nation-wide programme of events' that would boost public morale, inject a little gaiety – and win votes for the Labour Party. It was sponsored by Herbert Morrison. My own brief, which lasted until the Festival was officially opened by the King on 1 May 1951 (when I was made immediately redundant), was to sell the Festival project to a variety of audiences – Rotary and Young Conservative clubs, the Women's Guild, Women's Institutes, church societies and public schools. In a twenty-minute talk, which I learned by heart and was tempted to recite backwards, I suggested the sort of enterprises that would make a suitable contribution to the Festival year: local museum and art exhibitions, erecting bus-stop shelters or park benches, repainting the town hall, adding an extension to the public library, morris dancing, pageants. All my audiences asked the same questions. Who was going to foot the bill: the ratepayer? And were the Festival organisers justified in using vast amounts of cement and construction materials at a time when their supply was still rationed? My answer was that the Festival would pay its way through receipts from a multitude of foreign visitors. 'But we don't want foreign visitors,' some said. 'They'll eat our food.' The Festival organisers had their worries too. Casual labour was employed to prepare the South Bank site, and the men frequently went on strike. Some were spivs. Leaning on their spades in waisted overcoats, they looked like deranged waiters.

The Festival was a praiseworthy gesture as well as a political stunt. The South Bank architects and designers erected some hideous buildings, but at least they showed a spirit of innovation. For me, it was an opportunity to travel in parts of England I did not know and talk to a wide range of people I would not otherwise have met. What excellent people they were, these country parsons, Rotarians and public-spirited ladies with their quixotic schemes to give the municipal toilets a new coat of paint and to run sausage stands.

During the winter, in addition to my jaunts for the Festival, I spent many hours reading German literature, for I felt that my best chance of getting work abroad was to find a teaching post in Germany. My interest in Germans was still strong and I wanted to get to know the young German generation – an unknown quantity, neutered by tragic events, still shouldering the burden of their parents' guilt. Then, drenched with the best German prose, and armed with the addresses of a few friends, I set off in May on my uncle's bicycle down the Old Kent Road for Vienna hoping to find a job on the way.

I had no sleeping-bag and relied on my light blanket and raincoat to see me through the nights. My appearance at Bad Driburg as a poor cyclist did not impress the *Graf* von Oeynhausen or his relatives, who not so long before had been happy to drink my NAAFI brandy. The *Graf*'s *Kurhaus* had been derequisitioned and paying guests, stout, ruddy products of Erhardt's *Wirtschaftswunder*, were flocking back to treat their dyspepsia and liver pains at his mineral springs. '*Das blaue Wunder*' had gone, packed off in disgrace to stay with the austere family of a Swedish admiral in Stockholm. From Bad Driburg I turned through the Sauerland for Munich and Salzburg, and called on the *Graf* von Donnersmark in Wolfsberg. I felt shy wheeling my thirty-year-old bicycle across the great castle courtyard, and disturbed a retired British naval officer (he turned a fishy eye on me) taking tea with the *Gräfin*. The war criminals camp had been emptied.

I now faced a problem. To enter the Soviet zone of Austria I needed an inter-zonal pass, and I would have to be cleared by a Red Army frontier post at the Semmering crossing-point. But I was in no mood to confront a Red Army policeman, in case my name was indeed on the black list of Soviet Intelligence. So I had to leave the high road and find a way to cross the zonal border at an unguarded place. Soon after Mürz-zu-Schlag I turned off the Vienna road and humped my bicycle into the hills. It was hard work, picking my way up fir-covered ridges for an hour or more, and I was relieved to come at last to a small plateau where a few strands of barbed wire and a rough wooden fence marked the frontier. I was overlooking the Semmering pass. From somewhere below I could hear the ring of a woodman's axe. As I sat down to recover my breath, a young man came through the firs with a suitcase strapped to his back. I was delighted to meet a fellow law-breaker and gave him a cigarette. He too had no papers. I didn't inquire after his business, but he said he had already spent some weeks in gaol, 'cutting logs with a very small saw'.

Once inside the Soviet zone I bowled downhill through woodland and steep hayfields to Neunkirchen, and stopped at a village store. The shopkeeper followed me outside, shook my hand, and said 'Watch out for Austrian gendarmes. Nine out of ten are probably good fellows, but the tenth might run you in. If you meet Russian soldiers,' he added, 'take no notice of them and they won't bother you.'

Not far from Baden, after dark, I went into a country inn for a meal before looking for a field or wood in which to doss down for the night. The inn was filled with Communist posters of the 'Blood and Steel' variety, and the innkeeper was unpleasantly inquisitive, for he sat down at my table and began to question me. What was my business? Where did I intend to spend the night? Was I not afraid of the Russians? I noticed that the other customers were watching me. At that moment a gendarme came in. When the innkeeper got up to draw him a glass of beer I quickly paid my bill and slipped away. No one followed me. The road was bordered by patches of maize and vineyards outlined by moonlight. After a time I found a hollow among some vines, near a colony of noisy frogs. To my dismay, I soon discovered that I was at the edge of a Soviet military airfield. For an hour an aircraft circled overhead, pursued by the bright fingers of searchlights. Throughout the night they rotated, like a groping hand, round my sleeping place. Oddly enough I found I was enjoying the situation. The earth felt warm and friendly, frogs barked merrily, I slept well and, soaked in dew, left before the morning mist had lifted.

I didn't stay long in Vienna. The cobbled streets punished my uncle's bicycle, my old unit had folded up, and I was soon pedalling back through the ragged approaches to the city against a stream of Russian military vehicles that had a habit of stopping on the crown of the road. The Russians had closed Wiener Neustadt to through-traffic, but I ignored the diversion signs. The town was a mass of heavily damaged houses and piles of debris. Though the war had been over for five years, it seemed to be largely uninhabited. Little yellow-faced soldiers with bandy legs were trying the doors of locked houses or loafing round the railway station. The town cemetery attracted my attention, for it was sign-posted in Russian, and I went in. Here was a section of Red Army graves marked with five-pointed stars of flattened tin. I counted the names of thirty Russian officers with the rank of captain and major. From the inscriptions I saw that they had all died since the war, in 1946 and 1947. Affrays? Drunken driving? The effect of the little red stars in place of crosses was strikingly pagan.

I left the highway again at Wiener Neustadt and spent three days ambling through the valleys. I saw few Red Army soldiers: Austrians told me that Russian garrisons were generally confined to the main lines of communication and that 'Ivan was kept away from villages'. The hay crop had been good. Half a litre of *Most* cost one schilling (about 3*d*). I slept in the corner of a meadow or in a spinney, the long night stillness broken only by crickets, the rustle of cattle and the splash of a stream. Crawling from cover into the brilliant early morning sunshine, I felt as light and strong as a long-distance runner.

From Neunkirchen a woodman showed me a short cut through the hills that took me straight to the Styrian (British) side of the zonal border and I was soon free-wheeling down the long gradients to Bruck. Here the landlord of *Zum Schwarzen Adler*, an old friend, put me up for nothing and the ancient waiter filled me with veal cutlets, pancakes and wine. From Bruck I pedalled over the Tauern Pass and back to

Munich. It was now time for me to look for a job, and I was lucky. Through the Anglo-German Society in Munich I met a charming German who was about to open a new English-language school. He invited me to join his staff in September. I was also told of a newly inaugurated English department, affiliated to Mainz University, at the old Palatinate fortress town of Germersheim on the Rhine. I resolved to call there before making further plans, travelling via Würzburg. To see more of the countryside I chose side roads that took me through rustic corners of Bavaria unscarred by war. I was back in the world of Eichendorff. At Dachau, however, the romantic spell was interrupted. The concentration camp had been turned into a museum for ghouls and sightseers. Some of the Germans I spoke to expressed disbelief in the horror-stories concerning the camp. The young uniformed German guard at the gate told me that the Americans had been spreading lies (*Greuelpropaganda*), and when I asked a grocer's wife about the smoke that used to rise from the crematorium chimney she said 'We thought they were making sausages.' Beyond Dachau, along the winding Tauber valley, I was back again among the sun-cracked walls, the thatch and orchards of mediaeval Germany. When I got to Germersheim I was looking travel-worn. So I bathed in the Rhine, and hid my bicycle before calling on Professor Jaeger. He was delighted to meet an 'Oxford graduate and former British Army officer', and would be pleased to have me as *Lektor* when the college reopened in October.

By the time I had reached Düren, 300 km. from Ostend, I had nothing left but a few coins and the fare for the ferry. With my remaining pfennigs I bought a huge rye loaf and some cranberry jam. They lasted me to Notting Hill Gate. Looking back on this speculative attempt to start a new life, I could say that my journey had been worth while. It was, in a sense, a reversion to my undergraduate past.

I spent the remaining summer months tramping round London's parks, listening to the military bands and reading. I bathed once in the Serpentine – an unpleasant place used by body-builders and sly old men. One morning I chased some urchins who were vandalising a tree – I caught one and thwacked him with a broken branch. As I was walking away a man came up. 'That was brave of you,' he said; 'these days we look the other way.' Near Notting Hill tube station there was a café whose owner, a German Jew, allowed me to sit for hours with a book. I read Grillparzer and Jean-Paul Richter, de Vigny and Gide, trying to fill in the gaps left by a decade of neglect. Diana Dors used to visit the café with an escort of two vain young men.

In September I travelled to Munich and gave my first lessons. Through Bencke, the director of the school, I was given additional classes at a *gymnasium*, which meant that I had to register as a Bavarian government *Beamter* (official). At the end of the month the Oktoberfest was celebrated – a fortnight of fierce and noisy junketing in which thousands of visitors drained an ocean of beer in litre mugs and roared like lions; one could hear them a mile away. I liked Munich: its athletic young people and brown-eyed girls, its *Gemütlichkeit* and its proximity to the Alps. But Germersheim had more to offer academically. With regret I said goodbye to Herr Bencke and accepted the post offered by Professor Jaeger. Dunia and Gillian were to join me. I was to stay in Germersheim, with an interval in Düsseldorf, for over three years.

Chapter 9

Rhine and Alps

A t this time, in the early 1950s, the shadow of Hitler's infamy was receding, and the Germans were showing an almost neurotic eagerness to be readmitted into the cultural and economic life of their western neighbours. Commercial and business employees, officials and students flocked to English-language centres to qualify as foreign commercial correspondents, translators, interpreters and teachers.

The Foreign Languages Institute at Germersheim (*Auslands- und Dolmetscherinstitut*) had 700 students, and English, French and Russian departments (the last very small). The Institute had been set up by the French occupation authorities and was affiliated to the Johannes Gutenberg University at Mainz. The French lecturers enjoyed certain privileges – they had a families shop where they could buy coffee, Gauloise cigarettes and brandy, and they had no inhibitions about having affairs with the girl students. Professor Jaeger asked me to lecture on British economic history. This meant I had to mug up my faded memories of medieval tillage, the Mercantile Laws and Protectionism, the trade in slaves and opium, and the Anglo-Egyptian Sudan. The Institute library was inadequate: it consisted mainly of haphazard gifts from the Americans, and at first I took the *Encyclopaedia Britannica* to bed at night, starting with volume one (Aarhus, Aborigines, Armour, Artillery ...). The teaching staff was poorly paid. None of us owned a car. We rode bicycles up and down the cobbled streets and along the Rhine towpath, and shopped at small groceries – my standby for supper was pickled herring, sour milk and Mainzer 'stink-cheese', for less than a mark. I was given an attic apartment in a disused hostel with a small iron stove and a floor of bare boards. Dunia and Gillian joined me, and

Gillian attended the French children's school.

The students were delightful and I spent most of my time with them. With the tennis team I made jaunts to Landau, Speyer, Heidelberg and Trifels, where we played under a craggy ruin in which Richard the Lion Heart was once held captive. We swam in the Baggersee quarry or in the Rhine. The great black river swept rapidly by between rows of poplar trees, carrying barges loaded with oil and coal and family crews with dogs and washing lines. The sleepy little town was crammed with small frowsty inns run by ageing landlords who sat nodding behind the bar. *Glühwein* (mulled wine) drunk out of a bowl was a favourite among students. It was cheap, but left a vile hangover. Germersheim had once been a powerful Rhine fortress and in the nineteenth century it was rebuilt and enclosed by massive walls beyond which building was prohibited. Its thirsty Bavarian garrisons accounted for the thirty-eight inns in a town with a resident population of under 5,000. Photographs of the Kaiser's soldiers in spiked helmets and field boots, posed amid beer tents, flags and gun carriages, hung in the drinking parlours. With its jumble of small buildings and shops (many people kept pigs), the town smelled of sour wine and midden heaps. The nights were plagued by large gnats. Most of the older houses stood on their own cesspits, with 'long drop' latrines: a municipal lorry with a suction pump used to remove the night-soil.

Under the Allied occupation, Germersheim had become the administrative centre for an American vehicle park and supply dump. The American troops were reinforced by Polish and Bulgarian guard companies and German auxiliaries – 'Adenauer soldiers', as they were scornfully called by other Germans. The college compound had been put out of bounds to the GIs and they had to seek their girls elsewhere. The Poles and Bulgarians preferred their own nostalgic canteens. But I got to know a Russian soldier defector. He used to give away army clothes and hooch to the students because, he said, 'They have good hearts and their company makes me feel less lonely'. He disappeared one day, taking with him a pretty girl from the Russian department.

Dunia disliked Germersheim. She had an understandable bias against Germans, the town was too dull and rustic for her, and she longed to live in France where her mother had studied painting. In the summer of 1952 she took Gillian with her to a pension in the Black Forest. A year later she moved to Nice. Meanwhile I spent my vacations (almost six months in a year) getting rid of surplus energy. I cycled from one end of Europe to the other – to the North Cape on the Arctic Sea and to Salonica – and spent many weeks skiing over the Hochalp glaciers of the Vorarlberg and Tirol. The students too were enthusiastic travellers. Travelling rough, they would turn up in Inverness, Stockholm or Paris with their back-packs. They had little money and sometimes lived on bread and apples. But the only paid work they could find in England was at harvest camps, and girls had to take menial jobs in hospitals and lunatic asylums, or as domestic helps.

Then at the start of my third year at the Institute (October 1953) I was given the sack. I had just returned from my bicycle journey to the North Cape, and gave a party in my room. Along the corridor two girl students were living, a quiet and rather prudish pair. At midnight, fired by wine and the best intentions, we decided to invite them to join us. I knocked. There were protests. I tried the door handle and – being as clumsy as an ox – snapped it off like a chicken bone. Feeling silly, I retreated. Next morning I was on the mat. The director had been newly appointed and was not sympathetic. Molesting girls in the night, he said, was not on. I would have to go. Professor Jaeger, however, told me not to worry. 'I have another post waiting for you in Düsseldorf. The owner of the school is a rich widow. Be nice to her.'

At the languages school in Düsseldorf I had to face my first class at 8 a.m., which meant hurrying through the dark streets like a night-worker. In the evening I taught commercial correspondence and became expert on bills of lading, demurrage and the dollar gap. I also gave talks to the Anglo-German Society. At one meeting the members discussed Montserrat's *The Cruel Sea*. They were shocked by its 'English callousness'. Then the spring sunshine turned my thoughts to the open air. I packed my tin box, my tennis racket and skis, and returned to my friends in Germersheim.

To tide me over I took a navvying job. There were twenty men in our gang, rebuilding a country road that ran through tobacco fields and orchards. We were a mixed lot: three *Volksdeutsche* from the Balkans, two students, a gipsy who wore a ragged Bikini shirt and army field boots, a former parachutist, and a toothless ex-SS man. The roller driver and tar sprayer had worked for the Todt Organisation in the war, building strong-points in the Atlantic Wall under our present employer, Herr Steyer. Once a prominent Nazi and local *Bürgermeister*, Herr Steyer had been interned after the war but had prospered again through American army engineering contracts. Our ex-Navy foreman had a wooden leg – he was wounded in the siege of Brest – and a whistle. Most of the men had been recruited through the local labour exchange as casual labourers. They worked in the summer and went on the dole for *Stempelgeld* in the winter. The two students were earning the fees for further study, and (like myself) saw no social stigma in navvying with a spade, a *Japaner* (wheelbarrow) and pneumatic drill. Most of us, of course, were failures – uprooted by the war or untrained for any profitable trade. The pay wasn't very good: 1.42 DM (about 12½p.) an hour for a back-breaking 50-hour working week, excluding overtime, which brought in less than £6 every Friday ('*Lauter pfennige*, a few miserable coppers', the men grumbled when the pay packet was delivered by a clerk on a bicycle, and one of us was immediately sent to bring back beer or wine and cigarettes). The working day was from 7 to 5, with a 15-minute pause for breakfast and 45 minutes for lunch. We ate our bread and liver-sausage sitting on our jackets in a field. Tea was despised. Everyone drank beer or wine and we smoked the cheapest *Rothändle* tobacco, which was grown locally. I usually drank water. This made the others laugh. '*Du kriegst einen blauen Darm*', 'Your gut will turn blue.'

We worked with a relentless rhythm that seemed to suit the German disposition and method. The foreman was always on the prowl with his whistle. We were allowed to fall-out briefly to urinate against a tree but there was no break for a smoke, no hanging about. For hours at a stretch we hacked, shovelled, pushed barrows laden with hot tar and manhandled heavy pipes, in a state of perpetual motion. As my work comrades said when I paused to lean on my spade, '*Die Hosen müssen wackeln*, Keep your trousers shaking.' I used to cycle to work, sometimes up to 20 km., overtaking the early morning farm carts. I was never late. I didn't want to let my workmates down; and a hangover, a thumping heart and throbbing head would have made shovelling stone chips into a lorry all day a torment. After a few weeks my arm muscles stood out like oranges.

The English working man, in my experience, is notorious for his foul vocabulary. By comparison Herr Steyer's gang were paragons. But the toothless ex-SS man would brag about his virility. 'I woke up this morning with such an erection,' he would say, 'I could have cracked a nut with it.' When we had rebuilt our road, we laid sewage pipes and water mains in villages and built a hard-standing for army vehicles at the French Army barracks in Speyer. After finishing a job Herr Steyer would stand us a *Richtfest* – free beer, *Bratwurst* and television at an inn. The gang sneered at the French Army band that practised every morning on the barrack square in Speyer. Germans of the Palatinate hated the French. The province had a long history as a battlefield between the two nations. The Alsatian border at Wissembourg was not far away, and stories were still told of the brutality shown by the French native troops (*Goums*) to the German inhabitants – the arson, looting and murder. During army exercises the gang jeered at the convoys and dragged wheelbarrows across the road to annoy them. They thought French reliance on foreign equipment a humiliating sign of her poverty.

More than half the road gang had served in the *Wehrmacht* and would allow no criticism of its prowess. By crushing Germany in 1945, they told me many times as we sat on the grass during the meal break, the Western Allies 'had slaughtered the wrong pig (*haben das falsche Schwein geschlachtet*)'. With Hitler out of the way we ought to have joined hands with the *Wehrmacht* and 'driven the Russkis back to where they came from. Then all our problems would have been solved.' These men bitterly resented the charge that the German soldier was a war criminal. 'It was the Nazis and special units that carried out atrocities.' Reprisals? They were inevitable, a military necessity, the only way of checking partisan activity. What would the British have done under similar circumstances? And what about the Allied terror bombing (*Terrorangriffe*) of German populations in towns: and the pillaging by French troops when they invaded German territory? They were sceptical about Germany's planned rearmament under Allied sponsorship. In the event of another war they saw themselves being used to cover the retreat of the Allies to bases farther west. 'We shall be the cannon fodder.' As *Landsers* they knew what war meant: mud, snow, death – or starving in a barbed-wire cage with lice and dysentery and no Red Cross parcels.

In September I left the road gang for three weeks and worked on the grape harvest in the hills near Nüssdorf, on the Weinstrasse. There were three other hired labourers, and we slept in a barn among bundles of hay. Our employer was a rough farmer. He woke us at dawn by putting his head under a pump in the yard and belching like an animal. We were kept hard at work till dark. A big wooden *Hotte* (hod) was strapped to my back and I shuffled up and down the rows of vines while the pickers filled it with bunches of grapes. I then tipped my load into a great barrel on a cart. I must have gorged hundreds of grapes (they were rather sour), stuffing them into my mouth with my free hand. The next part of the job was unpleasant. The grapes were pressed in a huge vat. I then had to fill my hod with scummy liquid, full of grape skins, and empty it into containers in the cellar, where the wine was left to settle. Drenched and filthy, my hair matted as though dipped in syrup, I was glad when we were sent off to a field to dig a potato dump. I enjoyed my time at the farm. The coarse *Vollkorn* bread and thick cheese we ate squatting among the vines at the midday break had been earned by real sweat. Our evening meal of soup and fat pork which we shared with the farmer and his wife at a long kitchen table was consumed in a daze of strong Haardt wine. Among vine-covered hills I had taken part in one of mankind's oldest rites – a grape harvest; and I went back to Germersheim to rejoin Herr Steyer's road gang with £10 in my pocket.

In late December hard frost put an end to outdoor labouring work, the road gang was dismissed and went on the dole. It was high time for me to retreat to England, take stock and look for another teaching post. I had seen enough Germans for the time being. But I would go away with happy memories. My students had been delightful to teach and befriend. They were idealists. They didn't look back to the disastrous past, for which they did not feel responsible, but to the future and to West Germany's reintegration into Western Europe. On the question of Germany's projected rearmament, however, they had, like most Germans, strong doubts; and as for serving in a new West German Army, their attitude to the once-sacred principle of military service (*Wehrpflicht*) was summed up in the laconic phrase '*Ohne mich*! – You can count me out!' Like the road-gang labourers, they feared that in another war they would be used as America's sacrificial sheep. As for myself, I was not there to moralise. In the lecture-room I had avoided mentioning Hitler, as though there was a taboo on his dreadful memory.

Part of the charm of student life in Germersheim was, of course, that none of us had any money. The professors, like Victorian ushers, trundled their baggage to the railway station on the college trolley. Dr Kissling eked out his little jar of Nescafé for weeks. The students made do with the cheapest wine, ate their meals in the college *mensa* (canteen) – *Bratwurst* and potatoes soaked in gravy (*Tunke*) – and ran their own entertainments. There was no violence or ragging – the bill for breakages must have been infinitesimal. Poverty and the depressing effect of defeat had reinforced the inborn German respect for property and discipline.

My other debt to Germersheim was that the long vacations had enabled me to see a great deal of Europe by rough travel on a bicycle and skis. I had discovered that, viewed from a bicycle, the land-mass of Europe from the North Cape to Salonica is indeed an entrancing garden of slowly unfolding scenes rich in the hospitality of simple people, whether Lapps or Macedonian gypsies. I slept in fields. In Serbia I would wake to see staring faces of men with sheep or cows – they would offer me grapes or a lump of salty white cheese in a cloth, and ask me the cost of my bicycle; was I not afraid of snakes? In the Balkans there was little traffic – a few tiny red Fiats, some snub-nosed Russian-made lorries and farm carts pulled by water buffaloes. The 250-mile *autoput* from Zagreb to Belgrade, a gleaming ribbon of concrete flung straight as an arrow across a flat plain, had only just been built – by 'volunteers', many of them students – and had no petrol stations or pull-ups. When I reached the sea at Perea, across the bay from Salonica, the water, which today is covered in scum, was clear and the beach untrampled.

In Scandinavia, along the old Arctic highway through Finland to Hammerfest, I followed the Pole Star which glittered like a huge crystal and slept in little hay barns under the ghostly radiance of the Northern Lights. But having reached Honningsvag (North Cape), the thought of pedalling back to Germany along the endless rocky fjords appalled me. My host, a Norwegian house-painter, came to my rescue: 'Get a lift in a fishing boat.' This was soon done. A pilot took me out one morning to the *Kingston Onyx*, 350 tons, out of Hull. Leaning over the rail was a one-eyed sailor in a blue jersey. 'Can you give me a lift to England?' I bawled, feeling rather idiotic. Without a word he beckoned me to climb aboard with my bicycle. The trawler had been fishing for cod and haddock off Bear Island. I was given a bunk full of orange peel and old *Daily Mirror* newspapers, and a week later landed in Hull. I counted my money. It was 20 German marks and as it was Sunday I could find no one to change it, not even at the Seamen's Mission. There was a further embarrassment to come. I had to report to the Aliens Department.

What had become my real passion, though, were skiing journeys. I had taken my first skiing lessons at a Forces' skiing centre at Tegernsee in Bavaria while I was in Bad Driburg. Before the course was over I had learned enough to leave the pistes and wander off tentatively on my own. Here I had my first glimpse of a hitherto unknown world of beauty and solitude. For my subsequent cross-country trips through the High Alps I chose, as my starting point, Mittelberg in the Klein Walsertal. This was a German-administered Austrian enclave on the Bavarian border with the Vorarlberg. Mittelberg had an inn, a white-washed church with loud bells, and was said to be in an avalanche-free area, though just before my first visit a *Staublawine* had blasted a students' ski hostel, killing twenty of them. From here I made my first ski journeys, which took many days, through the Vorarlberg and into the Tirol, skiing down into Italy from the Oeztal, and traversing the Silvretta glaciers to Klosters–Davos in Switzerland before turning back to Bavaria via the Parsenn run and St Antonien. My final aim was to ski once more into Switzerland and cross into France before catching a train to England. It might be my last chance to see the High Alps before tourism took over the humble villages. Dunia and Gillian, in the meantime, had settled in Nice. Dunia had no intention of leaving France, and it was clear that our ways had taken different directions. Within a few years, indeed, Dunia was to introduce Gillian to the Paris film world of Vadim, as a young actress.

I was used by now to skiing alone and sleeping in mountain refuges. For me, a complete amateur, the journeys were an adventure. They were also a long, hard slog. Once among the high peaks far above the settled valleys and the tree line, one might spend most of the day toiling in zigzags up a mountain pass with skins tied to one's skis for grip and with no immediate hope of a sustained run down at speed. There were hazards: the possibility of an injury far from assistance; a sudden change of weather transforming the mountains from genial giants into a wilderness of tearing winds and blinding snow. I was once caught in a snow storm and second-degree frostbite turned my fingers black and swollen for days. Avalanches could occur in unpredictable places and might be set off by the skier's own clumsiness – the big ones roared past like express trains, peeling great swathes in the snow, and if there were trees, smashing them like matchwood. Among the fractured glaciers one had to negotiate crevasses and ice-falls that glittered like blue-green marble cliffs. But the joys far outweighed the pain. The moments of tension or of downright fear sharpened the appetite for more. I was never bored. Landmarks and snow conditions were always changing, there was the constant effort of finding the best route, and from time to time the thrill of swooping for miles down a great glacier slope unmarked by anyone else's ski tracks. Finally, there were the wonderful moments of relief: sitting down on my anorak among the white peaks, a tiny dot under a sky of rich blue velvet, eating *Knackwurst* and a lemon; and as the sun dipped and darkness approached, turning the brilliant mountain light into grey shadow, that first glimpse of my refuge for the night – a hut with a lantern, warmth and companionship. For the High Alps were not entirely deserted. Mountain huts were spaced at intervals like friendly pickets in the more accessible areas, with a keeper to provide hot meals and bunks.

The *Hüttengeist* (hut atmosphere) bred convivial memories. As the refuge filled up towards dark, the long tables disappeared under food containers, tea-cans and ski maps. Socks, boots and seal-skins hanging up to dry hid the glowing stove. Everyone shouted at once for goulash and tea-water. There was singing and accordion music. Many of the guests I met were good-natured Germans of the artisan class from as far afield as Hamburg, who had saved up for months to enjoy their winter jaunt. Yet few of them were young. A retired official from Vienna, looking round at the middle-aged and greying heads bent over Alpine journals in the Ulmer Hut, told me, 'Our young people have no ideals. They care only for racing down prepared runs like madmen a dozen times a day – exploring the mountains is too dull for them.'

Now, at the start of my last ski trip before leaving Germany, I plodded slowly on skis past the massive Witterstein and over the Hochalp Pass from Klein Walsertal into Austria. There was a mountain hut at this point, where I had once spent twenty-four hours lying in darkness on a plank with a bout of snowblindness (the eyes seem choked with grit and cannot bear the light). On a fine day green-uniformed gendarmes sometimes patrolled the pass looking for petty smugglers. One of them called me over. He laughed when I told him I was English. '*Die Engländer*', he said, '*sind unverwüstlich* – the English are indestructible.' From the saddle I trekked over the lonely Auenfelder to

Lech-am-Arlberg, where I spent the night in a grocer's store-room. From Lech it took me the greater part of a day and a long traverse to climb to Zürs and the next major pass over the Valluha. The reward was a long, swift descent past the Ulmer Hut and down the Kandahar-Strecke, one of Europe's famous ski runs, to St Anton on the Tirol border.

The Silvretta range now lay ahead, three days' journey via the Ferwall and Fasultal and the village of Ischgl. I was warned that the route up the valleys was unfrequented, and there was a danger of avalanches as it was already March and the snow was loosening. But well before dusk I reached a small untenanted hut – a delightful discovery, for it had ready-chopped logs by an iron stove, mattresses, blankets, and candles, a shelf of nineteenth century mountaineering journals, and there was no one but myself to enjoy them. The rest of the valley climbing up to the Schafbuckel pass was narrow and eerily silent, and as I threaded my way under the great overhanging névés I had an uneasy feeling that I was tempting fate. I was much relieved to look down at last into a wide glittering bowl. By nightfall I was at Ischgl, eating noodle soup in a small inn. The landlady sat with me in the parlour – I was the only guest – darning socks.

The Silvretta range is well suited to ski-touring. For several days, in a glittering white world of glaciers, I travelled in an arc from one refuge to another. Here were no narrow valleys menaced by avalanches, no sudden descents, losing hard-won altitude, to the tree-line where a skier must slither along crooked paths; no tedious spells of road-skiing, hopping over buried fences and ditches – but wide, slanting snow fields ringed by peaks under a sky that altitude and the clear air had painted a vivid blue. I met few other travellers on the way: two Swiss in knickerbockers, who guided me through a crevasse area, and a party from Munich. Like all Germans they were splendidly equipped and laughed at my old army rucksack and hired skis. Then, leaving the last of the Silvretta huts behind, I skied down to Gargellen, and early one morning before the sun was high enough to loosen the snow I hurried up the Schlappiner pass and from the top looked down a tapering valley into Switzerland. The only indication that I was standing on a frontier was a half-buried wooden post with the word 'Zoll'. Half an hour later, many hundreds of feet lower down, I was picking my way through the debris of old ground avalanches which littered the slopes like huge lumps of dirty porridge. Farther down I came to the Swiss village of Schlappin. It was deserted for the winter, the café locked, the only sound the gurgle of a stream under melting ice and the boom of a distant avalanche. Soon I was among trees and shuttered cottages. Then I struck a country road and merged with the holidaymakers in coloured sweaters thronging the streets of Klosters. I spent the night sleeping on the floor in the front window of a paint shop. The owner, whom I met by chance, rigged up a screen and told me to leave early.

In Davos, a few kilometres away, I found my old acquaintance Captain Sanders drinking his morning coffee. I had met him during the previous winter when I first emerged from the Schlappiner pass with my rucksack and mended skis, and he liked my idea of treating frontiers as though they didn't exist. The captain had lived in Davos for years. He owned a Rolls Royce, which he sometimes parked in front of his flat, but rarely used. Years ago, before the war, he had been companion to the Prince of Wales on some of his foreign travels and he showed me an album of press cuttings and photographs. Captain Sanders was well known in Davos as an ultra-English eccentric. He stood me a meal of snails with green sauce and took me to the cinema where he caused a disturbance by rising suddenly to his feet and calling out in a loud voice, 'The picture is rubbish'. We then left. His wife was a tall lady with fiery red hair and ten cats. They invited me to stay for the night, and when I went to bed she warned me to make sure no cats were left in the bedroom. I made a careful search and put out the light. Alas, I missed one of the creatures. In the morning I found it had pissed in my toilet bag, and I had to throw the shaving brush away.

From Klosters I pointed my skis in the direction of Zermatt, hoping to cross the Swiss border into France somewhere near Chamonix. I spent two dull days skiing through broken snow-cover below the tree-line, traversed a mountain to get height – scrambling up the funicular railway track and its tunnels – then started off again into the lonely world of high Alpine snow. My memory of the next days is fuzzy. But an unposted letter to a friend has survived the loss of my papers, and it has this passage:

Zermatt, 26 March 1955. In the last four days I have tried three passes. All were closed because of avalanches, which have suddenly set in and are rolling down the mountains like thunder. I crossed the first pass (Oberalppass) to Andermatt, and pushed on to the second (Furklapass). Here the villagers got in a group and shouted to me to come back. Of course they were right. While I was making up my mind, a huge *Lawine* came down right across the valley. The *Föhn* is loosening the snow and shows no sign of abating. So I had to turn back, and took the train for Zermatt. Here in Zermatt the avalanches are worse than ever. I might have to wait a week before conditions change. I asked the guides whether they would go up with me. They refused. So I must make one more effort to find another crossing into France – perhaps near Argentières . . . One must be careful not to set off these damned avalanches. Some are just big enough to sweep you off a slope over some wretched precipice – the snow breaks under the skis and slides downhill, taking you with it. Others roll down of their own accord once the snow has been loosened – they may be small, or enormous, enough to bury a village. The *Grundlawinen* bring down the earth, rocks and trees with them, like giant rakes . . .

So I took another train, got off at Martigny not far from the French border, and set off alone up the Trient valley. The border post was not manned. After a long day, as I was swooping down the reverse side of the saddle, I saw a cottage and knocked up the owner. He was a French peasant, living alone with two cows, which he kept in the back of his kitchen ('they keep me warm'). He shared his bowl of soup and bread, and I slept well, comforted by the sweet smell of the cows and the splashing of dung.

I left my skis with the station-master at a small railway stop near Chamonix and waited for the connecting train to Paris. It was the end of my trip. I looked rough and scruffy in my worn battledress jacket and anorak. The mountain sun had burned me as brown as a gipsy and I was alarmingly fit – legs like iron, and a sense of mental elation. Perched on a pair of wooden boards (*Brettl*), I had slipped over the frontiers of three countries. If I had had more money I could have gone on for days touring the wastes of snow. But it was the end of March, the season was already late and the snow, except at the highest altitudes, was rotting. Perhaps my luck was running out. As I waited for the train I asked myself what I had done during my three and a half years' absence from England. I hadn't saved any money – no more, indeed, than my return railway fare. Dunia, losing patience, had left me. It was a record of disorganised if not aimless achievement. Nevertheless I had started to re-educate myself, to read again, after the intellectual deprivation of the war years: and in bridging the gap with our former enemies, I had overcome an important psychological barrier.

Chapter 10

Turkey and Iran

I n England I stayed with my brother in Dorridge, on the edge of
Warwickshire farmland. His house was an anchorage, safe, warm,
with a soft bed and tea-cake. But I had no intention of staying for long.
I hankered after far countries – Greece, perhaps, or Turkey. My wartime
glimpses of the Golden Horn and the purple gorges and wild mountains
of eastern Anatolia sliding pell-mell down to the sand and date palms
of an Arab world had left evocative memories. Africa, with its blacks
kept in check by white men, didn't appeal to me. As a temporary mea-
sure I took a job as schoolmaster at Hallfield preparatory school in
Edgbaston. It had excellent playing fields. The headmaster, Mr Vaughan, who owned a powerful Jaguar, agreed to pay me £40 a month
to teach Latin, French, English and arithmetic and to run the Colts
cricket team.

I liked teaching these small boys. They were always ready to laugh.
I taught them weird Latin sentences ('*Nautae ad casam filias portant*'). Fig-
gins Minor wrote in his composition on 'The Ideal Home', 'I would
have Airwick in every room, and several dog kennels.' Mr Vaughan
disliked fat boys, and boys who didn't eat up their lettuce leaves at lunch.
Egged on by Soames Major, I sometimes tipped mustard into the trifle.
Most of all I enjoyed the cricket. No one objected when, as master in
charge, I scoffed half a dozen anchovy sandwiches and four doughnuts.
Twice I disgraced myself. Once, while umpiring a match against the
rival boys from Bromsgrove, one of our batsmen slipped and lay in the
middle of the pitch like a dead duck. 'Get up, you little bugger, and run!'
I shouted in a voice that carried to the pavilion. In the School versus
Fathers match I ran out Mr Fisher the Latin master (he was related to

the Archbishop of Canterbury) for nought, hooked a prominent solicitor for several fours ('they were my best balls', he said to me after the match), and in my first (and only) over bowled a barrister first ball and then struck Dr Burnside on the jaw, the ball having slid up his bat.

Sometimes I took Mr Greenwood's geography class. He was very old. He would start each lesson with the words 'The Golden Gates of California . . .' and then dry up. I told the boys about St Bernard dogs and the flasks of brandy tied to their collars, and about Venice (pigeon droppings, canals full of banana skins, and a Lido where bathers caught jaundice). Their compositions showed that these were the only things they remembered of Italian geography.

One morning I read that the Turks were looking for English teachers at a mixed school in Ankara. I informed Ingrid of this. Let me now introduce her to my story. I had met Ingrid in Germersheim. She was fond of cycling and the countryside; one occasion she had traced me to the hole I was digging in the Speyer road and, to the envy of my work-mates, handed me a beautifully packed sandwich lunch. Ingrid had just finished her diploma course at the Sorbonne. She immediately came to London, we were interviewed by Yuzuf Mardin of the Turkish Embassy, and we were accepted – though there was a slight snag: on the strength of my rudimentary arithmetic teaching at Hallfield. I was to be employed solely as a mathematics teacher. I put my skis, my leather cricket bag stuffed with books, and my German bicycle onto the Orient Express and with Ingrid set off on the three-day journey to Ankara. It welcomed us with a cloudless blue sky and an enormous orange-red sunset swollen with the dust of the Anatolian steppe. I had arrived in Turkey on impulse. I was to prolong my stay for over eight years.

Cesmi Bey, the headmaster, was a delightful person with ferocious white eyebrows and a bone disease that was slowly killing him. Ankara College had about 4,000 pupils and a staff that included fifty teachers from Britain. As a maths teacher I was a gross misfit. I could manage Pythagoras, mixed equations and logarithms, but could get no further. Still, I found that I could make my pupils laugh, and I set them outrageous sums (divide 97.506 into 9897.6430879 and convert the answer into a fraction) and problems (how long would it take a man to wash an elephant, allowing for intervals for prayer?) The school had a code of rules for teachers. It was forbidden to take a weapon into class – an American teacher, I was told, had appeared in the class-room one day wearing one Wellington boot and carrying a dagger. Teachers were allowed to twist the boys' ears and to bang them on the head. Yet there were few disciplinary problems as the pupils had been brought up by their parents, in the traditional Turkish way, to respect authority. But they cheated like mad and were not ashamed to be caught out.

Cesmi Bey told me not to get angry with one idle boy – 'His father is minister for railways, and if we offend him he might stop the college's reduced fare privileges.' There were a few scandals. One of the new teachers was a hopeless alcoholic. He drank throughout the day from a bottle of Turkish cherry brandy he hid in his satchel. Eventually he blew up, shattering the peace of the British Council reading room. 'I hate the Turks,' he shouted. 'Down with Turks!' He was gently removed, and sent back to Chelsea. A later arrival, Higgins, had a reputation in London literary circles as a promising poet. He also hit the bottle, and didn't last long. A few years later I read in the press that through self-neglect he had died in penury in a London attic.

After the First World War Atatürk had chosen the obscure caravan centre of Ankara as capital of the new, truncated Turkey because of its remote situation in the Anatolian interior (Istanbul was strategically vulnerable), its railway communications, and as a symbol of Turkey's break with her corrupt and disastrous Ottoman past. When winter came the high Anatolian plateau froze and snow covered the great mountain ranges that ring Turkey. I got out my skis, slid down the hill to school on them, and felt the urge to explore. Skiing and mountain climbing had few adherents among the Turks, who saw no point in pounding uphill for fun or being set on in remote country places by vicious sheep dogs and unfriendly Kurds. But there were two skiing centres, one at Uludag (the Mysian Olympus) overlooking Bursa, the other on the lower slopes of Mount Erciyes (Argaeus). At Christmas I spent three weeks with Ingrid at the Erciyes mountain hut, which had cubicles and an iron stove, and provided Spartan meals of cold black beans for breakfast, hunks of bread with sheep's cheese and olives, pilav (flavoured with pine kernels) and little tumblers of lime-blossom tea. The Turkish national skiing team was already there, practising for the Winter Olympics on a prepared piste under Hans, an Austrian coach. Their standard was not high, and their best performer, a thickset lorry driver, eventually achieved only twentieth place in his cross-country event. I went off on my own to explore the surrounding ridges and valleys. The thin snow cover made skiing hazardous but the boulder-strewn wilderness, the silence and the solitude, were awesome. The Turks did not object to Ingrid, Pat (a colleague) and me celebrating Christmas, and helped Ingrid to improvise a Christmas tree made of sticks hung with lichen beards. But they declined to share our bottle of cognac ('we are in training'). Slim, moustachioed, dark and handsome, they looked like Georgian bandits. Later in the evening the Christmas tree caught fire. Pat, when she went to bed, found that someone had drilled a peep-hole through the cubicle wall. 'Bad luck on the boys,' she told me in the morning. 'I went to bed in my long-johns and pullover.'

When I went back to Erciyes the following winter (1956–57) I was invited to join a team of four Turkish officers and NCOs who planned to climb the mountain carrying skis to speed them on the descent. No one had climbed Erciyes in midwinter, they told me, or used skis. They were cheerful but apprehensive, and trusted to Hans to see them through. Erciyes's crater-torn crest bristles ominously with pinnacles of red porphyry that shine as though stained with blood. Using crampons we climbed gingerly up a steep gully covered with treacherous ice – a fall would have meant spinning helplessly into rocky outcrops many feet below – while Hans hovered about us like a worried shepherd. At the top we opened our tins of tunny and looked down over a lava-strewn wilderness at the ruined battlements of Kayseri. On the way down, my experience of skiing over rough country stood me in good stead, and I was the first to get back to the hut.

One of the climbing party, Muzaffer, was a young army sergeant from a tank repair workshop in Kayseri. He knew a little English, and we agreed to meet in the summer and climb Ararat together. But first I had to get permission for the trip. The government did not welcome foreign visitors in eastern Turkey, the British Embassy couldn't help, and it took me several weeks, badgering police and Ministry of the Interior officials, before a letter from one of the school governors persuaded them to give me a travel permit. The fact was that the Turks did not want inquisitive strangers prying into the backward conditions of their eastern provinces and the extent of their Kurdish security problems. Access to Ararat (Agri Dag) was expressly forbidden. Wandering Kurds used its lower slopes as a grazing area, and above all the mountain stands at a point where the frontiers of three countries – Turkey, the USSR and Iran – converge in a cartographer's nightmare. Here, at the edge of Soviet Armenia, Russian and Turkish border guards faced each other across the Aras river, the Russians in watch-towers behind a massive barbed-wire fence, the Turks with patrols and army posts. The Russians were especially sensitive about the great volcanic cone that towered over its border, suspecting their rivals of using it for surveillance and espionage activities.

The Ararat trip turned out to be a team expedition in which Muzaffer and I were joined by three companions: Dr Bozkurt, Kazim, a sergeant from Kayseri barracks, and Ahmet, a journalist from an Istanbul newspaper who was to chronicle our doings in a series of dispatches. He brought with him a large metal plaque with the name of his newspaper on it. His editor had told him to plant this horror on the snow-capped summit of Ararat and to photograph it. Dr Bozkurt looked formidable in Victorian gaiters, motor-goggles and a woollen helmet. His crampons had been made by an Ankara blacksmith, and when he tried them on they did not fit. Kazim had been chosen because he was strong and could be used as porter and handyman. At Dogubayazit, our start point – a small Kurdish village and military station at the foot of Ararat – the garrison headquarters detailed a lieutenant ('a Korean veteran') and two soldiers armed with rifles to escort us, 'in case of trouble with Kurds, wolves, bears or snakes', as far as the snow-line. Ascending the southern face, we made our first halt at a Kurdish encampment where a rug was spread on the ground and we were given bowls of yoghurt. Our hosts refused to believe that Agri ('their mountain') could be climbed. 'Some claim to have been to the top, but where is the proof?'

By dusk on the third day, at about 14,800 ft, well above the snow-line, we scraped a resting-place in a jumble of rocks, pitched our tents and looked forward to an early start up the ice-cap to the 16,916 ft summit. But Ararat is a moody mountain. Not long after we set out, leaving the two soldiers behind, there was a mighty thunder-clap, a storm blew up, a bitter wind tore through our clothes and we were blinded by driving snow. We took shelter behind a pile of rocks. After an hour Ahmet and the lieutenant turned back to our night bivouac ('I have no orders to climb to the *very top*', said the Korean veteran). When the storm eased a little, we peered through the swirling clouds and suddenly caught glimpses of the ice-cap soaring above us. '*Gitmek lazim*,' I said. 'Let's go.'

The top of Ararat levels out into a gently-rounded dome with a hump on it. When we reached it we remembered that we had forgotten the journalist's plaque. Thick cloud obscured the view and we felt too miserable to stay long. So we photographed ourselves, haggard and snow-streaked, holding our ice-axes like spears, then glissaded down the ice-cap to our bivouac among the teetering stones. Our five-day jaunt ended twenty-four hours later in the garden of an officers' mess down in the valley. Ararat was now on its best behaviour again. The crest wore its usual bonnet of motionless white cloud, the glittering cone was bathed in brilliant sunshine. Relaxed, dry and fed I felt happy with my Turkish companions. Nothing had upset their composure, not even the horrors of the Dogubayazit doss-house with its bedbugs, its snoring peasants who slept with their clothes (and their caps) on, and the ghastly latrine-hole at the end of the landing. Ahmet's editor also served us well. For the next ten days our 'Ararat Expedition' was serialised with pictures on his newspaper's front page. Even the three sad bullocks which the soldiers had coaxed to carry our kit as far as our first bivouac were honoured with a picture and a caption.

Meanwhile I was settling down to life in Ankara. Though teachers weren't paid very much – none of us could afford a car – we were allowed to remit part of our Turkish salaries in sterling, and I eked out

my earnings by giving evening lessons for the British Council. Its library
and reading room were invaluable, though it is a pity, I think, that the
British Council does not stock foreign classics and that its librarians, as
I have noticed on my travels, have a penchant for the anti-Conservative
Guardian and *New Statesman*, and the esoteric *Encounter*. Freddie Tomlin,
the Director and cultural attaché, became a friend. He was a ponderous
man with large feet (he wore boots) and looked like a country policeman
in mufti. I later climbed Hasan Dag with him.

Through Ingrid I met many Germans. Germans were the Turks' favourite foreigners, their *arkadaslar*. England was ranked as a prime enemy,
having driven the Ottomans from the Holy Land and encouraged the
Greeks to invade Anatolia in 1922. Even now the British were resented
for opposing Turkish claims in Cyprus. German visitors and residents
delighted in the Oriental *Romantik*. More important, Germany had
re-established herself in her pre-war position as Turkey's leading trade
partner. German engineers had built the Cubuk dam that supplied
Ankara with piped water; and factories in Germany were recruiting
thousands of Turkish workers at standard wage rates and with family
allowances. After two years' hard slog on an assembly-line in a German
plant, a thrifty Turkish peasant could return home with enough money
in his pocket to buy a plot and build a house.

I soon grew to like the Turks, their formal manners and old-fashioned
courtesy, the unselfconscious gravity with which they prostrated themselves in prayer in the most unlikely places – in the back of a moving bus,
for instance, or in the crowded changing room of a sports club. But there
was little night-life in Ankara, and Turkish social gatherings were dull.
As a guest, one sat at a low table eating honey and almond cakes with
tiny cups of freshly ground, strong Turkish coffee and a glass of sweet
liqueur. Not much was said. The Turk is a man of few words and stands
on his dignity (he never smiles when posing for his photograph). One
had to be careful not to embarrass Turkish women by showing them
too much attention, which might be misconstrued as familiarity (a hand-
book issued to American servicemen advised them never to help a Turkish woman with her coat). In essence, and from a historical perspective,
we were foreign and Christians, *Firangi*, to use the old term, or *Ghia-
ours*, while the Turk, a Muslim, was the True Believer. In the past
Turkish armies had laid siege to western Christendom. The fact that
their Ottoman ancestors had founded a great empire which lasted
for centuries, and had governed and taxed millions of subject peoples,
gave them an inner self-confidence and a contempt for their less martial
neighbours, such as the Arabs.

Turkish does not belong to the Indo-Germanic family of languages.
Its vocabulary is unfamiliar and is not easy to learn. In time I knew

enough to fend for myself, and before I left Turkey I had spent many
weeks on long journeys among the Kurds or the Turkic-speaking herdsmen of Azerbaijan relying entirely on my basic stock of words. I had
no ambition to be more proficient, for when the time came for me to
leave, Turkish was not likely to be of any further use to me.

It was five years before I bought a car – a 1960 Beetle which I drove
back from Hamburg. Travelling in a country bus or the back of an open
lorry was an ordeal, yet it had enabled me to mix with Turks of every
class, from minor officials to peasants and soldiers. A long road journey
was a shared adventure. A tyre would burst, or the engine overheat; a
landslide, a heavy snowfall or ice would block the road; a cow would
get knocked down and smash the bonnet. Once I became a car owner,
trapped in a metal box like a fish in a tank, I found that I missed my
fellow travellers. I missed their smell, their voices, their rough warmth.
On the other hand I was free to stop, to put up my tent, to go off and
wander at will whenever I felt like it.

Football in Turkey was a people's sport, arousing strong regional
passions and sometimes knifing and brawls. Tennis was for the élite,
and was expensive to play. I joined Ankara Tennis Club. The Turkish
national team were members and I improved my game sufficiently
to play with them. I was, I think, the only English playing member,
and I was constantly challenged by opponents who wanted to beat an
Ingiliz. As national pride was at stake in these miniature duels I determined never to let the 'enemy' win. Two persistent opponents were
an Egyptian military attaché and a commercial attaché from the Soviet
Embassy. A Russian colleague in a square coat used to come with
Ivan to give advice and encouragement. After a game he would treat me
to raki and a diatribe against British colonialism in Africa – 'You are
murdering gallant Mau Mau freedom fighters'. He had a plump, elegant
wife and was a nice fellow. He wanted to see more of me, but I declined,
knowing how easy it is to compromise oneself once one gets involved,
even in a small way, with a Soviet embassy.

In addition to my mountain-climbing trips, I took Ingrid skiing to
Uludag, the Mysian Olympus (8,900 ft). There was a mountain hut at
the start of the main piste, and a hotel further down the valley. Few
skiers bothered to climb to the top of Olympus. From it one looked
down on blue Marmara bays; and having traversed the crest, one could
shoot rapidly homewards over several kilometres of untracked snow.
We stayed in the hut with two teacher colleagues – Cole, a New Zealander, and Barlow. The latter deserved a medal for valour. Having
dropped his dentures into a Turkish squatter-type latrine, he fished them
out and popped them back into his mouth. Our old friends the Turkish
national skiing team were also lodging in the hut. With Cole, I returned

to Erciyes in the summer of 1956. We had to keep a sharp look-out for falling rocks which ricocheted down the *couloir* when detached by the sun's heat. From the top we looked down over miles of brown, Central Anatolian plateau, dry and bare of woodland. Yet the emptiness was deceptive. Among the stony ridges and coarse tufted grass, countless flocks were grazing, and dozens of hamlets hid in sheltered places along trickling streams lined with poplars and willows.

The following summer (1957) I went to Iran to climb Demavend (18,603 ft) in the Elburz range not far from Teheran. The bus stopped at Dogubayazit, and as I looked up at the great ice-cap of Ararat high above the sweltering plain I had an irresistible impulse to break my journey and climb it again. On my earlier visit with Muzaffer, bad weather had cheated us of the view from the top that Lord Bryce, eighty years before, had so enthused about – 'the whole cradle of the human race, from Mesopotamia in the south to the great wall of the Caucasus'. This time I was determined to wait for a fine day before making the final ascent to the top. I was also better equipped. I had bought in a Munich sports-shop a light sleeping-bag, a new ice-axe and a small primus, I had my little bivvy tent, and a 700-page Barchester novel. Dogubayazit's Kurdish doss-house was at its worst. Bedbugs swarmed from the blood-stained walls, men with beaked noses and stubble were spitting in the hand-basins and there was the same sickening smell from the latrine-pit let into the landing. Fuad, a young Kurd, agreed to carry my kit on his donkey as far as a Kurdish camp in the *yayla* (summer grazing) area and we set off at midnight across the 12-mile plain of black lava dust leading to the south face of Ararat. Maddened by mosquito bites, our little grey donkey bolted. At last the morning star glowed brightly, and the sun, climbing from behind the mountain's eastern shoulder, threw a bar of gold into the sky and then projected Ararat's huge shadow far over the plain.

We were still below the snow-line when Fuad left me and went back with the donkey to his friends. I told him I would be back in three days. But the weather was turning foul again, and soon thick mist blotted out the whole of my surroundings. I secured my tent under a cairn of stones and slept out a violent thunderstorm which lit up the night like a battlefield. Next day the weather was little better. Huddled like a toad within the dripping walls of my tent I ate sardines with a penknife and tried to forget my misery in the gentle intrigues of Trollope's love-struck clergymen.

On the third day, at noon, the clouds at last rolled away and revealed the glittering ice-cap, still far off and, 3,000 or more feet below me, the black flecks of Kurdish camps. I climbed rapidly to the edge of a ravine, slept till dawn, and awoke to a cloudless blue sky. Stuffing raisins and

boiled sweets into my pocket, I was off. The snow was firm and by midday I had reached the top. This was the moment I had looked forward
to. Opening my most prized food item – a tin of Ankara sausages – I
gazed at the enormous panorama of the earth's weathered crust. I felt
that, far from being inhospitable and savage, it was a homely place of
nooks and hollows, of small brooks and lichen-painted stones, wrapped
in a carpet of immortelle flowers and cosy grass, where I could have
flopped down anywhere and, using my rucksack as pillow, slept soundly
through the blackest night.

I sucked snow-crystals to scour my mouth, lay back and dozed off.
Then, with a last look at the Maku gorge through which the road to
Tabriz would soon be taking me, I glissaded down the ice-cap until I
reached the zone of jumbled igneous rocks. At last the tiny speck of my
tent grew into a yellow mushroom. An eagle flapped away as I rolled
into my sleeping-bag, lit a candle and ate the last of my raisins.

As I went down towards the Kurdish camp in the morning, Fuad
suddenly poked his head over a ridge. 'My donkey has been set on by
wolves,' he called out. 'You will have to buy me another.' He explained
that he had left the donkey tethered to a stone. The wolves that roam
the grazing grounds after dark had immediately seized their chance.
At the camp I found the little grey donkey, its torn and bloody rump
buzzing with flies, dying miserably under a dirty cloth. I promised to
recompense Fuad and we left. It was late at night when we reached the
inn. I had lost weight, and my eyes, strained by snow-glare, were
distorting the shape of the stars into tiny Chinese lanterns. Fuad seized
a melon and roused a boy to brew tea. Two Pakistani army officers,
stranded for the night, called 'Welcome to the Hilton Hotel' from the
tottering balcony.

As I was waiting for the bus to Teheran next morning, a dozen
prisoners from the local gaol filed past, carrying buckets. I asked one
of their wardens what crimes they had committed. 'Murder,' he said
blandly. 'In these parts, if a man suspects his wife of being unfaithful
he'll cut her throat like a chicken.' The bus, a powerful Mercedez Benz,
was full of Iranian students on their way home from Germany, but I was
given a small folding stool to sit on. For two days, in a whirl of dust
and flying stones, we belted along through an arid plain, stopping for
pilav and tea at Khoi, Tabriz and Kazvin and sleeping on string-beds
at a wayside *khan* with a fountain splashing in the yard to sweeten the
air. The Elburz range, which curves like a great scythe-blade round the
southern shore of the Caspian sea, ran alongside us to the north.

Demavend, like Erciyes and Ararat, is associated with a legendary
cult. On Erciyes a fabled 'gold plant' was said to grow on the summit,
with a guardian serpent which destroyed anyone who went in search of

it. Ararat has the Garden of Eden and the Ark. On Demavend, the Iranian hero Faridun is said to have chained the cruel tyrant Zahak upside down in a cave, where he breathes out sulphurous fumes from the mountain's crater. At a Teheran Sports Club I was advised to sniff garlic and herbs to counteract the noxious gas.

Demavend was a morning's ride from Teheran. I camped in an orchard next to a decrepit tea-house. It was the time of *Muharram*, when Shiah Muslims mourn the slaying of Husain, Muhammad's grandson, with wailing, flagellation and drums. The cries of lamentation from the village sounded angry and hysterical and the owner of the tea-house told me to keep away from the mourners – 'You are a Ghiaour and they will beat you'. Ali, a Turkic-speaking herdsman, agreed for twenty tumans and some tobacco to come with me. We set off at dawn up stony slopes sprouting thorns like pincushions. At midday we stopped to rest at a goatherds' camp – a circle of rough stone walls enclosing hovels plastered over with mud. A single ragged family was at home. We were offered tea and a hard grey lump of sheep's cheese.

Ali was a small, bent man with bandy, matchstick legs, a woollen skull-cap and home-made *lastiks* (shoes) whose soles had been sliced out of an old motor-tyre. He hopped over the stones and scree at a great pace, like a clockwork imp. At dusk the cold struck sharply. We pitched my tent by a small stream and Ali, having washed his feet, ears and face, put on a clean round cap and prayed for several minutes. He then ate a round of flat bread, filled a long-stemmed *chibook* with tobacco dust and smoked it happily. He refused at first to join me in the tent, but he had a chronic cough and crept in later.

By noon next day, at about 13,400 ft, we had reached the spot whence I intended to climb to the summit. It was a jumble of rocks patched up into cave-like shelters for goat herds, reached by tongues of snow. From one gushed a stream of ice-cold water that tasted strongly of sulphur. The yellow sulphur cap of Demavend, streaked with ice, pierced the brilliant blue sky over 5,000 ft above us. When the dawn mist had rolled away I left Ali to smoke his pipe and started up a steep ridge of stones which swept up the south-east face to the massive volcanic cone. Crampons were out of the question, as the ice-covered gullies were serrated by row upon row of sharp ice-pyramids. Soon the long rampart of the Elburz range, which had dwarfed me in the valley, sank below to the south. Then I smelt sulphur and found myself treading a carpet of soft granulated stuff into which my boots sank a couple of inches at every step. Plumes of smoke were spiralling out of the ground. But I had no difficulty in breathing.

I sat on the top to enjoy myself. The grey wasteland below me was dominated by the vast curve of the Elburz. To the north a long violet bar marked the edge of the Caspian sea. Immediately behind me the mountain fell away into a gloomy crater partly filled with a frozen pool. In the strong glare, the sulphur rocks of the peak gleamed bright yellow as if freshly sprayed with paint. High above the earth's crust I looked for signs of life in this world of stone and ashes, but I could see none: no flocks, no camels, no gleam of water or herdsmen's tents. I felt utterly alone, and would have stayed longer to enjoy the solitude, but Ali was waiting for me and would be growing impatient. I finished my tin of *dolmas* (rice stuffed in vine leaves) and started to descend. It was after midnight when we reached the tea-hut and set the village dogs barking.

I spent next day talking to shepherds, beggars and soldiers from a pack-mule company who used the cramped little hut as a club. They grunted when I told them I liked working in Turkey ('A rich country, but wasted on the Turks'). The owner, who looked like a fowl that had been lying in a dust-bath, spent his time hammering a stone-hard cone of sugar into tiny fragments, which he rationed to two per small tumbler of tea. He confined his women to a mud-brick shed and yard behind the tea-hut, and shouted when he caught them peering over the wall for a glimpse of the Ghiaour with an ice-axe. I had my last sight of Demavend from a *khan* where the bus returning me to Teheran stopped to change a wheel. The massive fist of snow clenching the giant shoulder was a poignant reminder of keen air and ice-cold gushing water. Here, in the roasting valley, stream beds were dry. The poplar trees, grey with dust, gave only a thin pencil of shade. Motionless, the black flag of mourning for Husain drooped sadly from a mosque. In Teheran I bought a bus ticket to Erzurum, intending to travel north over the Pontic Alps to Trebizond on the Turkish Black Sea coast and from there reconnoitre the little-known Kackar massif whose snow-capped peaks, I had learned from the Alpine Club in Ankara, would be a good place for adventurous mountain climbing. For miles the road followed the line of ancient water canals (*qanats*) tunnelled underground and marked by banks of spoil. In the burned cornfields the harvest was being cut by sickle and cattle were treading out the grain. The *Muharram* month of mourning was not yet over. Schoolchildren, sallow and solemn, were marching about in black shirts. Holes had been cut out to expose thin shoulder-blades, which they slapped with little flails in imitation of the savage flagellation practised by grown men. The Red Army was on large-scale manoeuvres in Transcaucasia, and in response, near the Soviet border on both sides of the Iranian–Turkish frontier approaches, roads and hillsides were jammed with Iranian tanks and guns. My fellow passengers told me they weren't worried. 'The Russians', they said, 'are always manoeuvring.'

In Erzurum I went to a cabaret show, wondering how far the Kurds tolerated the belly-dance, but I was disappointed – not an inch of forbidden flesh was to be seen. In a smoky room men in thick suits and cloth caps, chewing hazel nuts and drinking *gazos* (mineral water), were staring at three plain young women in long dresses standing on a dais. The women sang a few songs to a violin and lute, gyrated, then left the stage to change their frocks. No imam could have objected to their performance. Back in the hotel dormitory room I found my room-mate prostrated in prayer.

From Erzurum the country bus to Trebizond followed the old caravan route that crosses the Pontic Alps over the Zigana Pass (6,640 ft). It is a remarkable watershed, separating Europe from Asia. On the Asian side are the dust and thorn scrub of ochreous uplands where women in black crouch over dung fires. On the European side, dense forests smelling of resin and wet ferns tumble down to the coast, and cloud banks sweeping in from the Black Sea empty themselves over the peaks, leaving the Asian side dry. We got out at the top of the pass to stretch our legs. Some old men with scarves round their heads were sheltering from the keen wind in a tea-shed. The grass, spotted with gentians, was as green and fragrant as a Swiss *alm*; chicory, delphiniums and purple crocuses crowded the verges. For the first time in many days I felt my appetite returning. From the pass, the road spiralled down through mountain mist to the market gardens that surround the Byzantine ramparts of Trebizond.

At Trebizond I wanted to bathe. A mile or so to the west I came to a little Byzantine church on a grassy mound at the edge of the sea. The water was warm, and some melon rinds were floating in it. I was sewing a button on my shirt when I heard English voices. Two young men in bathing trunks, with towels and dressing gowns, appeared from behind the mound. They had a proprietorial air, as though the beach belonged to them. Teachers? Poets, perhaps? Or the honorary vice-consul and his assistant? I looked like a hobo. However, I introduced myself, and they told me they were archaeologists restoring the church, which had been used for centuries as a mosque and contained some splendid Byzantine wall-paintings hidden under a coat of white plaster. I envied them, polishing their ancient pictures and gazing from their little grassy mound at the brilliant red sunsets that flamed over the green-black sea and the Crimean coast. One of the two men was David Winfield: over the years, he and his family have become dear friends. His travels too have taken him far afield, from Serbia, Istanbul, Cyprus, Canterbury, Oxford and Tiflis, to his new home on the Isle of Mull.

From Trebizond I took the coast road to Ardesen, fifty miles short of the Soviet watch-towers outside Batum. I was now entering the old Lazistan of nineteenth-century maps, the home of Laz fishermen and herdsmen settled along the humid seaboard at the foot of snow-tipped mountains. Traditionally this has been a wild, neglected corner of Turkey, with a history of brigandage, the blood feud, and a shifting frontier under Russian influence. At Ardesen I squeezed into a *dolmus* (a battered car with several paying passengers seated on wooden benches) and we turned inland up the Firtina gorge through a heavily forested mountain-gash bisected by a torrent that leaped and thundered between cliffs of almost impenetrable bramble and rhododendron tickets. I slept the night in a grassy clearing and woke to find myself in a sunny fairyland. The mist had lifted, revealing huge stands of beech, fir and pine, roaring water and cascades. Walking upstream I passed boys catching trout in cast-nets or spearing them with sharpened sticks. The first settlement I came to seemed to be inhabited by trolls. It was a primitive spa with a hot spring where very old men in beards with towels wrapped round their heads came to cure their rheumatism. Some of them spoke Russian or Polish – they had picked it up in 'the good old days of the Tsar' while following their traditional Laz calling as bakers and cooks in Tiflis or Warsaw. When the forest thinned I came to Kavrun *yayla*. Here scores of crude wooden shanties with roofs secured by loose stones – the summer quarters of herdsmen and their families – were huddled along a stream. The herdsmen were astonished to see an Ingiliz effendi prowling about their most private haunts. Was I a *mühendis*, a mining expert, prospecting for precious metals with my ice-axe? Was I looking for gold? They refused to believe that I wanted to climb Kackar for fun. No one they knew had done so. What was the point?

With no map I found it hard next day to orientate myself among the snow-covered peaks that pierced the skyline of Kackar like rows of jagged teeth. As I slipped and slid and forced a way through rhododendron thickets, I decided I must come again, with maps and food and Muzaffer as companion. The ruddy faces of the Laz herdsmen and their strong, nimble women appealed to me. Their crocus-studded pastures and the cold damp air would be a delightful change from the bare Anatolian plateau.

Chapter 11

Lazes and Kurds

In the summer of 1958 Muzaffer got ten weeks' leave from his unit
in Kayseri and we arranged to visit the Kackar massif. From Kackar
we planned to continue our journey south through Ararat, Kars, Van
and old Armenia to the Hakkari mountains in Turkish Kurdistan.
Muzaffer had a camera, field glasses, pitons and climbing rope, and
maps. I provided the film (it was old and grainy, and had been difficult to find in Turkish shops) and the tent. We went by bus to Trebizond and spent the first day scrambling over its ancient ramparts.
Their crumbling masonry was choked by fig trees and creepers, in which
tiny cottages and vegetable plots were embedded. Window-boxes strung
with eggshells kept out the Evil Eye, and there were Muslim graves with
prophylactic rags tied to them. I called on David Winfield and found
him and June, his assistant, perched on a rickety platform cleaning a
plaster-covered section of wall paintings high up on the vault of the sanctuary. Underneath the superimposed plaster and whitewash a splendid
Ascension of Christ, figures of the Apostles and of the Virgin Mary were
springing to life for the first time since the Turks converted the church
into a mosque in the sixteenth century.

Muzaffer and I turned up the Firtina gorge at Ardesen, halted at Ilica,
and from Kavrun were directed to Sano *yayla*. We reached it after midnight, soaked by rain and mist. An old Laz herdsman with a white beard
and makeshift turban let us stay with him until the weather cleared. He
and his family, like all their neighbours, lived in intolerable discomfort,
with mud floors and leaky wooden roofs held down by heavy stones.
We ate slabs of maize bread baked in the embers of his smoky fire – it
tasted like sour pudding – and drank milk warmed in a blackened pan.

During the day the old man's womenfolk and children were out with the flocks or collecting wood. After dark, a chattering rag-bundle in striped aprons and men's jackets, they crouched round their own fire until they fell asleep.

The Lazes are a Muslimised Caucasian people and Muzaffer was offended that, amongst themselves, the herdsmen spoke only their own Caucasian tongue. In the past, the Lazes had a reputation as wild and violent people. Tucked away in their mountain fastnesses and wooded shores they thrived on banditry and kidnapping. In modern Turkey I was to find their reputation paradoxical. Though people generally looked down on them as boorish and backward, the butt of popular jokes, there were others who admired the Lazes' skill in trade and the professions, their cunning and cleverness. The root of these prejudices is, of course, that the Lazes are not regarded as 'true Turks' – whatever that means. Like other ethnic minorities – the Georgians, Kurds, Armenians and Greeks – they are not, says the Turk, to be trusted.

Two Laz guides led us to the north face of the Kackar massif. Alte Parmak (11,900 ft) was a daunting sight: a wall of precipitous turrets soaring like the outspread fingers and thumb of a giant hand. To gain it we decided to climb the ice-slopes on the north-east face, then switch to the reverse or Asian side where the pitch was less and the face eroded into a mass of crumbling rock. We reached the top on the third day. It gave us a fascinating glimpse of two worlds. To the north, a rain-soaked European coast hidden under banks of cloud; to the south, beyond the corn patches of Georgian hamlets, the dry, ochreous uplands of old Armenia and Asia. We were sitting on the very edge of the cloud barrier, and I was enthralled to watch it at work. As the cloud mass mounted slowly towards us from the sea, it began to thin, then suddenly scattered as if melted by an invisible ray. The broken shreds fled past our perch and vanished like ghosts in the deep blue sky behind. Two yellow butterflies came fluttering in their wake. It was like coming across spotted ladybirds on an ice couloir.

Descending through jagged rock debris bright with alpine flowers – gentians, saxifrages and primulas – that would have delighted a Kew botanist, we forced a way through the dense rhododendron belt and made for the nearest Georgian hamlets two miles down the valley. Soon, above the drumming of water, we could hear the tinkle of cowbells and cries of herdsmen. Our two guides were waiting for us. We paid them off and watched them hurry away. Wretchedly clothed in torn shirts and rubber pumps, they had humped our heavy packs over the pass without a single grumble. We had just pitched our little tent on a stubble patch near some Georgian huts when a volley of stones thudded against it. A dozen ragged boys with slings and dogs appeared

over a ridge. Tousled women with bundles of firewood shouted at us
to go away. Muzaffer took out his loaded pistol and went to deal with
them. He was soon back, with a shame-faced youth who offered us a
bowl of thick cream (*kaymak*) mixed with honey. 'The men are away,'
he said. 'We feared you were Lazes. They are thieves and we don't want
them here.'

Ahead lay a two-day march down the valley to Sarigol, along a
bridle-path that followed a rushing stream. The Kackar range which had
blocked the horizon behind us like a sea of black breakers gradually disappeared. We were sorry to leave those forested giants. They guard
one of the last strongholds of ethnic division in Turkey, and are a
botanist's and climber's paradise. Yet the range and its passes are almost
unknown to travellers, who prefer to cross the east Pontic Alps by easier
routes. Coming down to Parhal, on the way to Sarigol, we were surprised to see below us a large building with a conical roof that towered
above the surrounding hamlet. It turned out to be a beautiful monastic
basilica of smooth, cut grey stone built by Georgian Christians a thousand years ago. But it had long been used as a mosque. At that very
moment, the imam and his helpers were in the process of daubing an
extra coat of whitewash over the ancient murals and stone reliefs.

Our journey to Kars took us through Artvin, Savsat and Ardahan.
In the absence of regular buses, travellers are dependent on lifts in country lorries. Crammed with villagers and dangerously overloaded with
bundles, vegetables, goats and food sacks they skid and swerve up and
down the dizzy ravines, driven by silent, dazed-looking men in cloth
caps and from time to time, when the brakes or steering fail, end up in
a mass of broken metal at the bottom of a cliff. The road to Artvin was
a narrow ledge of sharp spirals cut into the mountain face. Standing
precariously in the back of an open Ford truck, we peered down at the
Coruh wriggling and foaming in the bed of the gorge until it dwindled
to a minute brown string hundreds of feet below. From the crest we
sped downhill to Artvin and, yellow with dust, got out under a bust
of Atatürk. The Armenian church was padlocked and full of rubbish.

At Artvin we crossed the Coruh and climbed again into the clouds.
We had entered the corner of Turkey, split by the valleys of the Coruh,
Oltu and Tortum rivers, that, through my subsequent journeys to
the old Tao churches (see p. 195), I have come to love best. Strings of
pack animals were zigzagging up the gorge along crazy bridle-paths
lined with scarlet cornelian cherries, heavy quinces and apricots. Fruit
grew in confusion – vines twisting round fig trees, pomegranates glowing orange-red among tangled blackberries. The mud roofs of huts
gleamed with piles of corn cobs and peppers drying in the sun. Green
woodpeckers and golden orioles scuffled in the walnut and mulberry

trees. And the air rang with music – the grating of the magpie, the clucking of red-legged partridges in the screes and the splash of dyke water. From Savsat, given a lift in an army Jeep, we were slowed up by squealing ox-carts (the axles turn with, not on, the wheels). Then suddenly we mounted a pass and found ourselves on the threshold of a new and transformed world. The snowy Pontic peaks lay behind us and there, stretching ahead, was Asia – a huge treeless plain, straw-coloured and spotted with Kurdish cattle. A Kurdish camp with grazing saddle-horses stood before us like a guard post. Shivering in the strong cold wind blowing from the Caucasus, we all got out to urinate, the Turks, as is their fashion, kneeling to do so to avoid staining their clothes, and for modesty.

The Kurdish steppe people live in hovels dug for winter warmth into slopes and angles of the plain; the roof-vents stick out of the ground like little chimney pots. Muzaffer was upset to see Turks 'living in caves, like the old barbarians.' Ardahan, where we joined a group of peasants squatting among staling horses, was not welcoming. Like Artvin and Kars, it was a key point in the exposed NATO frontier zone facing the Soviet Caucasian provinces. It was closed to the tourist for security reasons, and from the authorities' point of view I had no business to be there. Army learner-drivers were steering American gun tractors round and round the square; as soon as we sat down in a tea-house, a policeman came up and told us to accompany him to the *karakol*, where an official checked our identities in a file. He gave us an hour in which to leave, and put us in a lorry with an escort. As the sun faded a keen wind blew up, whistling through the broken windscreen of our truck; the purple hills merged into the stony steppe, and it was dark when we reached Kars. Our inn was crowded with Kurdish farmers. They stank of garlic and slept fully clothed with the lights burning. We were awoken at dawn by their ablutions: the splash of cold water poured from little tin ewers over faces black with stubble, and a crescendo of hawking, spitting, spewing and throat-clearing that sounded like a chorus of demented frogs.

Kars, strategically placed on the Armenian plateau facing the approaches to Tiflis and Transcaucasia, has a history of sieges dating from the Seljuk invasion and its sacking by Tamerlane. In the last century it was captured three times by the Russians, who held it till 1921. I found the eleventh-century Armenian church padlocked, and used as a junk store. A second Armenian church had been converted into a cinema, with a poster of Tarzan over the vestibule.

Although Muzaffer and I were impatient to get to Hakkari, the great snow-covered ribs of Ararat were a challenge too tempting to resist. An excursion up the northern slopes would be a new experience and a fascinating lesson in frontier geography. As our start we chose a State

Farm Centre forty miles to the east of Igdir, at a point where Turkish
territory, hemmed in by the converging boundaries of Russia and Iran,
starts to taper and expire in a tongue of boggy grass and reeds. A hay
cart took us from Aralik to the Farm Centre along the line of Russian
watch-towers. We stared back at them through Muzaffer's field glasses.
I was wearing my red and white British Embassy football shirt, and
wondered what the Russian guards made of us. From the Farm Centre
we looked directly over the wire fence to the stacks of a Russian cement
works in Develli. Next day a water engineer took us in his Jeep to the
junction of the Aras and Karasu rivers, where the frontiers of three countries exactly meet. We got out at a tiny clearing and stood at the end
of a three-foot wide embankment, on the very tip of Turkey. Here, feeling absurdly conspicuous under the eyes of a Russian watch-tower 150
yards away, we watched the Karasu glide into the Aras among banks
of sedge. A few paces behind us Iran rose gently to the gleaming red
slopes of Little Ararat. The spot was marked by a single boundary stone.
We had seen no signs of Turkish border guards. 'We don't dramatise
our frontier,' the engineer told me. 'It's the mighty Russians who are
fussy.'

Our climbing route was up the south-east face of Ararat. We passed
through the State Farm's *yayla* (7,500 ft) and at dusk came to a Kurdish
encampment whose headman, a rosy-cheeked fellow, invited us to stay
the night. 'I am ninety years old,' he said, 'and I have had five wives
and ten sons.' A barefoot woman with black tresses baked us strips of
unleavened bread on a metal disc placed over glowing pellets of dung.
We asked the headman if they were bothered by wolves. 'You will
hear them tonight.' Cattle thieves from Iran, he added, were another
nuisance. We pitched our tent among the dogs. The night was quiet at
first, as the oil lamps were doused and the chatter of women and children
ceased. Then pandemomium suddenly broke out. The first howl of
a wolf set the dogs barking till dawn. The horses stampeded. From
above, where the sheep were folded, rifle shots echoed through gullies.
At sunrise there was a clamour of shrill voices. The headman was shouting abuse. 'Four horses were stolen in the night – by now they'll be over
the border in Iran.' We hurried away.

We spent the day climbing a great ridge of volcanic boulders that led
to a steep ice-slope. Dawn brought a biting wind and cloud. Clearly we
would have to race the weather. Roped together, we stepped out on to
the glittering ice mass. The surface was rotten and crusty and broke off
under our ice-axes; a slip, and without the rope one would have spun
helplessly to probable destruction. As the clouds closed in, I felt like
an insect in a world of white ghosts. When at last the pitch eased we
paused, until a sudden break in the clouds showed the summit 400 yards

away. We reached the top together, and for half an hour crouched on the gently rounded platform hoping that Ararat would reveal the magnificent view I had enjoyed a year before. Ararat refused to lift her veil. Disappointed and cold, we returned slowly down the ice-field and the causeway of boulders to our tent. It had been submerged in fresh snow, and there was nothing to eat but tinned tunny and scraps of bread.

We halted next day at the Farm Centre, relishing the warmth of the sun now that the cloud had lifted and the ice-cap, looking serene and harmless, glittered under a brilliant blue sky. The farm manager, a powerfully built, good-natured Turk in a cloth cap and leather jacket, gave us a supper of pilav and melon, and a quilt to sleep under. We sat on the ground watching twilight blot out the valley below. Suddenly, on the Russian side of the frontier, the lights were switched on. Erivan glowed like a great lighthouse and a chain of electric eyes marked the line of Russian watch-towers. The manager shook his fist at the lights. 'There they are,' he said, 'with their comfortable houses and electric current – and here am I with an oil lamp in a draughty tent.' He pointed to the Farm Centre's grazing slopes and cluster of ragged bell tents. 'Milk!' he said in disgust. 'It's guns our country needs – not milk.' And turning to me he added, 'you and the Americans are to blame. Your generals slaughtered Germany – the wrong sheep.'

Our final stop was at a gendarme post in the foothills, manned by a corporal and five men who had a donkey for transport. They lived rough, baked their own bread and slept under thin army blankets. I marvelled at their patience, for they had no radio, and nothing to read. We left Igdir in the back of an old Austin lorry, sitting on a pile of water melons which split and cracked under our weight. But we had a Kurdish musician for company. As we lumbered up the hills and stopped from time to time to let the engine cool, he twirled his drum and sang, looking at us with sightless eyes.

Our next plan was to spend a month walking through the mountain valleys of Turkish Kurdistan (the Hakkari *vilayet*) from Yuksekova to Colemerik, the administrative centre. We had a climbing map, drawn in 1937 by a previous Austrian expedition (one of whose members had collapsed and died), and our first aim was to explore the Cilo massif. The *vilayet* was not only difficult of access and lacking roads; it was the ancient stronghold of truculent Kurdish clans (Marco Polo's 'bandit people') whom the Turkish government had always found it difficult to govern, let alone tax or conscript as soldiers.

We found an old Perkins diesel lorry to take us from Van to Yuksekova. It had no bonnet, and the back was crammed with villagers and sacks of salt. We drove through the night along a dizzy mountain

ledge. Immediately below I could see the moonlight flickering on a
fierce torrent, the Nehil Cay, foaming through a narrow gorge. Our
driver, who looked exhausted, kept up a wailing chant ('He's singing
to keep himself awake,' said Muzaffer). At dawn, streaked with salt, we
stumbled out into the dusty lanes of Yuksekova.

The *kaymakam* was a young gendarme captain who kept us waiting
while he got out of bed. He told us he had never visited the valleys. But
he found us a guide, Raschid, with a strong mule, ordered him to accept
25 lira (£1) a day and warned us not to pay him extra for any food he
scrounged on the way ('He will get it for nothing'). Raschid was a
lanky, flat-footed Kurd with sloping shoulders and a lugubrious face.
We set off at a great pace over the flat Gevarova plain, overtaking a file
of girls loaded with hay and brushwood who called to each other like
starlings. At dusk, in the foothills below the Cilo peaks, we put up our
tent at a Kurdish camp. We woke to find a circle of children peering
at us through the tent flap. Muzaffer had neglected his usual precaution
of tying his gear to his feet, but except for a *chargol* (canvas water-bag)
our things were intact.

When we reached our next camp site, at Serpil *yayla* – it lay at the
foot of Resko (13,680 ft), the main Cilo peak – children cast stones at
us from slings and it was clear that we were not wanted. But next day
a small procession of women and children called on us, led by the headman's wife, a short dumpy figure in a long black skirt looking very much
like Queen Victoria. She apologised for our cold welcome – 'the men are
away, and we don't trust strangers'. We brewed tea and I passed round
our bag of precious sugar lumps. These sun-scorched matrons had the
wiry bodies of lean goats. They wore bulky turbans; trinkets and gold
discs twinkled on their throats; their strong brown hands were never
still. Each had a roll of wool round her wrist, which she spun onto a
wooden spindle dangling from the other. The children looked thin and
sickly. On their ragged clothes they wore an astonishing variety of buttons – buttons of the Metropolitan Police and Royal Air Force, buttons
of the Turkish and Iraqi armies, buttons stamped with the crest of the
General List, even one with the head of their arch-enemy, Atatürk.
'Your children need vitamins,' Muzaffer said to the headman's wife in
his self-important way; 'you should send to Van for lemons – and soap
and aspirins.' She looked offended. 'We have lived well enough in the
past without such things.' Another visitor called in the evening, a young
man whose foot had been clawed by a bear. He wanted a bandage.

We stayed three days at Serpil *yayla*. On the slopes above it, leading
to the east face of Resko, beautiful flocks of goats and sheep were grazing. We came across many traces of bears: the gory remains of a goat
seized in the night, the mangled roots of shrubs, piles of blackish drop-

pings, rock walls soiled with lairs. Just before we set off for the climb
a goat was slaughtered in the camp to honour the return of a young
soldier after twelve months' service in Korea. He arrived on horseback
with embroidered saddle-bags and a carton of American cigarettes (King
Size) sticking out of his tunic. 'Korea was fine,' he told us, 'plenty of
food and five dollars a month.' We were given the goat's kidneys and
some liver and a lump of sheep-tail fat to fry them in. I was sorry
to leave the camp and its simple pastoral routine: the thud of butter-
churning in sealed goatskins rocked to and fro on a tripod of wooden
stakes that woke us at dawn; the rising sun, alighting on the glacier and
turning it from dirty grey to brilliant white; the stillness of noon; and
as brushwood fires ushered in the evening star, the bustle and shouts
as the great bulls came swaggering and bellowing home. With them a
throng of girls, as colourful and tattered as rag dolls, would file back
from the pastures with fresh sheep and goat's milk in skins on their
backs, and a spindle in the hand, which they twirled like Yo-Yos. Then,
when the mountain choughs had gone to roost, the darkened tents slept,
silent under brilliant stars.

We set off for Resko before dawn, climbed a steep ridge into a parallel
valley and rested briefly at noon at a small cascade, which fell into a
grassy glen sprinkled with buttercups and mountain veronica at the foot
of the summit route. There was much evidence of bears. Overlooking
the glen three dung-stained lairs faced us like dirty eye-sockets and we
had the uneasy feeling of being watched. Two ibexes leapt across our
path as we began our final ascent, hauling ourselves up smooth grey slabs
between snow-filled gullies. The crest itself required an extra effort. It
could only be reached by a narrow ridge of rotten stone spanning an
abyss of terrifying depth. The view was magnificent. The craggy peaks
and steep-angled valleys of Kurdistan stretched over the frontiers of Iran
and Iraq in a wild medley of spikes and pinnacles, haze and shadows.
At our feet Resko glacier hung down like an immense carpet, rent with
crevasses, to the boulder-strewn moraine at the edge of Serpil *yayla*.
Perched on our eyrie, with our backs to space and our legs dangling in
the air, we felt like aviators.

We had told Raschid to wait for us at Serpil village, where the Kurds
had their winter quarters. The village was several hours' march away and
the sun already setting when we looked down into a black glaciated
valley with ice-streaked walls, narrowing to a deep gorge blocked by a
conical mountain. A shepherd boy had recommended this grim place
as a short cut. We were soon disillusioned. Thirty yards away, facing
us on the narrow track, we saw the first bear. For a few seconds neither
of us moved, hoping that the bear would not charge. Then Muzaffer
gave a loud shout and fired his pistol into the air. To our relief the bulky

brown animal turned and lolloped away. Good for Muzaffer! The next hours were a painful scramble in the night down a dried-up watercourse fouled with bear droppings. At the bottom of a rock chimney we had to abseil like awkward spiders. From time to time Muzaffer uttered a cry which he hoped would deter bears, until I asked him to stop, for it sounded less like a challenge than a cry of distress. 'Don't look, and they'll go away,' I told him, quoting nanny's advice.

Raschid, who had prepared a stew, grinned horribly when early in the morning we limped bruised and scratched into Serpil village, having forded a racing stream at the base of the conical mountain. We had come the wrong way, he said. No one ventured into *that* gorge. It had no grazing and was overrun by bears. Bears, explained the headman, were a plague. They raided the rice and maize fields, ate up the grapes and carried off sheep, and were increasing in number. Yet the bear was a coward. He kept away from bright fires and was scared by resolute dogs and loud cries.

Two days later we came to the beautiful Sat lake at 10,000 ft. We might have been in the Alps. Fat brown cows were grazing the fresh grass, snowfields fed the lapis lazuli lake with pure icy water. We jumped barefoot on the turf in relief from the jarring stones. Raschid performed his ablutions with a tremendous spitting and hawking that echoed round the lake and startled the wildfowl. I lay in the grass and watched a girl pour goat's milk down a funnel into the throat of an inverted goatskin and begin to shake it. After back-breaking labour, a lump of white butter would form. When darkness fell, brushwood fires lit up the snow-covered walls of our mountain bowl. The flames red-dened the fleeces of the folded sheep and the goat-hair tents stood out like Red Indian wigwams.

Muzaffer envied the Kurds their magnificent mountain scenery but shared the Turkish view that they were a troublesome, backward and clannish people – 'they're all law-breakers, and they live more like gyp-sies than Turks.' At Sat village, as we sat round a fire eating walnuts and boiling a stringy cock, our grey-haired host was joined by Raschid and a former soldier. Muzaffer, who said that the Kurdish women smelt like goats and that their children were covered in flies, now began to attack the incompetence of the Kurdish economy, the illiteracy and lack of medical provision. 'Experts should be sent from Ankara to teach you how to live, and you would all become rich.' His listeners looked aghast. Educating girls would be a waste of time – 'they are too stupid'. As for toothbrushes and reading glasses, 'who needs such trifles in the moun-tains? Government officials', they said, 'bring nothing but trouble. Let them leave us alone.' 'So you prefer to remain as you are?' '*Dogru*,' they exclaimed, 'you are right there, by God.'

I retain a clear memory of that night – the fresh, spicy walnuts and spreading trees, the uneatable cock, the smell of dung and toasted earth, our host's lined brown face and collarless shirt. The Milky Way (*Saman Yolu*, the Straw Way as the Turks call it) hung like a bright sword over the gorge, pointing to the Iraq frontier a few miles away. A shooting star flashed over the dark mountains and before it vanished I had time to make a wish. All of a sudden a hubbub broke out from the terraced fields and huts. Dogs barked, tins were beaten, there were shouts and moving lights. Our host smiled. 'The bears have come to supper. *Vallahi!* May God keep them out of my tobacco field.'

Three hours down the gorge, in a rocky wilderness of dwarf oaks and thistles, we came to a single boundary stone which marked the frontier that has severed the historic heart of Kurdistan in two. We rested here, with one foot in Turkey, the other in Iraq. Muzaffer spat on the stone. 'This is the boundary line that has cut Turkey from the oilfields at Kirkuk and Mosul,' he said. 'But for the Ingiliz, Turkey would be rich instead of begging aid from the Americans.' I sympathised with Muzaffer. When the frontier was finally ratified in 1926, Britain had successfully argued that without the rich Mosul province Iraq, for economic and strategic reasons, would not be viable.

Approaching Oramar village from above we looked down on tiers of rough stone cottages built into the valley sides with a stream running down the centre and untidy terraced fields bordered by hedges of wild vines. Raschid's home was here. It was a soot-blackened cavern without furniture, with a flat mud roof laid over thatched poplar beams and a floor of beaten earth. He had two wives. One was much older than the other, a shy girl nursing a baby. They cooked a great bowl of stew which we shared with the local *mudur* (district official) and a gendarme sergeant. When Muzaffer began to hold forth on the necessity for Kurdish reform policy – 'We need idealists, doctors on horseback, compulsory schooling' . . . – the *mudur* smiled and said '*Yavas, Yavas*, not so fast. Nothing will be improved till roads are built.' The gendarme sergeant complained that he and his detachment of ten men had been stuck eighteen months in Oramar with only a month's leave. In winter they were snow-bound. As well as being responsible for law and order and frontier security, they delivered call-up papers for army recruits – they were often difficult to trace. During the meal two ruddy-faced gendarmes from Sat came in, and with one hand still holding on to their rifles they dipped their fingers into the rice bowl. They had brought call-up notices for four Kurds. Three of the conscripts were ready to report, the fourth had vanished. 'They will get him sooner or later,' said Muzaffer. 'Some men are quite old by the time the army catches them.'

I had grown so used to the march routine – eight to ten hours a day – that I could have kept going for weeks. The day's heat was tempered by cool nights that refreshed the body like a cold bath. Partridges were clucking and scratching in the scrub. From the highest *yaylas*, flocks were already being driven down in clouds of dust that coated the cumbrous tails of the sheep. The villages were all built to the same pattern: little stone cottages perched one above the other like swallows' nests, with their backs against a mountain wall. Many were empty and despoiled. Below them lay terraced fields, most of them abandoned and overgrown. There were no mosques – each man's prayer rug sufficed for the act of worship. The ruins of little stone churches, built like small forts, showed that all this patient terracing and cultivation had been the work of the Nestorian Christians who had settled, farmed and worshipped here for centuries till their cruel eviction and flight to Syria at the end of the First World War. The highland Kurds were by tradition more concerned with livestock than with cultivation; but even if this had not been so, not enough of them had settled in the abandoned Nestorian villages to fill the gap left by their predecessors.

At Talana the village chief was a small, toothless man who chain-smoked green tobacco and asserted that he was 105. He took me to see the church. It was a simple flat-roofed rectangular building of rough-hewn stones scratched with Syriac inscriptions. To enter, we had to duck through two small openings – they were built low, it is said, so that worshippers would bow their heads on entering the Temple of God (and to keep cattle out). The interior of the church was wrecked, the sanctuary recess had been used as a fireplace and the churchyard was strewn with broken grave slabs finely carved with encircled Nestorian crosses. 'The Christians built well,' said the old chief, tapping the walls. 'But they sided with the enemy, with meddling missionaries and the Tsar who wanted to take our land, and they were punished for their treachery.' For the Kurds, the flight and dispersal of the Nestorians was the final triumph in this long-standing feud between two rival mountain communities and faiths.

We picked our way along a foaming stream to Medi village. The *hodja* was at home. He wore a cloth cap and had a pistol in his belt. He spread a rug at a camp fire of crackling scrub and began to question me. 'Did *Isa* (Jesus) claim to be God? If, as you Christians agree, there is only one God, how can you believe in the Trinity?' He asked me about the hierarchy of prophets ('of whom Jesus was one'). He said he admired the Germans ('enemies of Communism'). British support for Israel was 'treachery'. He had heard of Scotland but not Ireland or Wales. Polygamy, he asserted, was a law of nature. Without a husband, a women was useless, an 'abomination'.

Muzaffer and I pitched our tent close to the folded flock, and were half asleep when we were suddenly roused by a wild commotion and barking. Dogs were tearing past, followed by a youth with a stick. Muzaffer shone his torch through the tent opening and its beams fell straight on a black bear standing at the edge of the flock. As the beam lit up its yellow eyes, it hesitated with one paw raised, looking like a pantomime ogre discovered in a misdemeanour. It growled and vanished into the dark. It did not return and we said no more about it. But at breakfast the *hodja* gave us a friendly smile and offered to sell me his carpet for a small sum. I gladly took it. Its vivid colours of faded ochre and black were to brighten my room in Kampala for several years; until one of Amin's armed policemen took it for his own use and, I do not doubt, fouled it with beer, grease and spittle.

Gehi, our last halt before Colemerik, was a straggle of empty cottages, its terraced fields, once laboriously scraped from the bare rock face, now covered in thorns. Its only inhabitants were a man with three wives and a solitary neighbour. They slaughtered a kid for us. Cattle thieves, our host told us, had recently stolen eighty of his sheep, and bears invaded his fields – 'they come right up to my door at night.' After supper he took a rifle from a hole in the thatch and led us into the night to shoot one, with Muzaffer and me gripping our ice-axes like halberdiers. The stalk was in vain. At the edge of a stubble patch there was a rustle and crashing in the bush. But our torch shone on shadows and we came back with empty hands.

Now, as morning dawned on the owner's rice field and melons, our last day had come. We scrambled through a gorge shaded by huge plane trees and climbed to a high col. The col was a landmark – the edge of civilisation. From here we looked down on the Great Zab gliding along a gentle gradient to join the Tigris some 200 miles away – how tame it seemed, after the noisy, chattering torrents shooting eel-like through the defiles of Cilo! We passed a road-making camp with heavy earth-moving equipment, the spearhead of an invading army bent on breaking down the privacy of the mountains. This – the main highway from Van – was planned to push on south into Iraq, turning aside from the wild region we had lately crossed. As soon as we entered Colemerik a policeman asked to see my papers and took me to the Police Chief. He was a stout, friendly man and spoke English. ('I attended a police course in Eltham,' he told me. 'I am a Spurs and Fenerbahce fan.') He opened a file. 'Ankara has sent a letter about you. It states that Mr Hills will not after all be permitted to travel in the *vilayet* of Hakkari. When he arrives from Van, he must stay within the boundaries of the town while arrangements are made for his immediate return.' The Police Chief smiled. 'Since you have already done your tour, the letter is no longer important. But you must obey it now you are here.'

We slept the night in a school classroom and in the morning said goodbye to Raschid, who had tethered the mule to a poplar tree. The amiable Police Chief joined us at our breakfast of small boiled eggs and honey. I asked him if he visited the highland valleys. 'Good God, no,' he replied, 'I suffer from phlebitis.' From the open lorry returning us to Van, I looked back at Resko and the great limestone peaks receding into haze and little woolly clouds. They had opened up for me a page of savage beauty. It would be tempting to romanticise the herdsman's life of freedom in such grandiose scenery. Yet it was a life based on dirt and drudgery, an endless struggle to survive. One could not ignore the work-worn shrews who ran the summer pastures while their men smoked in tents or roamed the valleys on horseback; the enteritis and deaths of infants; the illiteracy and superstitions; the violent feuds. Mobile, clannish and superstitious, merciless to their enemies, the Kurds have never been easy subjects to handle. Yet their greatest enemy is not the Turkish gendarme or government official, but the bulldozer, grinding its way into the heart of their mountain fastnesses.

In 1959 I put away my Pembridge's school primer and took a more demanding post as lecturer in English at the newly opened Middle East Technical University in Ankara. The university was heavily subsidised by the Americans, and I was somewhat put off at first by the American dress, speech and mannerisms affected by some of my students. The following year (27 May 1960) a sensational military coup toppled the prime minister, Menderes, and his government. For many days army units, some mounted on big Kentucky cavalry horses, continued to patrol the city. It was during this chaotic time that Ankara Radio – which was still under armed guard – asked me to read evening news bulletins on its English programme, and later to give a series of travel talks on my journeys in Anatolia.

In the autumn of 1960 after visiting Ingrid's parents we bought a Volkswagen Beetle in Hamburg, and, with an ice-box strapped under the bonnet and our two-year-old son Hansen, drove back to Ankara. To my alarm I found that in my absence my post had been given to a Turkish major's wife. This called for immediate action and the intervention of Turkish friends; and within a fortnight I was driving north over the Pontic serpentines to take up a new teaching job in the small Black Sea port and coal-mining centre of Zonguldak. Again I was miscast. I had to teach biology in addition to elementary mathematics! My Ankara friends commiserated with me. They warned me that there was no central heating in Zonguldak, no Armenian grocers selling bacon and porridge oats, no night bars: nothing but rain and coal-dust in a cultural wilderness shut off from the rest of Anatolia by high mountains and dependent on a single bad road wriggling through lonely forest. Even the name Zonguldak, I was told, meant 'place of trembling,' an allusion to its former reputation for malarial fever. Yet I stayed for over three years in Zonguldak, and I have never regretted them.

We lived in the lower half of a cottage that stood on a cliff looking over the Black Sea. The landlord, an old-fashioned and courteous Turk, had a small glazier's business and used the cottage as a summer retreat. It had a rainwater tank and an untidy garden with a duck pond. The house was surrounded by woodland and wild plants – dense rhododendron thickets, myrtle bushes, strawberry trees and cornelian cherries. In winter we were buffeted by cold winds that dislodged the tiles, and the sea had a savage look with its flaming sunsets and screaming gulls swooping on shoals of silvery fish. Frequent snowfalls made it impossible to drive without snow-chains, and when the road over the mountains to the Anatolian plateau was blocked by drifts, lorry drivers would be stuck for two or three days, crouched over a log fire beside their vehicles. In spring the grey seaclouds lifted, and with the first fruit blossom hundreds of small black bulls would be brought out to plough the peasants' humps of soil. Rows of women followed the iron-sheathed wooden shares to break up the clods with hoes. Tortoises crawled out into the sun, butting each other in courtship with a noise like little hammers. They were tormented by children, who kicked and tossed them about like footballs. Maize was the main crop of the narrow coastal strip, and one-eyed sunflowers, nodding and staring to the south-east.

The Pontic foothills were covered with beech and Spanish chestnut that tumbled down to the sea and merged towards the top into fir and pine. Below, in the country lanes, wild roses gleamed among fig trees. Hairy water-buffaloes – their creamy milk was favoured for butter and yoghurt making – wandered like sleep-walkers through the brambles and rhododendrons. Even in midwinter, when the mountain pass was closed, I found cyclamen, primroses and snowdrops sheltering among moss and leaves.

Scarcely anyone came to the beach below our cottage. The country Turk dislikes (and fears) sea bathing, though men would sometimes sit in their underpants on the grey sand near the harbour and soap themselves. I used to swim round a headland, ploughing my way through jelly fish and disturbing cormorants, and in my last year, driven by some sort of masochism, I kept up the habit till Christmas Day. In winter the icy shock of the waves made my body tingle as though electrically charged. Once I came across a sad little scene. A boy had been carried out to sea and a group of people was waiting for the body to be recovered. His mother, an elderly woman in a black peasant gown, sat tearing her hair and screaming in lamentation while her husband stood in silent agony beside her.

The Zonguldak–Eregli coal basin had a mixed history of foreign management and exploitation until the mines were nationalised in 1940. Many of the Turks who now run the mines were trained in Germany and America; and the school where I taught had been expressly founded to give their children an education based largely on instruction in English. The mines had not yet spoilt the rustic character of the Zonguldak coast. Thick undergrowth soon covered the scars of old workings, and new ones were screened by wooded hills. Labour was recruited from seasonally unemployed villagers, who trudged home from work with coal-blackened faces and bundles of pit-wood and loaves. The coal trains twisted through steep woodland, scaring bony cows off the line. Ragged gypsy women picked up the coals spilled from the wagons. At night, jackals howled behind our cottage, and down by the water meadows frogs croaked like castanets.

Zonguldak's situation on the Black Sea coast made it a convenient start-point for journeys eastward along the seaboard to Trebizond, thence inland over the Pontic mountain chain to old Armenia, Erzurum and Azerbaijan. In my second summer I bought a bicycle from a junk-shop owner who had patched it together from odd parts. The frame had been roughly welded and it had cheap Taiwan tyres. But it was a lucky find, as bicycles were almost unknown in Turkey – no gentleman would sit astride a saddle like a frog, while the peasant had his pack-animal and his womenfolk to carry loads, and roads were stony and rough. My plan was to cycle from Erzurum through Azerbaijan to the Caspian (Pahlevi), then turn back along the Soviet border with a visit to Lake Urmia before heading for Tabriz and Trebizond. The journey would take several weeks; I carried my small tent, light sleeping-bag, primus cooker and rucksack.

At Agri, where Ararat first appears as a cloud in the sky, Kurdish boys threw stones at me from behind mounds of dung-fuel. But once on the road to Kazvin, over four hundred miles away, with a bag of biscuits and boiled sweets, and my legs pounding the pedals, I felt the elation, the *weightlessness*, of being alone. For me the key to a landscape is to move through it slowly, savouring the tiny details. As I pedalled along the plateau from Khoi, skirting the southern rim of the Elburz mountains, I was awed by the solitude: mile after mile of arid, khaki-coloured plain bristling with thistles and thorn bush, semi-deserted except for scattered villages whose mud walls crumble when it rains. The simplest things became objects of diversion and delight: a wayside graveyard of crudely shaped stones pitched together like a jumble of petrified corpses;

peasants laboriously sickling the corn while Egyptian vultures sailed overhead; a row of poplars by a trickle of brown water. Often the only relief from the sun's glare was the pencil of shadow thrown by a crooked telegraph pole with a bright bee-eater eyeing me from the wire. The earth smelt like burned toast. The few passing vehicles sprayed me with dust that settled over the thistles like volcanic ash.

A welcome sight were wayside tea-houses with their patches of colour – a shiny samovar and painted hubble-bubble stems stacked against a wall, an old rug, a horoscope, and a picture of the Shah in uniform. No one believed that I was bicycling *for fun* along the bone-shaking roads of Azerbaijan. I was generally taken to be an underpaid foreign scholar or expert, or the slightly comical victim of some mischance. The invasion of western junkies and hitch-hikers with their unkempt, ugly girls, hitting the hippie trail to the Orient, had not yet set in. The night arrangements I left to chance. Sometimes, at the edge of a village, peering from my sleeping-bag at dawn, I would watch my neighbours come to life – boys driving cattle out to graze, and tattered men and women shuffling to a greasy ditch to defecate, rinse face and arms, and loudly clear their throats of the night's phlegm. I boiled my drinking water, for it might have flowed through dung heaps.

From Kazvin I turned north over the Elburz mountains. I had been looking forward to bowling effortlessly down their reverse slopes to the sea. Alas, the descent through a steep gorge wriggling between high rock faces was so tough that I often had to trudge through drifts of broken stones. From the tea-huts, egg-shaped heads in yellow pudding basin caps turned to watch me with black, unblinking eyes. My humble status brought out a delightful trait among these simple, ragged men, for when I came to pay I often found that someone had quietly put down the money and disappeared.

Below Rudbar the gorge widened and levelled out, and the first specks of greenery thickened into sour-smelling rice fields where egrets stood like fluffs of white cotton and small humped cattle wandered between hedgerows bright with orange-red pomegranate flowers. What joy it was, to bowl along the tarred roads of Resht to my first glimpse of the sea. But Pahlevi was no good for swimming. Its long grey strand was lined with rows of bathing huts that teemed with families from Teheran. Paddling through a tideless scurf of melon rinds, they stood or sat like sea fowl in a bowl of tepid, indigo soup. Before I left Pahlevi I visited the Polish cemetery. This was a special moment for me. It was here that my wartime connection with General Anders's army had really begun. Weakened by typhus, malaria and malnutrition, the refugee soldiers ferried from Krassnovodsk had left their first dead here.

Forty miles on I was turned back by an army post. I was entering a

restricted frontier zone, and would have to return to Pahlevi for a
permit. I was in trouble, for the permit needed a referee, and I knew
no one. However, I learned of an American missionary doctor in the
neighbourhood. A phone call to him was enough to unravel the red tape.
I was off again along the coast road to Astara, through rice fields and
cool forest that smelt of damp ferns. I revelled in the shade. Unseen and
unobserved I could flop under an oak or acacia or a giant hornbeam, and
doze off amid the sweet, crushed mint. A rice farmer invited me to stay
the night on his verandah. He gave me *chalo kebab* (rice mixed with a
raw egg and strips of grilled meat) and *mast* (curds) for breakfast. His
son, who was a student, said that if I had been an American they would
not have asked me to their house. 'The Amis have money,' he said, 'but
no morals.'

At Astara an army officer in pyjamas stamped my pass. Here the
Iranian littoral collides with the Soviet seaboard and the frontier curls
up a forested ravine bisected by the Astara river which marks the boundary line. For the rest of the day I had to push my bicycle up a steep,
winding ascent with an unhindered view of Soviet Russia on my right.
How little there was to see! Wooden watch-towers on stilts, a few
clusters of military buildings, a double wire fence, and parallel to it,
ducking and swerving over the contours, a dirt road and a sandy track
which, Iranians told me, Soviet guards, like gamekeepers patrolling a
vast estate, regularly scrutinised for footprints. It all seemed dead but
for an occasional wisp of smoke, a snub-nosed military lorry grinding
round a bend, at night the howl of jackals. 'No one lives over there,'
said the tea-house customers pointing to the clearings behind the watch-
towers; 'the people have been moved out.' How hostile it was, this
apparatus of watchful suspicion, the spy-box rising high on its metal
legs, whence unseen eyes stared ceaselessly at the donkeys, the country
buses and tea-house idlers on the free side of the world. To amuse myself
I would sit down opposite one of the towers, kick my legs in the air
and shout 'Shit Russians!' On the Iranian side, there was a delightful
lack of restraint. The Kurdish guard posts gave me tea, and cucumbers
sliced with a bayonet, and chatted about their homes in Mahabat and
Hamadan.

From the top of the pass I had a following wind and skimmed
downhill as though levitating, until the gradient flattened out again and
I had the long grind to Arderbil and Tabriz to face. Before heading back
for Turkey, however, I made a detour to Urmia (Rezayeh). Urmia had
been a haven of Nestorian refugee settlement after the community's eviction from the Hakkari mountains in 1915. In the fertile plain of Urmia,
at Gavalan, I was delighted to find one of their simple churches standing
like a small fort on a ridge looking over the milky-blue lake. The church

must have been occasionally in use, yet it was completely bare except for the burnt remains of incense and some obscene graffiti scrawled in candle fat over the sanctuary. The town was largely Christian. But it seemed as dirty and ramshackle as any other.

Some days later, the baking brown spaces of Asia behind me, I trundled my bicycle up the steep Zigana pass. According to Xenophon's *Anabasis* it was from the crest of the pass that his exhausted heroes had cried 'Thalassa! Thalassa!' on catching their first glimpse of the sea. I spent an hour or two exploring the grassy saddle, but the mountain masses in the foreground blocked any view of the sea, and it was clear to me that Xenophon's men must have caught sight of it from a different vantage point, a supposition that David Winfield confirmed. I found him and June at home in their cottage by the grassy mound in Trebizond. David put a loaf, a huge jar of Marmite and a bottle of red wine on the kitchen table. Alas, while we were feasting, Professor Talbot Rice – the eminent Byzantinist and David's supervisor – arrived from Ankara. He would not have been pleased to find David carousing with a tramp. 'I'll hide behind your bed,' I said, retreating with the bottle. David joined me. We crouched there for half an hour before June persuaded the professor to leave. 'We get some strange visitors here,' David told me. 'Herbalists from Kew looking for rare flowers. An occasional solemn German. Freya Stark called once – a splendid eccentric – she hides her valuables in parts of her dress where no Turkish official would ever dare to look.' David disapproved of hitch-hikers. 'Instead of paying their way like gentlemen, they exploit the simple Turk's hospitality and good nature even though they're much better off than he is.'

I left Trebizond with a hangover, speeding along the coast road between flowering hedges and hazel-nut plantations, with the sea on my right. Perched on two iron wheels, with bare knees, I must have seemed like a portent of the Evil Eye to the peasant women, who hid their faces and ducked into ditches as I passed. I completed the last leg of my journey sitting comfortably on a load of melons in a boat that carried me from Amasra to Zonguldak. I arrived home just in time, for my clothes were falling to pieces. It would not have done for Selim Bey and my pupils to see their teacher pushing an old bicycle like a tramp.

David had been interested in my account of the old Georgian church at Parhal. I learned from him and from local villagers that a number of other ancient Georgian basilicas were hidden away in the wild side valleys of the Coruh, Tortum and Oltue rivers in north-east Turkey. They date back to the ninth to eleventh centuries, a notable period of church building under a branch of the Bagratid family which had extended its rule over this former borderland province of Tao after the Arabs occupied Tiflis and the Caucasian homelands of the old Georgian monarchy in the seventh century. The churches were very little known. Security restrictions kept foreign visitors away, and the rugged Tao gorges were difficult of access except on foot or horseback.

In the summers of 1962 and 1963 I spent several weeks tracking down these churches. This meant a good deal of walking up steep mountain paths used by pack-animals. The villagers welcomed me. I was not a spy, a tax collector or a government snooper, but in their eyes a 'historian studying old churches' – a sort of *hodja* or scholarly person. Among the striking features of these cruciform Tao churches were handsome conical glazed roofs mounted on sturdy drums set off by powerful columns, slender blind arches, wall-paintings, and stone reliefs of animal or Biblical scenes. Despite grievous wounds they had tenaciously survived centuries of icy winters, earth tremors, war and alien occupation.

The church at Dortkilise was being used as a barn and sheep pen. At Osk Vank the tenth-century building was divided between a threshing-floor where bullocks, dragging a flint-studded sledge, were treading out the grain, and a walled-off part for Muslim worship. The church at Haho had a small cloister and wall covered with remarkable reliefs in blackened stone – one of them a crude representation of Jonah being spewed from a whale's mouth. Ishan church stood on a mountain ridge high above the Oltu. I went there with the *muhtar* of Yusufeli and we had to ford the river. The church, with its animal figures and frescos, and its russet and blue-grey conical roof, seemed to have been dropped miraculously amid the jagged rocks of the defile, like a jewelled plant sprouting from a seed dropped by a bird. It was dark when we left and the rising moon had cast a copper glow over the gorge. I still remember that unearthly light with its hint of ghosts and dragons, the sun-warmed path down the red cliff and the cold river swirling round my knees.

Seven hours' march up the Oltu from Ishan, along a path that wriggled between steep rock faces with the river frothing below, I came to Tavusker village. It was dark before I got there and I was about to roll over in a hollow near some sunflowers and go to sleep when a man with a lantern called me over. '*Memleket?*' he asked. 'Where are you from? Your profession? *Cocuk varmi*? Have you children?' He threw a blanket on the floor of his poor hut and said, 'No one journeys in the night. You will sleep here.' He gave me a bowl of *ayran* and in the morning some peaches. All I found in Tavusker were some arched walls and a tiny chapel stuffed with hay. The headman told me to go on to Nikoma. This remote place was hard to find. It lay hundreds of feet below a rocky spur with a ruined castle on it. The inhabitants – a handful of old people and children – were startled to see me and hid in the trees while I prowled among the ruins of a tall yellow church with magnificently painted columns and a chapel with murals joined to a cowshed. When I picked up some tiny fragments of blue-glazed tile from the ground, they came out of hiding to join me. 'Did you find any coins?' they asked. 'Any gold?'

Then, not far from Tortum, I went in search of a 'tall church' at Ekik, a lonely hamlet high above the Erzurum road. Alas, the church was gone. 'We pulled it down three years ago,' I was told. 'We needed stones for our new mosque.' I was given a horse and guide for the descent. When I looked back, I saw the imam watching me from the new mosque like a fierce old bird guarding its nest. In the tea-house by the road a grave old man in a crimson turban greeted me. '*Memleket?*' '*Ingiliz.*' He thought for a few moments. 'The English,' he said, 'are not to be trusted. You change sides. The Turk has either friends or enemies, and they stay that way for ever.'

Travelling by road through Azerbaijan between rows of grim mountains it is hard to believe that above those bare, glaring walls of rock are hidden green pastures, great herds of beautiful cattle, and the encampments of thousands of wandering herdsmen. Their high summer *yaylaks* are a boundless field for exploration, merging one into another as the ridges that dominate the plateaux fall back and the sky empties but for the highest peaks.

Ever since, a year earlier, I had seen the snow-capped peak of Savalan (15,784 ft) floating like a white cloud above the hot settled valleys, I had wanted to explore it and to meet the Turki-speaking herdsmen who grazed their animals on its slopes. Now, travelling in my Beetle, after a bumpy journey via Ardebil, Lore and a fifteen-mile cattle track to Gotesu I had reached the base of the mountain. Gotesu was a little place of melon stalls and hot sulphur springs where camels, horses, their owners and families were solemnly soaking themselves in a dingy medicinal pool. A four hours' climb above Gotesu brought me to a *yaylak* encampment tucked under the south wall of Savalan's snow-streaked cone. Here in a grassy hollow cleared of thorn bushes was a ring of mushroom-shaped brown felt tents (*yurts*) spiralling smoke through the flaps in their domes. The Turki-speaking herdsmen, who came from the Aras valley, let me pitch my own little tent fifty yards from their lines. After dark, when the compound was crowded with livestock, the howl of wolves set off an uproar of men and dogs. My position in no man's land was precarious. Whenever I coughed or stirred, a dog barked savagely through my tent flap.

I found it an easy scramble up the south face to the top of Savalan. It has a snow-filled crater encircled by tower-like knobs of russet rock, and I recognised details familiar to me from other volcanic mountains I had climbed: ridges of lichen-stained igneous boulders enclosing snow-drifts, the trickles of ice-cold water nourishing tiny mossy glens and wild flowers, an eagle starting a hare in a snow-patch. From the summit I could see the Caspian Sea, its bright azure faded to a livid streak against the rice fields and dark forests of Gilan. But immediately below me the little *yaylak* encampments, so conspicuous at ground level, had vanished amid the enormous chaos of debris sprayed by the mountain over its foothills. Savalan has destroyed as much grazing as it has created.

I took a different route on the way down and as night fell, having met no one all day, and being uncertain of my direction, I was more than relieved to find a small encampment with a row of camels crouched outside the headman's *yurt*. I joined him at his samovar under the wooden ribs of his felt shelter, where a woman gave me scorched sheets of bread dipped in yoghurt as we squatted round a fire of horse dung and thorn bushes. The shepherds had been astonished to see me arrive out of the blue. They asked if I was looking for minerals – why else should a foreign *effendi* go to the trouble of toiling up a mountain? Behind me in the acrid smoke, amid the tent gear and swinging babies' hammocks, whispering red-eyed women were preparing for the night. I was given a quilt and rug, the *yurt*'s leather flap was rolled down, and I slept outside next to the camels. The night wind blew sharp off the snow fields. Down in the mud villages of the plain the air would be heavy and sour over the dykes.

From Savalan I went to Mount Sahand (12,172 ft), which I approached from Livan village, twelve miles off the Tabriz–Bostanabad highway. The landlord of Livan, who lived in a big stone house decorated with plastic flowers, ordered a labourer to accompany me as porter (the only preparation he made for four days' absence was to change his sickle for a stick), and we took our place in a file of horsemen moving up to the high pastures. Gradually the muddy ditches, corn fields, willows and poplar groves of village land fell below and a mass of grassy hills opened out. There was no food problem. Whenever we wished a shepherd wearing a flat fur cap that sat on his head like a wig would grab a sheep and squirt a stream of milk into a tin bowl, which was offered with a round of flat bread kept fresh in a cloth.

The top of Sahand is a long, easily climbed ridge with two humps. Camels were grazing a few hundred feet below the topmost snow patches, a herd of several hundred horses was corralled lower down, and lying against the green stain of brooks were the round *yurts* of the herdsmen. The green slopes shimmered with blue delphiniums, and over them crept great flocks chivvied by yodelling boys. The herdsmen were a mixture of Turki- and Kurdish-speaking families from the Maragheh and Mahabad areas. 'Which country is better,' some of them asked me,

'Iran or Turkey?' 'Iran is larger,' I would say evasively, giving my stock answer to this familiar question, 'your bazaars are better, you have petroleum, a royal family – and Isfahan.' I didn't dwell on Iran's less agreeable features: the endlessly corrugated roads tended by solitary labourers poking at the pot-holes with little spades; the lack of wayside springs – how cheerfully they gush along the roads of eastern Anatolia; the scarcity of good eating-houses in small places; the Shias' dislike of foreigners approaching his mosques.

From Sahand I returned to Maku, a few miles from the Turkish border, and while an army post prepared a permit for me to ramble about the Kurdish frontier *yaylaks* ('You risk getting your throat cut by those bandits,' warned the captain), I joined some teachers and students in a tea-house at the bus stop where they gathered every day to watch the tourists go by. 'How we envy Westerners,' one of the students confessed to me as some blonde tourists in brief skirts stepped out of the bus. 'Lots of girls – and free love.' A teacher added, 'An unmarried Iranian like me has to make do with prostitutes – unless he's daring enough to climb up to some married woman's balcony and risk being knifed.' Our morning tally was an English botanist (an ex-Navy officer) from Kew, a car-load of French musicologists bent on recording Iranian folk-songs, and some barelegged German hitch-hikers perched on a lorry. 'We Iranians like foreigners,' remarked another. 'In Turkey they throw stones at your cars.' He was right there, and shepherd boys are good shots.

Maku gorge, as seen from above, narrows into a black gash through which the highway twists as though through a funnel. I had a long climb up a dried river bed to reach the Kurdish *yaylaks*. The herds-men had pitched their dark booth-like tents and butter-churning tripods wherever there was water, and their camels, silhouetted on the skyline like grotesque long-spouted teapots, were grazing against a magnificent background of the two Ararats, which rose like islands out of a cloud sea. Inquisitive and hospitable, the Kurds asked me without ceremony into their goat-hair shelters while their women quickly baked bread on glowing pieces of dung. Agile, colourful and tough, Kurdish women seem perfectly suited to the herdsman's wandering life, which is as rough as a soldier's on campaign. The Kurdish dogs also have their role. Power-ful, light-coloured animals, they are fed on bread and buckets of watered yoghurt, and hate strangers, whom they come bounding up to attack from a hundred yards away. One morning while drawing water from a spring I was surrounded and nipped in the leg. The Kurds laughed. 'Our dogs', they reassured me, 'are *temiz* (clean).'

Three days later, back in Erzurum, I went to a chemist's for a bandage. The chemist looked at the laceration and said sternly, 'All Iranian dogs are suspect.' He immediately telephoned the hospital, and

I was ordered a course of fourteen needles. The needle was like a horse-syringe and an orderly plunged it every day into alternate sides of my stomach. I spent the days sitting outside my tent in a stubble field, idly watching the dust storms blow like smoke over the towers and ancient earthworks of Erzurum. After a day or two some peasants came over to talk to me. We discussed religion, money and '*guzel*' (beautiful) Istanbul', and for a time I felt like a wandering guru.

After a last jab with the big needle I still had time to call on David in Trebizond and go with him on another mountain excursion. We camped beneath the seaward-facing wall of Kackar Dag (12,914 ft) and, while we waited for the weather to improve, explored the slopes at the base of Kackar's spouting glaciers. They were thickly strewn with gentians, crocuses and mushrooms – we stewed pounds of mushrooms on my primus and swallowed them like hogs. Oddly enough, the Laz herdsmen couldn't stand mushrooms. They preferred chewing crocus bulbs. They were guarding a huge herd of bulls, which were so docile that we wandered among them as though they were sheep. We made a half-hearted attempt to climb Kackar Dag but were turned back by torrential rain and had to retreat to a hut on the Asian side of the mountain. The owner let us strip and dry off on his floor. This proved to be my last visit to the eastern Pontic peaks and to the wild gorges and foaming rivers where red-legged partridges cluck in the screes and mulberry trees rustle over those forgotten Georgian churches.

Ingrid and I had now been eight years in Turkey, the last three of them in a Black Sea backwater. We decided it was time to move on. We had thoroughly enjoyed living with the tough, hospitable Turkish people. I had explored a great many of Turkey's most beautiful and less accessible regions, described them for *The Times* and other newspapers, and written a book (*My Travels in Turkey*). But the constraints of living in a Muslim society had begun to pall; and our son Hansen had to be sent to an English school. Through the *Times Educational Supplement* I applied for a teaching post in Africa. Addis Ababa University offered me a lecturership, which I turned down – life under the Lion of Judah and his warring princes, I thought, would be too unpredictable and operatic. I asked for a post in East Africa, and flew to London for interview at the old Colonial Office. Some weeks later, back in Zonguldak, I received a message from the British Consulate in Istanbul telling me to report to Makerere University in Kampala. I could take my Beetle with me.

I said goodbye to David Winfield in Istanbul. He had finished repairing the wall paintings at Trebizond and was now doing restoration work at the great Muslimised basilica of St Sofia. I was allowed to walk along the dizzy rail that curves under the ceiling of the huge dome. Seen from above, the great building seemed to be less a place of worship than an empty barn. There were no cries, no bells, no sounds of prayer, no rows of men pressing their foreheads to the ground, no tiaras or turbans or smell of incense. David took me out onto the roof of the dome and we climbed over the lead slats to a long rusty iron chain that dangled from the gilded crescent itself. We straddled the chain like two somewhat overweight steeplejacks and hauled ourselves up to the huge, shining Muslim emblem. Below lay palaces and ships, the Golden Horn, the gardens and the Bosphorus. As I leant against the crescent I felt like a schoolboy who had achieved a dare.

Chapter 12

Uganda and Amin

A t Port Said in December 1963 my Beetle was loaded onto the deck of *La Bourdonnais*, bound from Marseilles for Mauritius, and I settled down to a week of gigantic French meals before disembarking at Mombasa. From here it was three days' journey by road to Kampala, driving through Kenya and eastern Uganda, on a mostly untarred highway enlivened by 'Elephants Have Right of Way' signs. I took a week over the journey, noting in Kenya and especially in the White Highlands the ubiquitous evidence of a British presence: the flower shops with roses and geraniums in small towns, the English newspapers, red-faced men in khaki shorts driving vintage English cars, scones and Worcestershire sauce in the inns. But it was the black man, not the sahib or his memsahib, I was more interested in: and my first meeting with Africans was encouraging. Not far from Mombasa I had to change a wheel. A group of young women with shining bare breasts, wearing *kitengi* cloth tied round their waists, stopped to watch me. Turkish countrywomen would have made a detour to avoid a stranger, or looked the other way, hiding behind their head-cloths. There was no false modesty about these smiling brown African girls: they looked me straight in the eye. That, I thought, was a good augury – to be among people who smiled.

In Kampala I was given a government flat on Kololo hill and was joined by Ingrid, who soon gave birth to our younger son Johnny. I took over the garden and became expert with a long-handled African hoe and a slasher – a thin metal blade with a sharp curved end for cutting grass and undergrowth. Gardening – indeed, any physical labour – was regarded as demeaning for a gentleman, and Africans, seeing me sweat-stained and shirtless burning piles of mango leaves, would look aghast and say 'I am sorry, Bwana'. The garden had beautiful flowering shrubs – bougainvillaea, hibiscus, gardenia and jasmine – but through neglect they were being eaten away by termites whose mounds, like hard chocolate humps, would spring like magic out of the red earth. The little sloping plot, which in time I began to regard as my own, was alive with birds: bulbuls that started to sing at dawn in the tickberry bush below my window; sunbirds flashing among the hibiscus blossom; plantain eaters that cackled like imbeciles.

Kololo was one of the prosperous parts of Kampala. The residents were mostly Europeans, with a few African civil servants and Asians. Now that Uhuru had been granted (1963) the number of expatriates was being severely reduced, their jobs Africanised, and Kololo had begun to lose its character as a predominantly white suburb. Alas, I was still a misfit. I had been posted as mathematics and biology teacher for an African secondary-school teacher-training course at Makerere University; and it wasn't until over a year later that I was asked to teach English literature. Richard Poskitt, our new principal, a fine old warhorse recently retired as headmaster of Bolton Grammar School, asked me to build up a new college library. This enabled me to order books of my own choice and to catch up with the reading I had been deprived of for years.

My students were delightful to teach and eager to learn. The prize of a diploma was a magic wand that would lift them out of the primitive round of rural life into the glittering modern world. They had the African's inborn sense of humour, a gift for words – fireside talk and story-telling are part of the immemorial African tradition – and a talent for writing verse, much of which I was able over the years to get published by the local press or in African anthologies, or broadcast by the BBC.

The new school of African writing and thinking that burst forth in the 1960s following the retreat of white rule was at first strongly anti-colonialist and an outlet for bottled-up resentment of the white man. Among its models were the novelists Achebe, Oyono, Armah and Ngugi. Bitek, the Acholi poet, was the satirist, sneering and laughing at the old white establishment with its priests and 'suffocating paternalism'. The Makerere professor and political philosopher Ali Mazrui, who had studied at Huddersfield and had an English wife, supplied the dialectic. But in less than a decade it was seen that black rule in Africa was in many respects more violent, more chaotic and more corrupt than white government had been. In a succession of *coups* military leaders seized power, among them the formidable Idi Amin in Uganda, who ousted Milton Obote. Obote's Common Man's Charter and incoherent

socialism had made him many enemies; above all he had alienated
the Baganda, Uganda's most numerous and influential tribe, by burning their hereditary ruler's, the Kabaka's, palace and arresting their
leaders. In January 1971, taking advantage of Obote's brief absence
abroad, Amin sent his motorised troops into Kampala. Soon afterwards
he donned cap and gown as the Chancellor of Makerere University. In
his opening address he jeered at the students ('Many of you have gonor-
rhoea'); a dark cloud descended over student life in Uganda and the flow
of creative writing and debate was extinguished.

At first I was strongly conscious of the African's colour and the
physical differences between us. In a crowd of Africans I felt like an
albino, muscle-bound and ungainly. The African was lissom and relaxed.
His fingers dangled when he walked (the white man clenched his hands,
and was usually in a hurry). Africans liked a woman to have a large bottom. This enhanced a woman's status: it meant that she had parents or
a husband who could afford to feed her well. Baganda women – unlike
the leaner ones from the poorer northern tribes who scarified their toil-
worn bodies – were often massively built with a tendency to stea-
topygia, rolling their buttocks with pride under ample *busuti* gowns: a
church parade of stout, velvet-skinned matrons was a magnificent sight.
Among the Baganda especially and their neighbours the Banyankole it
was no compliment to be called 'very black'. Hence the craze for skin-
lightener creams, used by prostitutes and ministers' wives alike. Many
African women despised their own naturally dense, curly hair ('it's like
wire') and were constantly teasing it, straightening it with hot combs
or plaiting it into intricate mosaic patterns. Some women wore wigs like
birds' nests.

It was through my students that I began to get a closer understanding
of Africans. Several of them invited me to their homes. Kalisto Okwonga,
an Acholi, lived in a bush clearing near Adilang. He had his own
thatched 'bachelor' hut and was cramming modern European history
(Napoleon to Bismarck) by the light of an oil-wick. His father, an
old soldier who had fought in Burma, grew a little millet, cotton and
groundnuts. As Kalisto was destined for higher things he was excused
field work. His mother or sister, kneeling on the mud floor as they
entered Kalisto's hut, would bring us trays of gritty millet dumplings,
groundnut sauce or pieces of chicken. When the sun went down we sat
round a log fire under a wild fig tree with Kalisto's father and his drinking cronies. We drank the beer warm, from calabashes. It was yellow
and bubbly and strong enough to incite men to beer fights, which left
scars on their heads.

The small homesteads of the Adilang area were favourite targets for
Jie cattle raiders. Armed with spears, oiled and naked, they came at night

to murder people and drive off their animals. On one occasion, during a time of constant raids, Mr Okwonga said that it would be our turn next. He had already sent away his family and livestock. That night the half-dozen men who had stayed behind crowded into Kalisto's hut with their spears and bows and a calabash of beer. In the early hours we heard a commotion outside – shouts and whistles and a shot. Someone had lent me a spear and I remember gripping the handle. But no naked warriors thumped on Kalisto's flimsy tin-lined door. In the morning Kalisto and I went to see the raided huts. Broken hoes, pots and thatching straw were strewn about, guinea-fowl were pecking at spilled grain.

Despite his father warning him not to go with me into the mountains ('You are teaching my son to sleep in the bush like an animal,' he told me), Kalisto joined me on several safaris. And his cramming paid off at last. It was a happy moment to find him ensconced one day in his own teacher's flat at an up-country school, with a fridge, a sofa set, a reading lamp and chickens running about the yard. 'All I want now', he said, 'is a *bibi* (wife) to cook my porridge and warm my bed.'

Hesbon Lubega lived at his family home near Masaka, in Buganda. Villa Maria was a strongly Catholic neighbourhood with a big church, seminary and schools. The rich red earth was crammed with banana trees, coffee shrubs, pineapples and mangoes. Hesbon had for a time studied at the junior seminary with a view to joining the priesthood, but had rebelled against the discipline ('no mango stealing, no Congo music, no girls') and was now writing a novel about barmaids and bride-price. He also wrote verse, with striking lines ('O fat bellies are favoured most!' or 'Drunkards like sick dogs retch homewards'). His father, who had prospered through his coffee crops and long since replaced his that-ched roof with corrugated iron sheets, had an old gramophone and liked his guests to dance. These were solo exhibitions of bottom-waggling. To enhance the waggling effect ('Your buttocks are too small') he made us tie a jacket round our hips; it heightened the effect of threshing loins. Kalisto's people had lived on maize or millet beer and porridge (*posho*). Here the staple diet of the Baganda was plantains, steamed as *matoke* or fermented into a sour beer which made my stomach rumble. Mr Lubega and his friends didn't care for northerners, whom they called *banag-gwanga* (outsiders). 'They tear out their front teeth and mutilate their skins. Not long ago the men walked about naked. They are fit only to be night watchmen or soldiers.'

I spent a week exploring the neighbourhood with Hesbon. The valley quivered with banana groves which waved their long green fronds like windmills. Dark paths shielded from the sun led through the planta-tions to little cottages with scarlet canna lilies growing against the door and the window openings shuttered against 'thieves and wild animals'.

Everyone was well fed, smiling and courteous. Ibises were wailing
in the sedge and crested cranes flew overhead with trailing legs and
sad, mewing cries. Watching the sun go down over the banana gardens,
the cassava, and the white-flowering coffee shrubs shining like bridal
dresses, I felt that this was one of the world's most pleasant corners. A
warm climate, regular rainfall, women to do the work, schools, a church
and the unwavering support of the clan if one was in trouble – what
more could one want?

Respectable Europeans kept away from Kampala's back streets, from
Mengo and Kisenyi, especially after dark. There were the flies, the smell
of urine and rotting heaps of *matoke*, the troops of brazen tarts who
hung round the bars and markets, the pickpockets and violence. The cry
of 'Thief!' would be followed by the blood-curdling ululation of women
as the suspect (perhaps he was innocent) was chased, caught and beaten insensible or lynched and left in the road. Someone would grab the
dead man's shoes; an old woman holding a hand over her mouth would
sprinkle grass over the sightless face. I used to visit Mukasa, a Mukiga
student, who lived with an aunt in a two-roomed hovel at the foot of
Rubaga hill. To make ends meet he did odd jobs, helping in the market
or as barman. He slept little, and coughed. Once I took him to his aged
mother's village near Bombo, where she lived in a small broken hut hidden among banana gardens and pawpaws. Later, when Obote returned
from exile in 1980 to seek revenge on the Baganda for having spurned
him, the district was ravaged by soldiers and became a graveyard of butchered villages. Mukasa, I heard, was one of those who perished during
the troubles, gunned down perhaps by a drunken soldier who wanted
his wrist watch or his shirt.

One of my safaris through the mountain ranges of northern Uganda
took me to the Teuso village of Pirre, three days' march from the point
where the borders of Uganda, Kenya and the Sudan converge at Zulia.
The anthropologist Dr Colin Turnbull, whose lyrically written account
of the Ituri pygmies (*The Forest People*) upset the pedants by becoming
a best seller, had been living in Pirre for some weeks. He was now
writing a study of the 1,500 Teuso (or Ik, as they called themselves) and
put me up in his ramshackle little hut. It was protected by a barrier
of thorn bushes inside a stockade, and had a broken bed, a sloping
mud floor, and Colin's neatly rolled black umbrella hanging from a
nail. Colin was wearing elegant but grubby white shorts that were,
I thought, too tight, and unsuitable sandals (no protection against
thorns); he looked like a shipwrecked actor. He told me that the Teuso
were going through a hard time. Drought had ruined their few food
crops and they were starving and demoralised. 'They snatch food from

each other and go off into corners to eat by themselves. The old people can't manage and will soon die.' The real problem though was that the Teuso had no cattle wealth. They were hunters and gatherers by tradition. Yet they were no longer free to roam, as of old, in search of food, owing to stricter control of movement over the Sudan border and the encroachment of the Kideppo game park boundaries. They lived also in constant fear of Turkana raiders, of whom some carried firearms.

I set off for Zulia with three porters and Atum, the guide. My companions looked thin and undernourished but had surprising energy. They searched far and wide for berries, poked the termite mounds, and scurried after the chattering honey-guide bird when it led them to a honeycomb, devouring as a delicacy the combs that had grubs ('protein') in them. They knew exactly where to dig for water. At night they slept naked round a fire with their skimpy *shuka* cloths wrapped round their heads. Only Atum wore shorts (stolen, he told me, from a police post). Zulia, approached through protea bush charred by grass fires, was not a high mountain (7,048 ft), but it gave an immense view of the Didinga lands of the Sudan and, to the north-east, wild Turkana country – miles of bush like a scalp bristling with tufts of peppercorn hair over which the shadows of clouds moved slowly like the figures of giant reapers. On the way back the porters, Lochere and Locham, grabbed two young hornbills and a tortoise, which they cooked for supper while I scraped out my tin of steaming porridge oats.

Then the wind rose and black storm clouds swept towards us. Atum had a charm with him – a magic plug of wood given to him by the witch-doctor. He stuck it on the tip of his spear and pointed it at the streaming rain curtain – which hovered and then swerved away. Atum was delighted. 'The rain', he giggled, 'will now be striking Bawana Turnbull.'

When I returned to Pirre the following year, Colin told me that many Teuso had already died of starvation. The survivors were wretched and emaciated. The women's breasts had shrunk to flaps, their bellies were a mass of wrinkles and folds, the children were skinny and pot-bellied. Colin was depressed. 'Hunger has made them vicious and cruel to one another. They steal food from the mouths of the old and sick. "Goodness" means having a full stomach.' The book (*The Mountain People*) which Colin subsequently wrote about his experiences with the Teuso shocked its readers. Sociologists were appalled at the revelation that the noble savage, even in his pristine state, could behave so badly to his own kin. A dramatised version of the fate of the Teuso was put on the stage in London.

On another journey to the same area I took Kalisto along the Turkana escarpment to Kalapata and through the grazing lands of the Dodoth

to Kaabong. Kalisto didn't enjoy the trip. He had the Acholi farmer's
fear of the Dodoth and Jie ('thieves and cattle raiders') and the educated
African's contempt for a society where the men walked naked and
women wore nothing but a 'smelly animal-skin'. The tribes of Kara-
moja, he said, lived in a human zoo; they ought to be forcibly resettled,
educated, made to cover their nakedness, grow their own food and pay
taxes. 'They eat raw sorghum from the stalk and cook their porridge
with rotten fig-fruits.'

Nakedness never bothered me, indeed I admired the physique of the
men with their oiled and depilated bodies (removal of the pubic hair
made them look even more naked), their painted mud helmets and sleek,
agile limbs, and the grace of the women, their gourd-shaped breasts and
small neat heads framed by necklaces of beads and shining metal rings
which made them look like kingfishers. They wore nothing but a simple
cowhide trailing at the back with a small beaded leather flap (or a tiny
string of chains for young girls) in front to hide their private parts.

In addition to my journeys in northern Uganda I was attracted to the
Virunga chain of volcanoes that stretches along Uganda's western border with Rwanda and the former Congo (Zaire) and includes the three
Mufumbiro peaks. Tension on the Congo side – there were reports of
fighting in which white mercenaries were involved – had led to the frontier zone being sealed off by the Uganda army, and when I asked for
a permit to climb the Mufumbiro volcanoes, the white official in charge
of the Kampala pass office said 'You must be joking – you don't want
to get shot as a white mercenary, do you?' But I am usually lucky when
it comes to slipping over frontiers. So I drove to the border crossing in
Kisoro. Here the guard post told me that I could stay the night at the
Travellers' Rest hotel 200 yards inside the prohibited zone, but I must
leave my Beetle behind. I found Herr Baumgaertel, the proprietor, in
a foul temper. 'The soldiers', he said, 'are ruining me. No fresh supplies,
the officers drink in my bar and don't pay, no tourists – even the gorillas
have disappeared from the mountain.'

My intention – which I kept to myself – was to climb Sabinio, Father
of Teeth (11,900 ft). Early in the morning, I strolled past the African
guard post without disturbing the sentry (he was asleep on a chair) and
met Reuben, an experienced guide, who was ready to join me with two
stocky Bahutu porters carrying sickle-shaped pangas for hacking a way
through undergrowth. On the way we passed parties of smugglers trotting silently through the bamboo forest with hides, sacks and bundles. We were not expecting to see gorillas – Reuben said they had been
frightened away by leopards – but on the second day, a dark mass about
seventy yards away suddenly began to move. 'Gorillas,' whispered Reuben. We stood watching them. It was their size that impressed me,

the great powerful bodies, and their shyness. But they had already taken alarm. Dropping on their hands, they retreated slowly over a ridge: last of all a big female with a young one riding like a jockey on her back. The nests they had built like cradles among the tree heathers were soiled with half-chewed food and droppings. Towards the top of Sabinio the tree heathers that had taken the place of the bamboo forest gave way to a dense green thatch of giant lobelias and groundsels. Among the powder-blue lobelia flowers tiny malachite sunbirds flashed like jewels.

From Sabinio we crossed the Mgahinga saddle to climb Muhavura, The Beacon (13,540 ft). At dusk on the following day, while I was leading, a file of smugglers came round a bend in the track. They must have thought I was a government officer. In a flash they threw away their head-loads and bolted into the bush. The heavy bags were stuffed with tin grains. We carried them into our night shelter for the police to retrieve. No one had passed this way for some time and we had to hack a tunnel through thick brambles and hypericum forest. The top itself was surrounded by a weird barricade of grotesquely over-developed plants – groundsels like huge cabbages and tall lobelia poles. From here we could see Karisimbi, the highest of the Virunga volcanoes (14,872 ft), towering into the Congo's purple mist. I asked Reuben if he would come with me one day to climb it. He gave me a disapproving look. No, he said, 'the people over there are *kondos* (bandits) – they would murder us for the sake of your boots and binoculars.'

The Virunga chain of eight volcanoes stretches from Muhavura to Nyiragongo in the Congo. Nyiragongo (11,450 ft) was still active – a few years earlier it had pumped out a flaming mass of lava that had covered the approaches with a hard grey scab. To reach it I drove to Goma, just in the Congo on Lake Kivu. This decomposing collection of banks and poorly stocked shops had been ruined by marauding soldiers. It was littered with rubbish and overrun by touts and tarts. The tarts wore bulky turbans and *kitengi* cloth twisted round their hips. They had large, sad and beautiful eyes and lips that looked purple under the thick red paint. The few Europeans – Belgians and Greeks – walking about with parcels and briefcases had the woebegone look of spivs. The Tourist Office was a sham and I could find no one who knew anything about Nyiragongo. So I drove to the headquarters of the Albert National Park administration in Rumengabo. None of the officials was at home. But six women with babies – their wives – came out to ask me for sugar. The luxurious houses that the Belgians had built for the administration had been looted. There was no piped water or electricity, and chickens were hopping through doorways.

I could see the blunt cone of Nyiragongo smoking in cloud some ten miles away. When the Director arrived late at night in a battered Beetle he was immediately helpful, and detailed Jean and three porters to go up the mountain with me. It was a long, wet climb through dense podocarpus and hagenia forest festooned with creepers and lianas like trip-wires. When the tree heathers thinned out, a cindery slope took us to the crater rim and there, looking over the edge, I found myself craning over an abyss. From the bottom, some 1,300 ft down, rose and fell a thunderous sea roar. One of the fumaroles was tossing out gobbets of fiery matter with a thud and protracted echo which pulsated round the crater like the tolling of a gigantic bell. There was, I remember, a single flower, flame red, sticking out from the crater rim: a kniphofia.

Coming down we had to pick our way softly through a herd of elephants. 'They are *méchants*,' said Jean, looking at the great ears pointing towards us through torn trees and foliage. 'Poachers have made them bad-tempered. Some are wounded.' Back at Rumengabo I put up my camp bed under a tree, and woke to find a guard watching me. He wanted tobacco and sugar.

When I returned to Rumengabo some months later, the *Conservateur* told me that no one had climbed Karisimbi (14,782 ft) since independence. The mountain was strictly *interdit*. But he agreed to let me go, with Jean as guide. Three Bahunde porters came with us, reeking of beer – it took over a day for the smell to wear off. We followed a track that was so boggy, so churned by elephants and buffaloes, that I was soon coated to the knees with black slime. Beyond the bamboo zone we plunged into a magnificent rain forest of neoboutonia trees which, seen from above, looked like an impenetrable sea of glistening green umbrellas. Then came hagenias with moss- and lichen-covered branches from which rows of red-hot pokers stood up like exclamation marks. At about 10,000 ft we climbed through hypericum woodland to Kabara meadow, a grassy clearing with a small cabin in it. Forty years earlier Carl Akeley, the American naturalist and founder of the Albert National Park, had been taken ill and died here. His grave was marked by a cemented slab; an elephant had cracked it.

We camped for the night in a rough shelter a thousand feet above Kabara. I was cold and muddy, and as I looked up at the Plough dragging its tail like a weary kite I wondered what I was doing in this lonely far-away place. Running away from Nanny, as the experts would say, with her red hands and cough mixture? Or simply curious to see what lay beyond the warning notices, the Keep Out! signs that cramp and limit the law-abiding citizen's steps? Were Marryat, Stevenson, Rider Haggard and Buchan to blame? And what had been the rewards? An encounter with a man in a clay cap holding a spear, or a stork with a comical bill shaped like a shoe?

I set out early for the top, with Jean, who was wearing my spare socks as gloves. A bushbuck sped past us like a demented spirit. Then came a lava pitch and the black dome itself. There was not much to see. The splinters of a summit shelter lay among buffalo bones. Mist covered the green plain below, the mounds and craters of minor eruptions. We had climbed to the top; and we had to climb down again.

On the night of 25 January 1971 I was in a bar with friends in Bakuli, an African suburb of Kampala. When I left I heard distant firing and there was a smell of smoke and cordite as though the security forces were shooting *kondos* (armed thieves). There followed explosions. Dawn was breaking as I drove back to Wandegeya and the streets were already filling with poor Africans hurrying barefoot or in flip-flops to their jobs. It wasn't until I saw the armoured troop carriers grinding through Wandegeya and the faces of Asian shopkeepers peeping timidly through barred windows that I knew there had been a military *coup*. The workers trotting to town realised this too. They panicked and went into reverse. By now the soldiers had sealed off the city centre. I drove to Nakasero preparatory school, where my younger son was a pupil, and took two stranded white children home to Makerere. The Apollo Hotel was full of bewildered guests. I sat down with a party of Japanese fish-net experts and ordered beer for them.

In the evening, soon after supper, with the town under curfew and everyone indoors, the radio announced that Amin's *coup* had succeeded and that the political prisoners whom Obote had detained were to be immediately released. As the news broke an immense roar rolled over Bat Valley from the darkened streets and shanties of Mengo. It was a roar of jubilation, a howl of Buganda tribal triumph – yet, for me, a hysterical and malignant noise that boded ill for the future. The thought of Uganda being ruled by half-educated and bullying soldiers appalled me. They would want loot, promotion, revenge and above all power. Amin was generally regarded as an oaf. The status of civilians would be demeaned and diminished. I walked over to my neighbour's compound, where I could hear drumming and cheers. Normally a quiet and respectable inspector of schools, I found him in his pyjamas pounding a tin dustbin lid with a stick while his family and servants jumped up and down as though drunk. 'I'm so happy,' he panted, 'I can't control myself.'

For a time Amin ingratiated himself with the Baganda. He arranged for the Kabaka's body to be returned from London to Kampala and gave it a magnificent state burial over which he presided like a benevolent witch-doctor. He said nice things about 'my friends the British', who lost no time in recognising his government. He praised the Israelis. Soon, however, there were reports that Amin's followers were taking bloody revenge on their enemies, the Langi and Acholi. We heard of mass tribal killings, the settling of private scores by murder, the elimination of public figures. Michael Kaggwa, a prominent state servant and family friend, was found incinerated in his Mercedes Benz sportscar, his hands tied to the steering wheel. Bodies were ferried in lorries to be thrown like sacks of maize into the Nile at Karuma Falls or into Lake Victoria. One day I came across dozens of corpses heaped at the water's edge behind Kasubi school. There was a guard post nearby and I had to wait till the coast was clear before I could photograph them. They were young, strongly built men wearing khaki slacks and shirts and army belts. Their bodies, many of them turned piebald and their eyes blue through loss of pigmentation, were riddled with bullet holes. Then Kalisto arrived in panic from Moyo, where he had been teaching. His compatriots in Moyo – Acholi soldiers and civilians – had been butchered *en masse* by Amin's men, and he had run for his life, leaving his belongings behind. The shock had unhinged him and he had to have psychiatric treatment at Butobika mental hospital.

In August 1972 Amin produced the master stroke of his 'economic war'. He gave the Indian community of Uganda three months' notice to leave the country ('You are sitting on fire,' he warned). The British government weakly let him have his way. The departure of the Indians was to spell the economic doom of Uganda. Arriving as coolies and pedlars with the building of the railway from Mombasa in 1901, they had become the true founders of modern Uganda. They had supplied the drive, the capital, the goods and services, introducing these things into a rural vacuum. The majority of British expatriates, promised compensation for cutting short their contracts, followed in their wake, leaving schools and vital services understaffed.

In August 1973 I had to go to England for urgent surgery. Within three months I was back in Kampala with a shortened intestine. Alas, I found my job was gone. An African lady, elegant and self-possessed, was sitting at my desk. Still, I had months of accumulated leave pay and a gratuity to tide me over, and the ministry allowed me to stay on in my flat. Ingrid meanwhile had moved some months earlier to her own lecturer's flat on Makerere Hill, with our two sons. I was left alone with my small library, the Kurdish carpet given to me by the *hodja* of Medi *yayla*, my ageing Beetle (400,000 km. on the clock) and Bitlensi the servant. With time on my hands I settled down to complete the script of *The White Pumpkin*.

My first intention was that it should be a non-political book, dealing with happy experiences. But the violence that was crippling Uganda couldn't be passed over. People I knew were being murdered. Karuhanga, a quiet youth who had helped me run the college library, was roped to a tree and shot by firing squad in front of his family. The dismembered body of Kay Ardroa, a small jolly girl who had left my English class to get married to Amin as his third wife and had borne him children, was found in a gunny bag in August 1974. Not long beforehand, Amin had peremptorily discarded her, and thrown her cousin, the former Foreign Minister, to the Nile fishes. When her limbs had been sewn back, Amin went to see Kay's body. 'She was a bad wife,' he told her parents and children as he towered in a sports shirt over the remains. Then my neighbour Lieutenant-Colonel Arube was drilled with bullets; his servants fled in panic to my compound.

With such evil let loose I decided to rewrite my manuscript and to attack Amin. I referred to him as a 'black Nero', 'governing his tiny territory, like a village tyrant, by fear' and ruining the good name of Africans. Then, with my typescript safe in the hands of Allen & Unwin the publishers, I made my opinions known to acquaintances. This was incautious. But I had made up my mind to stay in Uganda when the book came out in June 1975 and to face the consequences. I reckoned on being given a prison sentence of a few months and then deported. Mistakenly, as it turned out, I thought the surviving British community, which had been remarkably docile, if not servile – some went so far as to kneel before Amin, swearing an oath of loyalty – would welcome the fact that one of them had stood up to protest against the regime.

On the night of Easter Monday, 1 April 1975, two armed policemen and two security officers arrested me in my flat. They put a bundle of my papers, including the 40,000-word script of a new book (a memoir I had been working on for several months) into the boot of their car and drove me to Kampala police station. At one point they had to stop because papers were flying through the half-opened boot into the road. In the morning another security officer took me back to my flat while he collected books, letters, photographs and my own copy of *The White Pumpkin* typescript. As I watched him take away my things I felt as though he were stripping me of my clothes. Those bits of paper and pictures were a record, the only record I had, of my life.

Kampala gaol was a squalid place full of unwashed, tattered men. I shared a cell with two Somali smugglers, who lent me a chair with only two legs. A man who had been flogged showed me the weals on his back. An epileptic roared all day. On 3 April, in the presence of the acting British Consul Burton, I was charged with sedition (for my book on Amin) and transferred to the maximum security block at Luzira prison. There were twenty cells along a corridor with a lavatory and shower at one end, a small exercise yard, and a warder with a big bunch of keys at the gate. I had my own cell and slept on the cement floor with two blankets (no mattress or bed) and a plastic chamber pot. My prison uniform was a shirt, shorts and wooden pattens that were too tight.

The eight weeks which I spent in Luzira prison before I was handed over in manacles to the army at Bombo barracks on 29 May gave me time to adjust myself to prison conditions; and there is something to be said for being institutionalised, whether it be within the four walls of a hospital or of a gaol. Neutered, relieved of all responsibilities – the daily grind, the decision making, the unpaid gas bill – one becomes morally weightless. My cell-mates (all Africans) behaved decently. We shared our cigarette stubs, played dominoes, and clapped the Church of Uganda parson who came on a bicycle and set up a cross and altar table in the exercise yard. Boredom and anxiety about one's future were the main problem. On bad days prisoners would lie down on their stomachs, cover their heads and not speak for hours. (Five of them belonged to a gang of car smugglers. They were later executed, and must have had more than an inkling that their lives were over.) The food was so awful – a bucket of boiled cabbage leaves, cakes of stale maize porridge, and black beans infested with white grubs – that no one was tempted to pinch any one else's portion. Luckily I had some books to read. These were left-overs from the disbanded British Council library in Kampala, which Burton brought me. Among them were Cellini's *Memoirs*, Waugh's *A Little Learning* and Fothergill's outrageously malicious *An Innkeeper's Diary* in which the landlord of The Spreadeagle in Thame describes the awful behaviour of some of his guests. His book renewed memories of how I had once taken eight Thame wickets in a cricket match. In my straitened circumstances the recollection filled me with an absurd sense of vanity.

Ingrid and Burton were allowed to pay me several visits. We had to converse through a glass panel with a guard listening. My small son Johnny was amused when he saw me carrying my pattens (the straps were agonisingly tight). The first thing he said was 'Mummy's car was stolen by gunmen'. Two armed *kondos* had stopped Ingrid after dark on Nakasero Hill, pointed guns at her and said 'Car keys or we'll shoot.' I got on well with Burton. He advised patience: 'You are not forgotten.'

The monotony was broken for me by several visits to Mengo District Court, where I was formally charged with sedition (the 'village tyrant' reference). On 5 May the public prosecutor told the court that the sedition charge had been withdrawn. I was to be charged with treason and tried by military tribunal. This was bad news. Treason was punishable by death: Amin, it seemed, was determined to get me. On 25 May I was manacled and, with an escort of two army officers and ten armed soldiers, handed over to Malire Special Mechanised Reconnaissance Battalion at Bombo barracks. 'You are a very dangerous man,' said the officer who took me to the guard room. Here soldiers threw me to the ground, tore my clothes and tried to force a second pair of handcuffs over my wrists. When they had gone I lay down on the cement floor of my cell to think things over. Someone had written on the wall, 'I shall not see again this world'. Whatever I did, I knew that I must retain my dignity (soldiers despise cowards) and avoid upsetting the guards (who might be half drunk). I noticed a long nail sticking in the cell door. If my situation became unbearable I could cut my wrist with it. I played with the thought for a minute or two, then rejected it. Wrist-cutting would be shameful.

Lieutenant-Colonel Sule, the Battalion Commander, removed my handcuffs in the morning and I felt I could relax. Ten men with Kalashnikovs guarded me, another section sat in the guard room at the end of the corridor (all the cells except mine were kept empty). The latrine was a nasty hole in the floor. Soldiers stood over me when I used it. I was handed an amended copy of the charge sheet to brood over and a few days later, on 9 June, given ten minutes to wash and hurried to the courtroom. My escort officer wore the glengarry and kilt of one of Amin's show units ('I respect the Scots. They are better and braver than the English.').

The trial, which lasted three days, was a sinister farce. The chairman of the tribune was a ferret-faced major, a promoted thug who didn't know English and was Amin's mouthpiece. The other four members were junior officers and mere passengers. All carried ceremonial swords. The proceedings were in English and Swahili. When Mr Wilkinson, who had agreed to defend me, entered the room the chairman said he had no right to be there and dismissed him. The last of the prosecution witnesses to be called was Ingrid. The prosecuting officer, a captain, as part of his tactics to discredit my relationship with Ingrid, had already referred to her as my 'former wife' (*bibi zamani*), and I had protested. Ingrid told the tribunal that in law a wife could not be made to give evidence against her husband, and that she would not do so. The chairman gave her a nasty look and said one word, '*Kwenda*! (Go away!)'

There were some awkward moments. I had called Amin a 'black Nero' as well as a 'village tyrant'. 'Who is this Nero?' asked the chairman. 'The cruellest of all the Roman emperors,' explained the prosecuting captain. The courtroom went silent and I looked through the window. But it was the reference in my text to 'spies' that the prosecutor seized on. Here is the passage:

> Amin is fond of calling us 'spies' (a white man seen bird-watching in a sugar-cane field or changing a wheel within a mile or two of a barracks had better watch out); and though the European bridles at the

charge, there is some truth in it, for we foreign residents, whether we like it or not, are the eyes and ears of a wider world. Our presence in Uganda must have some inhibiting effect on the excesses of government. The African feels less isolated and less vulnerable while there are white faces around. Corpses may be dumped in swamps, individuals disappear. But the word spreads. It reaches the news media, and a Nairobi or a London newspaper, though they may not always get the facts right, will announce their obituaries.

The prosecuting officer picked out a single phrase without its context, and misquoted it ('Amin calls us spies, and there is truth in it'), but it was enough for him to charge me and the British community with widespread espionage activities in Uganda. My book was deliberately intended to harm the Uganda government, which was treason; and I was a spy. By the time I had made my own address – no doubt to the ears of those imposters it must have sounded priggish ('I have written what I believe is true') – the tribunal had had enough. 'Words,' exclaimed the chairman, 'words, many, many words.'

My appearance in the courtroom next morning was brief. 'You have bad eyes,' said the chairman, 'a bad look in your eyes.' The verdict was guilty. I was taken out, and brought back to hear the sentence: to be shot by firing squad. The five officers then sheathed their swords and I was left among the scattered papers. I could see my typewriter, which had been produced as evidence, on a desk with its ribbon broken. It was an old-fashioned Remington given to me as a schoolboy and I would not see it again. I had no feeling of shock. The tribunal had shown itself so unsympathetic that the death sentence was not unexpected; and a firing squad was better than being hanged. A kilted sergeant and guards with fixed bayonets took me back to my cell. This was a painful moment, and I remember it clearly. Sun and shadow had cast a blue haze over the green valley below Bombo. Outside the thatched huts smoke was spiralling from cooking fires where women were preparing *matoke* and children chivvying livestock. For twelve years I had lived among these people as a friend. Now I was an enemy, and soldiers were hustling me away like a goat.

For several days I was left alone with my thoughts. I had not lost hope. The British authorities, though I had heard nothing from them since I had been moved to Bombo, would, I knew, be working on my behalf. On the other hand, I found that I could accept the death sentence without being too upset. I had only myself to blame for my predicament; indeed, in a sense I had virtually asked for it. And what is death? I had seen soldiers killed in war; and every second people were dying bravely and uncomplainingly in sick-beds. I tried to persuade myself that the whole affair – my cell walls spattered with the blood of squashed mosquitoes and despairing graffiti, the shuffle of army boots in the corridor, the occasional cackle of laughter from the guard room, the bugler in the yard whose piercing call chased away the devils in the bush – was a pantomime. Amin liked clowning. But he would joke one moment, and order one of his killer squad to cut off a man's head the next. One thing remained constant in my mind. At whatever cost to myself, my book had to be published. To achieve this aim was the challenge, the ultimate dare.

As the days passed the absence of any visitors – no duty officer, not even Lieutenant-Colonel Sule, who had once brought me a mango – struck me as ominous. Sudden noises in the night – a vehicle pulling up in the compound, the trampling of boots, raised voices – made my heart beat a little faster. I did not know at the time that at regular intervals Kampala Radio was counting the number of days to go before I was taken to Death Valley to be shot (by an irony, as I learned later, the announcer was one of my former students). Someone sent me a Bible, much used, with missing pages. The Old Testament, I found, was not for me. It read like a bloodthirsty oriental saga with its violence and acts of divine vengeance. The New Testament was different. Its message was one of mercy and forgiveness. Reviewing the balance of my life, I thought of the unpaid bills: the unfulfilled promises, the acts of ingratitude and egotism. One of the younger guards, who had had some English schooling, told me to read Psalm 88. Its verses were depressing, for David was in desperate trouble ('I am shut up, and cannot come forth.')

On 18 June I was taken out for an hour's exercise in the sunlight. The wired compound was partly overgrown with elephant grass and brambles. I counted ten guards, some hidden in the elephant grass, covering me with automatic rifles. I ignored them, did some exercises, and sat down to pare my finger- and toe-nails with a stone. Some soldiers' wives stopped to look at me as they passed, keeping their hands over their mouths – an ominous sign. Then suddenly, with no prior warning, I was hurried in my crumpled safari shirt and trousers to the officers' mess. 'Big men are coming to see you, perhaps the President himself.' Soon a helicopter landed with a clatter. Amin had two British officers with him: Lieutenant-General Sir Chandos Blair of the Scottish Command, and Major Iain Grahame. 'I have brought Amin a letter from the Queen,' Blair told me. 'This is an awkward mess, and Kampala is buzzing with pressmen.'

Amin was waiting for me in an ante-room. He stood up, a towering figure in an ill-fitting pullover that showed the bulge of his belly. As he looked at me with his muddy eyes and slightly drooping underlip I was prepared for wrath. But he began quietly, stressing his 'love for the Queen and the British nation.' 'You have been mixing with the wrong people,' he said. 'You have written a bad book, and your friends have double-dealt – they have betrayed you.' Then, speaking with deliberation, he said, 'I have signed the execution order for tomorrow morning.' This was the critical moment. I resisted the temptation to change expression. 'But because the Queen is my friend,' he went on, 'the order will be reconsidered.'

Africans say that the dog that smiles gets a kick. If I unsettled Amin now he might change his mind. I willed him not to, and said nothing. But he had wandered off on a rambling complaint about his economic problems, as though fishing for our sympathy. My attention strayed. Major Grahame was looking pale and concerned. General Blair, small and neat in a service uniform with campaign ribbons, was trying, I could see, to control his impatience. Amin's face looked very black in the dim electric light, his neck a thick band of unhealthy oiled flesh as though the glands were swollen. How much more impressive he was in his Field Marshal's uniform with a breastplate of medals stretched tight over the boxer's torso. Suddenly Blair interrupted Amin's monologue and turned to me. 'The President is a very great sportsman,' he said. The remark was well timed (hadn't Amin and I both played rugger at the Kampala Club?) and Blair now asked permission to speak with me alone.

Blair came straight to the point. 'You will have to write a letter to the President apologising for the remarks he has objected to in your book. Kampala is standing by to broadcast it and the press are waiting.' I took this as an order, and assented. Major Grahame also suggested that I might ask to be deported. We then relaxed. Blair complained that he and Grahame had been 'buffeted about in Amin's helicopter for hours'. They felt a little bewildered. 'The President is now taking us to a place called Cape Town something. Do you know it?' This, I explained, was a splendid villa by the Lake which Amin had requisitioned. 'I suppose you will retire now on the royalties from your book,' Blair remarked as he left to board the helicopter, ' – if it is not suppressed.' The remark worried me. I could not bear the thought of defeat. I went up to Grahame again and said to him, 'Whatever happens, the book must be published.'

At ten o'clock that night two officers, both drunk, brought me pen and paper and told me to write a letter to the President 'explaining everything'. They were in a hurry and tugged at my blanket. In ten minutes I had scribbled my letter and they took it away to be typed. There were four paragraphs. I expressed regrets for the remarks that the prosecution had objected to. I denied treasonable intent. I regretted the embarrassment I had caused to good relations between Uganda and Britain. Finally, I asked for magnanimity (but would Amin know the word?). Left alone, I thought about what I had written. It was a sort of surrender. Yet these were General Blair's instructions; I was in no position to criticise them; and they were a lifeline.

I was still closely guarded. No one came to see me and I heard no more about the results of General Blair's visit or of a reprieve. A corporal told me that Blair had been disrespectful and 'totally drunk'. (I heard later that when Blair first called on him the President, wearing a sort of cowboy's hat, received him in a grass hut. Blair had to duck through the low entrance and was caught by the photographers with his bottom in the air!) On 4 July Lieutenant-Colonel Sule told me that there was to be a government conference on press and public relations, and the President wanted to have my views. I suggested in a letter that the government should lift its ban on British newspapers and journals, allow foreign journalists to move through the country and meet its ordinary people, and recruit a new generation of expatriate teachers and social workers who were without mercenary motives. About now the guard was relaxed. I was allowed more time out of doors, soldiers invited me to fill my mess tin with soup and beans from their dixies, and I began to feel that the worst that could happen to me was a term of imprisonment in Luzira. Then on 10 July I was told to shave, my suit was returned to me and Sule drove me at breakneck speed in his Mercedes to Kololo.

Someone wrote that a 'dazed-looking man' stumbled into Amin's command post, led by Colonel Sule. Seeing a mass of photographers facing me, and behind them a row of dignitaries, I had put on my *sahib*'s face. Amin was grinning – he shook my hand and showed me his small boy, Mwanga – plainly a sign of truce. I still had no idea that the British Foreign Secretary had flown to Uganda, and it wasn't until he greeted me that I exclaimed 'Mr Callaghan!' Amin wanted to make another rambling speech but Callaghan interrupted him, and the meeting broke up in confusion. Ingrid came up, and a large Foreign Office policeman in mufti took charge of me ('the plan is to get you to the airport as soon as possible in case Amin changes his mind'). As we left for the High Commission, Amin was waving his arms.

Mr Hennessy, the High Commissioner, drove me and Ingrid to Entebbe airport. I was taken aback, when Ingrid told me that my reference to the British community as 'spies' – though I had ridiculed the notion – had been seized upon by Amin and that he had been threatening them with expulsion. It was a shock to hear that the British were accusing me of putting their jobs in danger and were angry and bitter about me. It was a further blow when Ingrid told me that she had no immediate intention of leaving Uganda. I felt crushed.

I was told to board the RAF transport plane a few minutes before the others, and walked alone across the apron to the gangway carrying my few belongings – books, a saucepan and towel – in a striped blanket. A crowd of whites was waiting at the barrier. I gave them a small wave but no one returned it. But I was heartened by the smiling faces of the African airport workers who crowded round the gangway and cheered. For them, Amin's conduct had been an outrageous breach of good manners.

Mr Callaghan was extremely kind – perhaps 'avuncular' is the right word. Over a steak and glass of champagne (he is a virtual teetotaller, I believe, and the bottle was taken away after a single glass) he put me at ease by telling me the cricket scores. He had seen the text of my as yet unpublished book *The White Pumpkin*; and he asked me about Poland, which he was about to visit. My note on Enoch Powell ('a pale, brilliant schoolboy who won all the prizes but never kicked a football') seemed to amuse him. He complained that he had not slept well in Kampala; barking dogs had kept him awake. Did I think Amin was mad? I said no – 'he started as an army cookhouse boy and power has gone to his head. He looks on Uganda as his own property – every blade of grass, every cow or woman belongs to him.' Like every successful African tribal chief, I added, he was extremely cunning.

Mr Callaghan then gave me a rueful look. 'Back to the economy,' he sighed, and told his press officer to take me to see the journalists, who were making a great din, like a rugger team, in the rear of the plane. 'Be careful what you say and don't talk to the BBC,' the official warned me. I was glad to meet Peter Snow. I felt we had something in common as he had at one time worked as a volunteer teacher in Uganda. I also met the *Daily Express* reporter. He stuck to me like a burr. He and his colleagues followed me in the night to my brother's home in Dorridge, and the press siege began.

My first concern was to say nothing that would embarrass the British – and Ingrid – in Uganda. I asked Malcolm Barnes, the editor, to postpone publication of my book for a month. Meanwhile I thought hard about the moral and diplomatic implications of what I had written. Barnes told me that the Foreign Office had been 'leaning heavily on him'. When I met them in London, Foreign Office officials were polite but disapproving. They reminded me of my obligation to Mr Callaghan 'after he rescued you from Uganda'. They pressed me hard to delete all the passages which the prosecution had objected to during my trial. On the other hand, they 'did not wish to impose any form of censorship on the book.'

In the end I agreed with Barnes to omit four words only ('like a village tyrant'); and I used the time to update *The White Pumpkin* with a hurried postscript outlining my experiences in prison. Amin in the meantime was continuing to threaten the British with economic and other sanctions. My own unshakeable conviction, notwithstanding Foreign Office fears, was that Amin had no intention of taking reprisals against the British community. They were his shop window and were too valuable for him to evict. I told the media that he was bluffing. On 16 November Amin, who had got hold of an advance copy of my book, attacked it on Kampala Radio as the work of a 'sex maniac, drunkard and debaucher of African students'. Publication, four days later, passed without any further outburst. Amin by now must have felt that he had won his little propaganda war: he had, in his own words, 'made the British quake'. A few weeks later he expressly disassociated the British in Uganda from my affair, and a group of British businessmen in Kampala was photographed carrying a gleeful Field Marshal on a palanquin (subsequently at least one of the bearers was murdered). On 16 December he re-graded the Acting British High Commissioner of Uganda to his old rank of High Commissioner. The joke – for the time being – was over.

My affair with Amin had been meat and drink for the media ('Black tyrant threatens to shoot white man'). When I got back to Dorridge I received hundreds of letters. Some were sympathetic, others critical. 'You are lucky to have got away with it,' wrote one correspondent; 'it has cost the Government a lot of money to bail you out and you have imperilled your countrymen in Uganda. You should now keep quiet.' Or as one Makerere professor put it, 'Why bugger us about any more with your wretched book?' An Irish lady, however, sent me a rosary from Cork. A South African farmer offered me hospitality ('I hear you're on your uppers, man'). And a kind stranger sent me his house key and the railway fare to London. I also learned from *Hansard* that Enoch Powell was the only member of the House of Commons to protest against the Government involving the Queen in my clash with Amin. When, fifty-five years after we had left school, I met Powell at a crowded party I recognised the pallor, the stare and the frown. He remembered me straight away. 'You were an outstanding sportsman,' he said solemnly. I told him I agreed with his protest. 'The risk of the Queen being humiliated, had I known about it at the time, would have been unacceptable.' Nothing more was said, and we drifted apart.

Chapter 13

Last Days of Rhodesia

From Dorridge I moved to my aunt's house in Leamington Spa. Ingrid in the meantime had renewed her teaching contract at Makerere and was to stay there another four years before finally settling again in Germany. My aunt had recently left for a nursing home. Until the age of 92 she had fended for herself, and her house was a museum of old furniture and hat boxes. My neighbours were two old maids and their cats, which scowled at me from behind an apple tree. The little church opposite chimed the hours. As a royal spa, Leamington was dead. The pump rooms were closed and for many years no military band had played in the Jephson Gardens. Indian families were taking over the cheaper housing and small shops along the canal, young West Indians in T-shirts hung about the pubs, and Irish tramps sat on the public benches with their big green bottles tucked away in the litter bins. When my aunt died in her sleep, the funeral was as she would have wished. We lowered her into the ground in Wasperton churchyard beside the moss-covered and eroded gravestones of her ancestors.

In the summer of 1976 a prolonged heatwave turned the Warwickshire meadows as brown as the East African bush. The milkman, the dustman and the road sweeper took off their shirts and exposed sun-reddened torsoes. 'If the weather stays like this,' a Sikh grocer told me, 'we shall all be black.' The sun reminded me of Africa. I was determined to go back there. But I was still under a cloud as the man who had offended an admired black African leader, and my applications for an entry visa to Kenya, Zambia and Malawi were rejected. Eventually I persuaded the Nigerians to let me in ('We want no more collisions,' the consul said, smiling), and I flew to Kaduna to stay with Terry Driscoll, an old Kampala friend, now teaching at a local school. My visit didn't last long. Unwisely, as it turned out, Terry took me one day to meet Jacqueline, an Irishwoman whose late husband, a colonel, had been one of thirty Nigerian officers recently executed by firing squad for alleged complicity in the assassination of the Head of State. The immigration officer from Kano heard of my visit. Policemen on motor-cycles came to take away my passport, and I was bundled on a plane back to London. Amin was turning into my albatross. Terry voluntarily followed a little later. The shocking and unexplained death of Jacqueline (she was found dead beside her car on the Kano road) had been too much for him.

As no black African state would have me I was left with a choice of Rhodesia or South Africa. In August I flew to Johannesburg and from there to Salisbury. The white immigration official at Salisbury airport was about to give me a temporary entry permit when he hesitated and looked again at my passport. 'Are you the Uganda Hills?' An hour later I was sitting in a dirty little room littered with cigarette butts waiting for a plane to take me back to Johannesburg. I had been declared a prohibited immigrant. In the morning I woke to find a policeman in a pith helmet standing under my window.

Back at Jan Smuts airport I found myself in a dilemma. As I had used up my South African entry visa by flying to Salisbury I was incarcerated in the transit hall with a batch of Portuguese refugees from Mozambique. In the morning, no longer able to control my anger, I confronted the three officials who were denying me my freedom. 'I won't be kept here like a rat in a cage ...' I began. Then I saw they were grinning. One of them showed me a headline in the *Rand Daily Mail*, 'Amin's "Friend" Banned from Rhodesia.' 'Take a seat, man. Tell us about this bastard Idi Ay-min.' They gave me a mug of tea, and one of them carried my baggage to the bus.

Armed now with enough money – £200 of my savings which I had obtained from an English bank department – to establish my credentials, my next attempt to enter Rhodesia was successful, and I felt immediately at home. The Salisbury boarding house rang with cheerful Yorkshire voices. The days were cold and sunny. The British, being a nation of gardeners as well as tradesmen, had built up this old settlers' outpost into a modern capital graced by splendid parks with ornamental trees and exotic flowering shrubs. The colonial atmosphere was still strong. Every white family had its black servants and nannies. Schoolchildren wore blazers and boaters and had superb playing fields, their fathers wore safari shirts and drove vintage cars. There was not much mixing of the races. Whites, Coloured, Indians and blacks had their separate residential districts and practised their own form of social apartheid. Sanctions had taught people to economise. There was little money for foreign travel, a restricted supply of foreign consumer goods, petrol was rationed, and Rhodesian soldiers and police reservists were to be seen everywhere. The terrorist war, though, was still largely confined to the bush. It had yet to spread its tentacles into the towns.

In reply to an advertisement in the *Rhodesia Herald* I soon found a job, and was sent by the Division of African Education to teach English and Environmental Studies at Gwelo Teachers' College. Gwelo was the centre of a white farming community in the heart of Rhodesia. The college, with a mixed European and African teaching staff, had some 450 black students who were being prepared to teach in African secondary schools. I soon noticed that the syllabus was painfully restricted. The students had no current affairs or debating societies, no social centre or canteen. The gym was closed and the playing field was rarely used as the college had no football or sports team. Cultural activities for black youths were regarded as an irrelevance (they also cost money). The emphasis was on cramming. The Irish headmaster, Mr Bragg, was a strict disciplinarian, and wore the little badge of a teetotaller in his lapel. Pullovers, shorts and wigs (for girls) were not allowed, neckties were obligatory. Senka, the nearby African township, was out of bounds. At 11 p.m. the student hostels were locked and the lights put out. When, after a time, I began to voice my disapproval of the restrictive regime and to ask, at staff meetings, for changes, I naturally upset Mr Bragg. 'If students are allowed into the gym,' he said, 'they will misuse the equipment.' I had some small successes, however. Black African literature, though it flourished and had been studied for years in schools in other parts of Africa, was scarcely known in Rhodesia. When I persuaded the Mambo Catholic Mission – it had a special allocation of foreign exchange – to import black authors, and gave my classes *Poems of Black Africa* (Soyinka's anthology) and Armah's *The Beautyful Ones Are Not Yet Born* to read, a new and exciting atmosphere invaded the lecture room. I also started a debating society in which matters near to the bone were discussed – the pitiless use, for instance, by both sides, white or terrorist, of teenagers to hunt down and destroy each other in the bush.

At Christmas I spent three weeks with Bucky Rowlands, a white farmer who grew potatoes on a 1,200-acre strip of high veldt a mile or so from the Mozambique border. Bucky's homestead was protected by a high wire fence and an extra brick wall. He had a direct radio link with the local security forces, four powerful dogs – two black Great Danes and two grubby bull terriers – and we carried weapons. Bucky had an FN automatic rifle, I was given the Sten. Bucky was a hard worker. He was out all day with his labourers, humping heavy sacks of potatoes and forcing his mine-proofed Land Rover, with a broken differential and no brakes, through the mud. Terrorists had so far left him alone, though they had a base on a small plateau on the Mozambique side of the valley which was clearly visible through his binoculars. 'Kaffirs', he said 'don't worry me. They are cowards. Just fire a burst at them and they'll run away.' By nine in the evening, after a few beers, Bucky fell heavily asleep, leaving the farm eerily quiet except for the crickets and the groans and scratching of the four dogs.

College routine, and walking in the surrounding thorn bush (Gwelo was five miles away), seemed dull after my taste of life on a beleaguered frontier farm. But there were compensations. Visits to schools all over Rhodesia to observe students on teaching practice were an opportunity to discover the remotest backwaters of the country. I knew, however, that my 'temporary teaching appointment' would be short-lived. Bragg, who didn't like me running a current affairs debating society or 'hob-nobbing' with students out of class, had told me 'You're skating on thin ice.' Whale, an education inspector, warned me 'to lay off culture'. So I was not surprised when early in 1978, on the pretext that I had reached retiring age, my contract was not renewed. My residence permit was still valid. With my savings I decided to buy a second-hand Beetle and use it for a year or two as a mobile home while I explored a country at war and watched the events that must inevitably lead to black independence.

By early 1978 terrorist gangs had infiltrated from their bases on the Rhodesian borders into the very heart of the country. The government's call-up policy had turned White Rhodesians into a nation of armed citizens. Most whites – including all farmers and many wives – carried weapons, and in areas where there was a risk of ambush white drivers (but not black) were instructed to travel in convoys under military escort. I decided to have nothing to do with the convoy system. I didn't want to shoot anyone; I had no passengers for whom I was responsible; indeed, the long hours driving alone through the bush and fenced farmland, the tension and uncanny stillness of the tribal trust lands, appealed to me. The outward scene – the black children playing outside their huts, cows wandering on the road, women with baskets – looked harmless enough. But the innocence was illusory. Terrorists and their sympathisers were hiding among the kraals, and there was the ever-present threat of ambush. When figures detached themselves from the shadows two hundred yards away, I felt vulnerable, and as I snaked round the narrow serpentines leaving a trail of dust I gripped the steering wheel tighter. That youth sitting under a tree watching me go past, what was he doing out in the blue? The homely shapes of baobab trees reassured me. I would get out of my Beetle to smoke and touch their smooth grey skins and crinkled elephantine feet.

In June 1978, as I was on my way to Umtali, terrorists seized the white teaching staff of Elim Pentecostal Mission School, lined them up on the sports field, and clubbed them to death – eight adults and their four children. I went to the funeral service at Umtali church. The five hundred mourners, almost all white settlers, were surprised to find that the ceremony – though the Pentecostal missionaries were known to be odd people – had been announced as a service of forgiveness and thanksgiving. When the mayor gave his address he bluntly stated that he preferred 'the teaching of the Old Testament, which demands punishment'. Settler opinion was that the missionaries had been unpractical visionaries. In their lonely hillside boarding school they had refused to take the most elementary security precautions. They had no weapons – not even a hunting rifle – no radio link, and had foolishly exposed their children to mortal danger. I went to see the deserted school. Among the scattered exercise books and overturned equipment I found on the sports field a single cricket bail. I put it in my pocket.

The Vumba range, forming the frontier with Mozambique immediately to the south and east of Umtali, was a favourite haven of retirement for settlers and small farmers. The war had turned it from an idyllic bolthole into a vital defence line against terrorist incursions and a dangerous place to live in. Bell, the headmaster of an African secondary school whom I met in a British Legion club, took me to stay at his farmstead high up in the green hills. Bell's friends were a resilient lot. Threatened with bullets, mines and ambush – they had all survived narrow escapes – they made a small income from coffee plots, kept pedigree dogs and Siamese cats, grew roses and prize aloes, and when it was dark sat in their wood-panelled lounges by lamplight with a gun on the table. Allen had been blown up in his Land Rover by a mine. The proprietor of the Leopard Hotel showed me a hole where a rocket had burst in a bedroom. The Mountain Lodge, from which one looked down on the Mozambique bush, was especially exposed. It was raided by terrorists who tied the owner to his bed and shot at him (removing a part of his ear). One of Bell's neighbours was the writer Doris Lessing's son, John Wisdom. 'His mother's a Commie,' said Bell, 'and we never mention her name.' Wisdom was convinced that the real danger to Southern Africa was Soviet Russia. As we sat on his *stoep* in our crumpled shirts and shorts, discussing the war, FN rifles resting against a wall, we must have looked like a parody of some old Kipling scene from the North-West Frontier; but instead of Pathans with firelocks the enemy were black 'Marxists' with grinning white teeth, automatic weapons and rockets.

An old acquaintance whom I met in Umtali – we bumped into each other on Main Street – was Rotmistrz Emil Mentel. I had last seen him thirty-eight years previously when he was a handsome lieutenant serving

with the Carpathian Brigade in the Western Desert. He took me
to his farm at the foot of Christmas Pass. The first thing I noticed
when I entered his homestead was a big painted Polish eagle with
a splendid crown. With a happy smile he put a scratched record of
Polish cavalry tunes on his ancient gramophone. Emil was sheltering
two Polish ladies – Princess Lubecki (née Sapieha) and her daughter
Maria – who had recently been driven from their nearby farm by terrorist gunfire. The army had arrived by helicopter just in time to rescue
them. Maria lent me her long-barrelled Spanish pistol and asked me to
escort her back to the farm to collect sweet bananas from the garden.
A mortar and rocket attack had wrecked the house. Maria pointed with
disgust to some African cattle grazing a few hundred yards away. 'The
munts', she said, 'are grazing our land. We shall never come back.'

In August 1978 my book *Rebel People* was published and at Allen
& Unwin's request I flew to London for interviews. It was a hurried
visit. I had written some hard things about Smithy's government,
and my main concern was to get back to Rhodesia before – as I thought
likely – the authorities declared me *persona non grata*. On returning to
Johannesburg a week later, I found that the *Johannesburg Star* had seized
on my reference to Smith as 'the biggest cheat in Africa', as well as on
other unfriendly remarks ('Is it for daddy's golf that teenage sons are losing their lives?'). As I drove my Beetle back to the Beitbridge border
crossing I felt certain that the Rhodesian immigration officers would
have my name on their blacklist. To my great relief I found three pleasant young men listening to a Springbok rugger match commentary.
'Returning resident?' one of them asked me, and waved me through.
In a state of euphoria I bowled away into the veldt on the road to Gwelo.

In Gwelo I went straight to my teacher colleague Hasebroek, the
Shona expert. 'Things look black for you,' he said. He showed me
a news item in the Bulawayo *Chronicle*. 'Denis Hills', I read, 'whose
new book *Rebel People* castigates Rhodesian whites and calls Mr Smith
Africa's biggest cheat, is believed to be still in Rhodesia. But yesterday he could not be traced in Gwelo, where he was recently living and
teaching.' Hasebroek advised me to go to the Mambo Mission for advice.
Father Plangger was amused. 'You had better keep out of sight for a few
days. Stay with us.'

I decided to go to Inyanga, forty miles from Umtali, and find a corner
in the game reserve where I could camp and remain invisible for a time.
While I was on my way news came of an outrageous incident. Terrorists
using a heat-seeking missile had shot down an Air Rhodesia Viscount
carrying fifty-two passengers and eight crew not far from Victoria Falls.
The pilot had made a brilliant landing in a cotton field. Of the eighteen
dazed and injured survivors, a terrorist gang had rounded up ten and

shot them in cold blood. This atrocity provoked further hatred and a bloody reprisal. In the punitive air and land strikes on Nkomo's ZAPU base camps in Zambia that followed, the Rhodesian security forces claimed to have killed 1,500 terrorists, many of them school-age fugitives.

I booked in at the Game Warden's office as 'David Wood, retired, of Salisbury', a shameless but I thought necessary deception that made me feel like a truant from society. Below a wooded ridge I found a beautiful and private camping place, hidden by rows of tall pines. A stream ran past with the gentle sound of rustling leaves. There was a water point, a disused ablutions block, and fallen wattle trees for a log fire. I stayed there, apart from a few short breaks, until the following summer. Dossing down under the pines I would listen to the noises of the night – crickets, tinkling frogs, the squawk of river duck, the howl of a jackal. It was the soft pad of feet that I feared. The Mozambique border lay a few miles to the east and Mugabe's terrorists roamed the neighbourhood, attacking farms and hotels and ambushing roads. I was a little nervous at first. But I soon felt at home. The pines stood round me like sentinels, shedding pea-green pollen dust over my Beetle, grumbling and creaking as they rubbed their branches together like nuzzling horses. The moon was a constant visitor, pausing to greet me before it sailed past the Southern Cross and over the *kopjes* into the western clouds. In the daytime kudu and duiker browsed in the sedge along the stream bank.

Inyanga was three or four miles away. It had a butcher's, a small store and a lending library, which was a boon – I was a castaway with books. It was some weeks before the postmistress, who handled my mail, gave me away. Now, when they saw me, the police reservists and shopping ladies turned aside, and soon afterwards the Warden sent Conroy, a young game ranger, to question me. He was delighted to find that I was not a 'Commie'. He came again, with steak to cook at my fire and a bottle of wine, and the ladies greeted me once more. New Year's Eve I spent alone. On my radio, Smith was castigating England ('Britain and America are guilty of madness on a scale never seen before in continuing to side with the terrorists and international Marxism'). I walked down to the stream. Throughout Rhodesia white people were singing Auld Lang Syne. Here in the hush of curfew the night was unnaturally quiet. More farmers had been killed, oil-storage tanks in Salisbury had been set ablaze, and Father O'Casey of the Carmelite Priory in Umtali had warned me that by staying in my present camping place 'you are running a foolish risk'. I put more wattle logs on my fire and watched them leap into flame and crackle and spit juice. In my bed roll I found some friendly visitors: some tiny frogs with striped legs, and a millipede.

In April 1979 news of Amin's flight from Kampala revived my old hopes of seeing Uganda again. I considered the possibility of driving there in my Beetle, and visited Botswana and Swaziland to see if I could get across their borders into Central Africa. But sanctions had blocked all land communications with the north. So I sold my Beetle to an Indian tailor in Gwelo and in July flew to Kenya. Again I was disappointed. The Uganda consular authorities in Nairobi told me 'You are a controversial person' and refused to give me a visa. Then I had a stroke of good fortune. Sharad Patel, an Indian film director, was making a film on 'The Rise and Fall of Idi Amin' and assembling his cast. He asked me to play myself in a few brief appearances on the screen. The script had been concocted by a local American journalist; the chronology of events was confused. Accuracy, though, was not Patel's concern. It was enough that he had portrayed Amin as a strip-cartoon monster wading in gore among corpses (including refrigerated heads) and killer squads; unsophisticated cinema audiences in Africa, India and Third World countries would revel in the violence. My own lines were so much out of character that without telling anyone I altered the most banal of them. The Kenyan government went out of its way to help. It loaned soldiers and equipment to represent Amin's army and there was one glorious morning when Nairobi's main thoroughfare was closed to allow Amin's victorious troops to enact his triumphal entry into Kampala. Amin's part was played by a good-natured Luo giant in a Field Marshal's uniform jangling with medals. Whenever we were seen together, a crowd of shoe-shine boys, street sellers and mystified tourists followed us.

When I returned to Emil Mentel's Rhodesian farm in December, I found that the political scene had radically changed. As a result of the Lancaster House Talks in London, Britain had lifted sanctions, Lord Soames was installed in Salisbury as temporary British Governor pending black elections to be held at the end of February, and a cease-fire had come into effect. The election result was a massive victory for Comrade Mugabe. I listened to the radio announcement in Mrs McIlroy's teashop in Umtali. She was in tears, and the four police reservists who had just sat down for breakfast grabbed their FN rifles and left without a word. A white farmer gave me a lift back to Emil's homestead. 'It's the end of Currie Cup rugby and cricket for Rhodesia,' he said sadly. 'Our kids will be made to play soccer and volley-ball instead.'

I watched the Independence Day celebrations on 17 April on an Afrikaner neighbour's television. His wife looked with disgust at the jubilant crowds and native dancing. 'If I had to sit among all those kaffirs', she said, 'I'd take my air freshener. And look at Prince Charles – he needs a haircut.' Mr Reinecke, a retired railwayman with a small farm and a shop, remarked bitterly that from now on he would have to pay his assistant a higher wage ('Bang goes my profit!'). But neither of them had the slightest intention of abandoning their beautiful little farm with its maize plot and grapes and prize pigeons. 'If Mugabe's boys want me to leave,' said Reinecke, 'they'll have to strangle me first.'

That night I drank vodka with Emil. The stress and strain of the past months, the constant threat of being attacked by terrorists (a gang had recently raided his labourers' compound and killed a neighbour's headman), and his work as security officer organising patrols, had lined his face. He was angry with Britain. 'First Churchill abandoned us to the Russians, and now Mrs Thatcher.' He had decided to sell his 1,100-acre property, and African traders would be coming to buy up his farm machinery for a song.

Chapter 14

Retracing Steps

N ow that Rhodesia's frontiers with her black neighbours had been reopened there was nothing to stop me from driving overland to Uganda. First I went to Johannesburg to look for a cheap vehicle. There I stayed with a friend, Jonathan – son of the writer Alan Paton – who was lecturing in English literature at Witwatersrand University. Jonathan had liberal views but, like his colleagues, feared the violent repercussions that would follow if government anti-apartheid policy were to be prematurely dismantled and 'the mob let loose to loot and burn shopping centres'. Through Jonathan I had already visited Soweto, the progressive Market Theatre where he acted minor parts, and the Ravan Press which had recently published the then unknown J. M. Coetzee's *Dusklands*. It was through Jonathan that I now met Izzie Kiloff, a Jewish car-dealer, who found me a 1964 Volkswagen camping van fitted out with lockers and a folding bed. I stayed for some days in Izzie's home at Norwood and had a fascinating glimpse of life among his Jewish neighbours. They had all prospered since the days when their grandfathers – the original 'Litvaks' – had arrived from Lithuania wearing the strange garb of Orthodox Jews. They had beautiful houses with swimming pools, and strapping children. Being realists, they had no mawkish feelings about the 'injustices' of apartheid. But they were worried about their long-term future in South Africa once the black population began to assume power.

My major worry was that my van had South African registration number plates, and under the existing laws I was unable to change them. So I expected trouble whenever I came to a frontier. The fact that I was setting out on a journey of many days on roads of varying quality, and that I was no mechanic, didn't perturb me. I had learned over the years that if I broke down a black man with a spanner would appear out of a hut. In the event, the frontier authorities of Zambia and Malawi let me through with no trouble, giggling when they recognised me as the author of the *White Pumpkin* – 'You must be crazy to be going back to Uganda.' The Tanzanians, though, were adamant. So I made a detour to Mpulungu, at the southern end of Lake Tanganyika, in the hope of finding a boat that bypassed the Tanzanian and Zairean coasts and would take me direct to Burundi. I was lucky. Standing on the quayside was a dapper little Greek, Captain Dmitrios, owner of the tug boat the *Indépendance*, which was loading bags of cement on two barges. As soon as I gave him my name he agreed to take me to Bujumbura in Burundi. 'You are welcome. I'll carry you for nothing.'

For four days we chugged at snail's-pace through the black water of the lake. At night the African helmsman glued his eyes on Cassiopeia. On the third day, which was Christmas morning, Dmitrios opened a bottle of resinated wine and we ate a prickly fish and a bowl of groats. Snug in my little bunk, I could have stayed there for weeks listening to the splash of water under the prow and reading my books.

If Dmitrios had not been there to help me – he knew all the port officials – the Burundi customs at Bujumbura would undoubtedly have impounded my illegal Transvaal van. But after some hours of suspense I found myself at last bumping down a pot-holed lane into the little town. A week later, covered in red dust and with the hairpin bends and pepper-pot hills of Burundi and Rwanda behind me, I arrived at Kyombo on the Uganda border. Beyond the barrier I could see the Uganda flag flying from a crooked pole. This was the moment I had been looking forward to for so long. Would my luck still hold?

The Uganda immigration official, a captain, grinned when he saw me. 'So you are the one!' After a little banter he fell serious. 'You are giving me problems,' he said. 'It is forbidden to bring a South African vehicle into East Africa. You will have to wait while I telephone Kampala for instructions.' He locked his office and walked away. I was still there in the morning. 'The *bwana* is deceiving you,' a police guard told me. 'There is no telephone connexion with Kampala.' But when the captain reappeared, freshly shaved and smiling, he had worked out a compromise. I could proceed to Kampala with a police escort and report to the customs there. Two days later I turned off the Jinja road into my old college compound and stopped at Colin Sherwood's house. My former colleague was sitting on his doorstep, in the same position I had last seen him six years ago, reading Betjeman's poems. 'I knew you would be back,' he said, and poured me a tumbler of *enguli* out of a square bottle.

Colin had a spare room and I stayed with him for several weeks. He and Father McKee were the last survivors of the former white expatriate staff of fifty teachers. Colin had been through hard times. One night, thieves had forced him to lie flat on his face while they ransacked his house and carried off the fridge, radio and furniture – even his bed and the curtains. A few months earlier, undernourished on awful food – rice, maize porridge and boiled plantains – he had collapsed, and had been flown in a coma to England, where the doctors diagnosed pellagra. Since the Tanzanian invasion in 1979, he said, college teaching had been erratic as lecturers had to spend much of their time searching the black market for food and currency. But the college library, which I had helped to build up, was intact ('Thieves and soldiers aren't interested in books'). I learned that Burua, the former college principal, had been murdered in Arua and his body gnawed by street dogs.

Kampala looked as though it had been ravaged by rats: peeling plaster, missing window panes, rusty roof-tops, roads a string of pot-holes, no buses, and everywhere a swarm of soldiers and armed police, hawkers, and unwashed people without work. The shops displayed only rub- bish – shoe polish, soya bean flour and sanitary towels; black market goods were kept out of sight. Soap, sugar and bread were immediately snapped up from the delivery vans and resold on the spot at high prices. Vultures stood sentinel on Parliament House and the British High Com- mission. Fruit bats, hanging from trees like blackened bananas, dropped dung on passers-by.

I went to see my old Kololo flat with mixed feelings, fearing ghosts. I had last glimpsed it in the night from the back of a police car taking me off to a prison cell. Amin's police had then rifled it. Apart from a few books retrieved by Ingrid, I had lost everything, from personal papers to my skis and my faithful Beetle. Now, as I turned into the drive, I had a shock. Broken window panes, strips of rag instead of cur- tains, the storm drains choked with rubbish, and the garden – where I had toiled with hoe and slasher – a wilderness of elephant grass and wild cassava. No one seemed to be at home in the block. But in the servants' quarters at the back I found Maria, the old drunken nanny, and the *enguli* distiller's wife. They did a little dance, giggled and gave me their scaly hands. '*Mungo* (God)', they said, 'has saved you.' My old servant Beatrice had gone back to her village.

When I called at the British High Commission Mr Fry, who was in charge, said with a smile, 'So you're back again. You must be a glut- ton for punishment.' At the High Commission's English Club, where members meet for beer and darts, I was given a cool welcome. This was hardly surprising. Even after my reprieve and return to England, Amin had persisted with his threats to expel the British community if 'the

British Government allowed Mr Hills to continue his unfounded and malicious propaganda against Uganda.' Further, at the time of the Entebbe raid the following year I had been quoted as saying that the British Government, instead of pandering to the fears of the small British colony in Uganda ('many of them are beachcombers'), should immediately break off diplomatic relations with Amin. It took a few more meetings at the Club to clear the air.

Meanwhile I had applied to the Ministry of Education for a teaching job. The officials were friendly enough ('How is the Black Pumpkin?'), but after several fruitless appointments I realised that they were not going to re-employ me. 'Your file is clean,' they assured me, but they wanted no more trouble. Several of my old students came to see me. The years that had passed since they were youths writing poetry ('Lapobo! The whiteness of her teeth/When I think of them/Makes food drop from my hand'), the strain of running up-country schools short of books, food and fuel, the fear of soldiers' raids and theft of school property, had aged them. One noticed the receding hair, the coarsened features, the frayed collar. Makerere University had suffered too. Its corridors stank of choked toilets, and the water-storage tank had been smashed by a rocket.

Then to my delight I suddenly ran into Kalisto in the street. Over the best meal we could find – rice soaked in gravy and sugarless coffee at the run down Speke Hotel – he told me of his problems as head of a school at Kalongo, not far from his Adilang home. He was short of teachers as there was no accommodation for them. Could I help? I could sleep in my van in his field.

Kalongo was a remote little settlement in northern Acholi, 300 miles north of Kampala, with a mission hospital run by the Verona Fathers. I parked my van under a wild fig tree in Kalisto's field – which was a clearing in the bush – made sure that it was safe from grass fires, and lived there for several months. Kalisto had a brick shed with a tin roof. He pointed to a heap of blackened stones a few yards away. 'That was my first house,' he said. 'Men came in the night and set fire to it – I might have been killed.' Kalisto's problem was that the local farmers objected to school development on what they considered to be their land. 'We want the land for our crops and cattle and for our sons. Schooling for girls? Their job is to carry water and firewood and earn bride-wealth.' 'Watch out for Ojong,' Kalisto warned me. Ojong was a powerfully built man, naked except for a strip of cloth round his loins, who carried a bow, arrows and a heavy *panga*, and had a small herd of cows. They brought flies and dung and I drove them off with stones. This angered Ojong. 'You are a *mzungu*,' he cried, waving his *panga*. 'Go back to Kampala.'

Kalisto's 130 pupils had a hard life. Not many had shoes; there was no electricity and no piped water, so we had to use the Verona Fathers' borehole and light oil lanterns after dark. I enjoyed teaching them. They had strong views about rampaging soldiers. In a composition on 'A soldier's life' they made comments such as: 'A good soldier in Uganda is the most daring thief.' Or, 'Soldiers are rude and cruel. They are a menace to their innocent brothers, and should not be allowed to mix with civilians.' Another pupil wrote, 'Before he joins up a soldier may have been an ordinary decent and kind man living peaceably with his family. But from the day he goes to the barracks his character will change, and there comes a time when he will kill his own parents.' Still, some of the boys were eagerly waiting for the first opportunity to join up. Armed with a gun, they looked forward to bringing back home a load of loot and sacks of Tanzanian bully-beef.

For me, the Verona Fathers, doctors and nuns at the Mission Hospital were the real heroes. They were overworked, patient and brave. As they might be carrying cash, they were always at risk of being ambushed and shot. Father Ambrogio preached every Sunday to packed congregations. His message was forgiveness ('the Acholi are a vindictive people'). Many of the worshippers took out an additional insurance – they visited the rain-maker and the witch-doctor too. The latter was a leathery old woman. When I heard the gourds rattling in her compound, the rhythmic incantations, and then shouts as the *jok* (evil spirit) was exorcised and chased into the forest, I knew that she had a client, who would pay her with a goat.

As I sat in the shade of my van watching baboons scramble up an escarpment and disturb the rock hyraxes that barked and whistled in stony caves, I felt as happy and contented as any retired gentleman who had the sun and stars as his constant campanions. Vervet monkeys ran across the clearing, casting furtive glances at me, and sometimes a bushbuck or a baboon with close-set, angry eyes. There was a day-long chorus of birds with strident calls: the bleating hornbill, opening and shutting its great hooked beak as though it were on hinges; the sharp cry of the go-away bird as it tossed its cockaded head; and at dusk the gossip of guinea-fowl under the thorn trees. After dark I sat with Kalisto round a burning log under the moon's Cyclops eye. The nights were so still one could hear a falling leaf. Occasionally a messenger from the Mission brought me a bottle of *waragi*; and I had my set of Russian classics, which I read slowly, savouring Oblomov's inertia and Dostoevsky's mad outbursts. When the season of grass fires started, necklaces of writhing flame incinerated the earth and plants, covering them for a brief spell with smoke and flying ashes.

It was Ojong who started the trouble that led me to leave Kalongo.

Hoping to embarrass Kalisto, he spread a report that Kalisto's white teacher had a secret wireless transmitter and was photographing military installations. Recalled to Kampala to explain my presence in his school, Kalisto returned in a dejected mood (on the journey back he had been held up by soldiers near Karuma Falls and they had taken his money). 'You had better go,' he said. 'Soldiers are coming to harass you and we don't want that Amin business again.' I left with regret. Kalisto filled up my tank with school petrol and Father Ambrogio gave me a bag of oranges. He smiled doubtfully when I said I would come back next year. 'We will take good care of Kalisto,' he promised.

I drove to Nairobi, and it wasn't until five months later (June 1982) that I managed to get back to Uganda. In the meantime I made a trip through Tanzania, and camped in Nairobi at Sam's Inn. Sam was a good-natured Scotsman with a hot tempered Kikuyu wife who sometimes threw beer bottles at him; his inn was a meeting place for an unruly collection of overland hitch-hikers from the Antipodes, Britain, Germany, Japan and Scandinavia. Many were rugged young men and women of piratical appearance, thinned down by the rigours of the road, moving in pairs with frame packs so heavy that it was impossible to hump them very far. Others were transported in the back of tarpaulin-covered ex-Army lorries. One admired their desire for adventure.

Nothing had improved in Kampala when I returned in June. The police gave me trouble, insisting that I renew my visa every seven days, and I was followed when I went into the city. 'Your file', an official confided in me (he was one of my old students), 'is held by the Special Branch.' Kampala was still lawless and unrepaired. Bedraggled marabou storks stood like witches on stilts near uncleared garbage dumps. The new black marketeers carried suitcases stuffed with banknotes. Road blocks were still a menace; soldiers would spring from cover waving their AK rifles and demand food or cash. By early afternoon city workers were already plodding home before Obote's armed rabble started to prowl at dusk. Colin was on sick-leave in Durham; his house was being used by jobless students who smoked pot. Kalisto, I learned from the Verona Fathers, had been temporarily suspended from his post at Kalongo, but was to be reinstated.

Uganda, once (in Churchill's words) 'the pearl of Africa', was now only a mockery of the well-ordered country I had known when I first arrived in 1963. The departure of the old British administration had led to disaster. Tribalism, unworthy leaders and half-baked ideologies had taken over and ruined the economy, and in the turmoil thousands of people had been shot, stabbed, strangled, tortured and burnt to death. With hindsight, perhaps, this outcome should not have been entirely unexpected: for in Uganda violence has always existed close to the surface.

The northern tribes had been brought up in a tradition of cattle-raiding, inter-clan fighting and vengeance. They were – in the eyes of the more civilised southern lake-dwellers, such as the Baganda – the illiterates, the hard men, with skins black as pitch. The charm, good manners and intelligence of the Baganda, on the other hand, which had captivated their white rulers, were deceptive. Under the old Kabakas, grovelling courtiers had pandered to the cruelties of the royal whim. Travellers have recorded the ritual executions of victims picked out at random by the Kabaka's secret police (they wore a rope twisted round their heads like a turban); the human sacrifices of office bearers and slaves; the burning by Mwanga in 1896 of the first Christian converts. Speke relates that nearly every day two or three palace women would be dragged through the palace grounds to execution; and his companion Grant, who was housed next to a place of torture, agreed that 'the shrieks of poor people, night and day, were quite heart-rending.' Sir Gerald Portal mentions the savage mutilations that were meted out for minor offences, such as cutting out the lips. During the collapse of law and order that came to a head under Idi Amin the bodies of his victims were left unburied, lynching was common and *kondoism* (banditry by armed thieves) put everyone's property at risk. Amin, by promoting illiterate Muslims to high rank, perverted his army by putting it in the hands of killers.

Yet the white old-timers loved this beautiful and sensual Lotus Land. Bishop James Hannington's last words, just before he was stripped and stabbed in sight of the Nile at Jinja in 1885, were 'Tell the Kabaka I die for Uganda'. In the European cemetery in Kampala there is a grave with this inscription: 'Hugh Ostler Crighton, 1948. The Old Man of Kikagati, Ankole, who lies buried here in the land he loved.' In this entrancing equatorial landscape, it is easy to understand such devotion. There were moments, when the flaming ball of the sun sank into the lake, and the earth's heat flew upwards to the stars, and the night sounds began – crickets, the squeak of bats in a mango tree, the scuffle of roosting birds – when the possibility of leaving Africa never crossed my mind. Nevertheless other things were waiting to be done, journeys to be undertaken. The traditional Uganda had fallen terminally sick, and loyalties had been rebuffed; the old love could not be revived.

I had set off from Johannesburg in October 1980 with £800. That was two years ago, and my money was running short. So I took a job as tutor at Coldham's, a Nairobi crammers, at £150 a month. I was put in charge of 0- and A-level English literature classes. The set books, which I treated as entertainment, included Chaucer's *The Pardoner's Tale*, *Othello*, *Jane Eyre* and Edmund Gosse's *Father and Son*. The books that I didn't care for, I rejected. No one could force me to teach *Look Back in Anger* or Bradbury's trifling *The History Man* to African students. I stayed at the crammers for two years, using my van as home, office and study. At first I camped under a grevillea tree in Sam's garden. Later, when creditors pulled down the inn, I moved to a field in Karen, where my companions were sunbirds and a flock of geese.

Sam's Inn was shunned by the sort of respectable white residents who lived with servants and guard dogs in Westlands and Hurlingham. They would have been alarmed by the rough overland hikers (a favourite T-shirt worn by the Aussies bore the logo 'Go Black. Never Look Back') and disreputable old-timers who used the inn, and by the nightly invasion of tarts with dreadlocks and junkie boots, who might nick their wallets and threw stones at the night-watchman when he tried to turn them out. The old-timers who called at the inn for their sessions of Tusker beer had seen better days. Among them were two wartime pilots, the retired champion jockey of Kenya (whose car had no battery), an alcoholic doctor who was studying cysts among the Masai, a melancholy Dane whose farm had been seized by his native wife, and Sam himself. Sam had written a book of war memories. It had been rejected by twenty publishers, but every guest was made to read it. After being captured at Dunkirk, Sam had spent his time as a prisoner in Germany 'eating Red Cross chocolate and screwing the fräuleins'. Other regular customers were a group of Indian storekeepers who came to spend their petty cash at the bar, and some Sikhs. They all drank neat whisky.

Every Sunday one of the Indians, a printer, brought parcels of food and a tin tub which he filled with chicken, rice, curry, chillies, onions and saffron and stewed over a charcoal fire. Everyone was invited – the tarts, the Sikhs and Goans, and any overland girls who would allow themselves to be pawed by men with curry-stained hands. The Sikhs, with their bearded leonine faces set off by puggarees, and their thick, sun-blackened forearms, were the most formidable of the Asians, and even the tarts were scared of them ('Singha-Singha gives the ladies a hard time'). They worked as builders, lorry drivers and carpenters, and were never worsted in a fight. No Asian wives ever came near Sam's Inn. Their place was in the kitchen with the chapattis and children.

So far in this book I have said nothing about the Asian community of East Africa. This is not to belittle them as mere intruders on the African scene. To Uganda they had brought immense benefits: trade, capital and skilled brains, filling a role which the British did not want and for which Africans were not yet ready. They had, however, overplayed their hand; and black resentment against the 'brown Jews', their wealth and influence, was ruthlessly exploited by Idi Amin when he declared his 'economic war' against them, seized their property – handing over their shops to soldiers and their wives – and deported them at the end of 1973. To their credit, in their adopted countries they have triumphantly succeeded in building new lives. When I meet Uganda Asians in England, we recall the 'good old days' under British administration, the absence of violence and the respect for law. But for the younger generation, the shock of their parents' brutal eviction has faded from memory.

In Kenya too the Asian community had felt from time to time the precariousness of its position. Suddenly, with no warning, a failed *coup* attempt by rebel air force officers on 1 August 1982 was the pretext for a plundering mob to loot Nairobi city centre and its mainly Asian stores and businesses and make off with everything they could load or carry. The speed and spontaneity of the operation was astounding. The Asian storekeepers stood amid the broken glass and empty crates in their looted shops, and lamented. Yet such was their resilience that, ten days later, they had managed to restock their businesses and the cash registers were working again.

When the time came for me to leave Kenya, I felt sad and yet strangely elated, as though I had broken the spell of Africa and exorcised a spirit that had been threatening to take over my life. One could have decayed gently into the red soil, a sort of vagrant, without enemies, without property, among cronies. I could have stayed on in my van, sleeping on a plank bed, eating smoked Nile perch and bird watching. But there was unfinished, long postponed business. I had to see Poland again.

I was lucky to find a splendid winter home in the village of Snitterfield, a few miles from Stratford. It was a fine old house, like a manse, with roaring log fires. Miss Barbara Parsons, the owner, was a clergyman's daughter. In her time (she was eighty) she had cared for her father's slum parishioners in Deritend, driven a Red Cross ambulance, run a dance school, and helped manage her brother's private school. Miss Parsons was partially blind. She employed three uniformed maids whom she had rescued from a mental home. They couldn't read or write, and had runny noses, but they were happy. During my stay I walked many scores of miles, in mist, drizzle, snow and winter sunshine, rediscovering the Warwickshire countryside. The ditches ran with black water, the leafless woodland bared its scabs and scars; sheep, monstrously swollen by the mist and their heavy fleeces, peered at me through hedges. I explored the village churches with their tiny stone war memorials, their cramped aisles and carved pulpits, and found gravestones where my mother's farming ancestors had been buried. When the snow melted from the fields and the days lengthened, it was a signal for me to prepare my journey back to Poland.

My first problem was to find money for the trip. The Polish authorities charged visitors £8–£15 for every day they stayed – for me,

an exorbitant fee as I hoped to spend six months there. I also had to
acquire a vehicle. The money problem was partly solved through a
publisher's small advance; and a carpet fitter in Henley-in-Arden sold me
his old Bedford camper van for £500. It had been lying out in a field and
was badly rusted, but had a sound engine. Early in April 1985 I waved
goodbye to Miss Parsons and her three maids – her parting gift was six
kilos of porridge oats – and was off to Warsaw via the Rotterdam ferry.
Two minor mishaps occurred immediately. The van's sliding front door
fell off – a Cotswold village mechanic welded it back; and somewhere
in Northamptonshire the skylight flew away over a hedge, leaving a gap-
ing hole in the roof. But by the time I had passed through the East
German frontier at Marienborn and got used to the laboured thud and
drumming of the engine, I felt confident that with a little coaxing the
old van would get me to my destination on the Vistula. The euphoric
moment came when the frontier officials at Frankfurt-on-the-Oder let
me through after a two-hour search of my baggage and books, and I
chugged off into the black Polish night. After an hour I turned into a
spinney, and rolled over on my stretcher-bed. I woke to the familiar
smell of damp woodland, rotting leaves and moss, and of little yellow
mushrooms embedded in mould. I was back in Poland.

In Warsaw a quick look at the three major hotels discouraged me
from spending any time there. The lounges had been taken over by
Arab spivs, beefy Americans of Polish extraction wearing baseball caps
and striped shirts, and raddled tarts in fish-net stockings. I drove to the
Gromada camping site, parked under a willow, and spent the rest of
my stay exploring the city on foot – the best way of mixing with ordinary people. The changes saddened me. Warsaw, which used to have
a Baroque elegance, was now, under Communist control, a grey jumble
of ugly rectangular buildings and tower blocks put up at feverish speed
to replace the vast tracts that had been turned to ashes and rubble during
and after the rising of 1944. Looking for places I remembered, I found
that my old landlady's apartment block in Hoza Street had vanished. But
Chopin's statue in Lazienki Gardens, which the Germans dismantled,
had been restored to its plinth near the pool. On Sundays I joined the
two or three hundred Poles who gathered there to listen to an open air
piano recital of his music. They listened in rapt silence to the chords that,
as Poles say, echo the beating of the nation's heart. Before the war, with
brilliantined hair and a book, I had sat there watching slim, laughing
girls eating cherries out of paper bags. Now, over forty-five years later,
I felt like an antique.

Through the British Council I met Emma Harris, an English history
teacher at Warsaw University. Emma was a phenomenon; during her
dozen years in Poland she had acquired an inexhaustible knowledge of

the country, and had great sympathy and understanding for the Poles; she was also bilingual. At her small flat in Zbawiciela Square I met many of her colleagues: Tomasz, a student of Lesmian's esoteric verse, which he was translating into English ('an almost impossible task'); a deputy who had recently been in prison; Bogna, who rented a holiday *dacha* where we sat on creaking chairs among cool leafy trees and wild flowers; Breeze (a Welshman) and Doyle (from Cork) – they had a curious assignment at the Catholic University of Lublin, where they were teaching the Celtic language and literature to bemused Polish students ('a rebel tongue for rebel people'). There was also an archaeologist, a professor of Ethiopian history and Amharic, as well as other delightful sages. None of them had any money, and no one owned a car. It was the state censorship, though, and the virtual impossibility of foreign travel, that riled and frustrated them. They made up for material deficiencies with the warmth of their hospitality. At their parties there was always something to eat and drink – vodka and cheap Bulgarian wine, bortsch, mushroom pie and strong cheese. With Emma I went to films and plays, art exhibitions and concerts. The much advertised Soviet film week, however, was a flop. Only a handful of people attended the films. In a Cossack epic, Budyenni was whirling his sabre at an audience of five, one of whom was asleep. It was usually well after midnight when I walked back from Emma's to the camp. It was eerily quiet. The streets were deserted but for cats and police patrol cars with flashing blue lights. The city was asleep, crammed behind the flower pots in congested little flats that smelled of cabbage, in jerry-built skyscrapers where the lifts didn't work and the tarmac petered out in sand and mud.

Warsaw, sealed behind its iron curtain, had indeed lost much of its former charm. No Paris fashions, virtually no night life, no riotous evenings at a cabaret. And no Jews. The absence of Jews struck me as remarkable. Their brass plates had vanished from the lawyers' chambers, the clinics and surgeries. The old ghetto had been levelled and built over, and the great Jewish cemetery at Okopwa was a neglected wilderness of tangled undergrowth and broken tombstones. Yet memories of the war dead were everywhere, in street tablets and shrines erected in places where Poles had been executed. The Old City (Stary Rynek), meticulously rebuilt stone by stone, was itself a memorial to Warsaw's shattered past. Not far from my camping site was the big Soviet war cemetery and memorial that honours the capital's liberation by the Red Army. How odd it seemed to me, as I looked at the neat plots and cement stars, that only the Russian officers' graves were named. The other ranks lay nameless and unknown, as though there was no equality even in death. The extensive cemetery with its beautiful trees was of course rarely visited by Poles. At the time of my stay, they were reserving their homage for the tomb of Father Popieluszko, the rebellious young priest recently murdered by government police agents and his body flung into a dam.

By the end of June I was looking forward to visiting the provinces, so I went to Okrzei Street to extend my visa. The woman who ran the visa office, a good-looking middle-aged blonde, gave me a friendly welcome. There would be no problem about a visa, she said. I could collect it in the morning. Late that night I was woken by a tap on my van window. It was Andrzej, a Polish acquaintance from the camp who used his small caravan as a weekend home. In the shadows his face looked white and anxious. 'Pani Denis,' he whispered, 'you are in trouble, grave trouble. You must be very careful what you do.' He refused to say more, but when I pressed him, added 'There is a spy in the American news office [ABC]. *They know about you.*' He wouldn't elaborate and I went back to my stretcher-bed to ruminate. What, I wondered, had I done to offend the Polish authorities? I had written nothing. I hadn't met any Polish politicians, and didn't want to (I found their quibbles and quarrels boring). My only contact with the Press had been a few friendly drinks with Kevin Ruane of the BBC and Roger Boyes of *The Times* – with Kevin I had talked about Everton football, and Boyes had been amusing about his Oxford days; he was at Keble. Boyes had taken me to one of Urban's press conferences. Urban, the official government mouthpiece, was widely disliked as 'a liar and a rogue' and I remember telling Boyes that he 'looked like a bat with donkey's ears'. We then ate a sandwich at the American news centre.

Andrzej's warning had alerted me, and when I walked to the bus stop in the morning I realised I was being watched by a young man with a satchel and an umbrella. He stood behind me when I changed trams twice, and followed me through drenching rain to the visa department. The blonde woman was no longer smiling. She gave me a severe look, and two officials with note pads came in to question me. For an hour and a half they gave me a relentless interrogation. Their manner was entirely humourless. What was my *real* purpose in visiting Poland? Who were my contacts in Warsaw, who was paying me, and what was I writing? The ramifications of my wandering career made no sense to them. That I had gone to work in Germany after the war, and later lived in Smith's rebel Rhodesia, were not in my favour. When I told them that I had been with the Poles at Cassino, they merely grunted. Clearly they thought me a snooper and a spy.

The result of this unfriendly meeting was a deportation order (*wiza administratcyina*). I was given forty-eight hours to leave Poland. Before I left I spoke to Andrzej again, and asked him to tell me the truth. What had the police against me? 'You are', he answered, slowly, 'a *korespondent* (a newpaper man).' After a pause he added, 'And perhaps more than that.' He declined to say anything more. Emma and some of her friends saw me off from the camp. Bogna gave me a cold roast duck with rich stuffing to eat on the way. As I turned through the camp gate I said to myself, 'The Poles can't get away with this. I will be back.' The final blow came at the Frankfurt border crossing, where the Polish customs confiscated my unspent zlotys (a substantial sum, which I had earlier been paid for sterling) and kept some of my books. Among them were a guide to the stars and *Memoirs of a Consul's Wife in Turkey*, a gift from Emma.

I spent the rest of the summer travelling through East Germany, living and sleeping in my van. This enabled me to see how socialism worked there as compared with the Polish model. The old German aggressiveness, the citizen's respect for law and authority, even the obsession with orderliness, had gone. Communist propaganda continued to ram home the message of military defeat and war guilt; thrift, and the poor quality of goods and services, had led to dejection and shabbiness. The question of war crimes perturbed me. When I saw the wounds inflicted on Dresden in two days of Allied bombing (135,000 people were killed, compared to 60,000 in Britain during the whole of the war) I felt shame, not pride. Buchenwald, on the other hand, tipped the moral scales heavily against the Germans. Weimar, four miles from the camp, once famed for its poets and culture, had watched idly as slave labourers were driven to perish on Ettersberg hill. The presence of Ivan, the Russian soldier, with his scrubbed face and ill-fitting cap, was depressing too; it took me almost two hours to drive through the huge Red Army training area in Thuringia. The culmination of all this neurosis was The Wall (*die Mauer*). You came up against it suddenly, round a street corner or behind a housing block – a whitewashed barrier where soldiers of the *Volksarmee* peered from guard towers into the citizen's private life. Cut off and institutionalised, the East German led an existence without honour.

In late autumn, after several attempts, I finally persuaded the Polish Consulate in Cologne to give me a new visa, and set off again over the Oder. In Warsaw the lime trees were shedding their golden leaves, Gromada camp was closed, and I stayed at Emma's before departing for Cracow. After Dachau and Buchenwald I was curious to see the death camps at Majdanek, Auschwitz, and Treblinka in the northeast. Majdanek, I found, was a big grassy enclosure only a bus ride from Lublin. The entrance was marked by a repulsive slab of concrete, cracked and shapeless, representing nightmarish thoughts of chaos and death. The perimeter fence, sentry towers and a few wooden sheds were still standing. In the sheds were stacked the pitiful relics of some of the

350,000 people who had perished there: their rotting prison pyjamas and jackets, a pile of human bones, bundles of thick hair ripped from the scalps of victims, and sets of cyanide gas containers with poison crystals. Next to a crematorium was a great mound of compacted human ash covered by a domed roof – the camp memorial. Countless local citizens must have seen the columns of doomed Jewish families trudging with their suitcases and bundles past Lublin's ghetto and along Droga Meczenikow (Street of the Tormented) to the black tombs and furnaces. Just outside the camp fence villagers were working in a beet field which (I imagine) had been fertilised by scattered bones and ash. During my stay I was put up at the Catholic University of Lublin. Few of the students, I was told, bothered to visit the death camp. For a Pole, what had happened to the Jews in Majdanek was not their concern. Only tourists, relatives and organised school parties went to see its ghoulish memorials to the holocaust.

It had been a clear frosty morning. Approaching Cracow, the sun disappeared behind a smoky haze as I entered Poland's most notorious pollution zone – the heavy industrial complex of Nowa Huta centred on the Lenin Steel Works. Sadly, the sculpted stones of historic Cracow, the churches and palaces, were bearing the brunt of this onslaught of smog and acid. I spent the night as a guest of the Dominican Friars. They gave me a pallet bed in an attic under the curve of the thirteenth-century dome of their basilica and I ate supper in the vaulted refectory. The Friars were a splendid sight – fifty handsome men magnificent in their long white habits and white cowls, eating hot potato pancakes (*placzki*), cottage cheese and stewed plums washed down with glasses of scalding tea. But my most vivid memory is the poignant sound of the bugle call (the *hejnal*) which is sounded every hour from the clock tower of St Mary's in Cracow's main square. The call originates in the legend of a Polish watchman who blew the alarm at the approach of a Tartar horde; he was struck by an arrow that made the call die in his throat. But the alarm had been heard, and the city was saved. Like the Last Post, the pure notes floated through the great stone square and died abruptly, as though the bird that uttered them had been suddenly strangled.

Auschwitz–Birkenau (in Polish, Oswiecim–Brzezinka), a little over an hour's drive from Cracow, was not only a place of extermination for Jews – and many non-Jews, too – from Poland. It was an international murder factory. Victims, packed in sealed freight trains without food or water, were ferried there from all over German-controlled Europe, from Athens and Amsterdam, Budapest, Prague and Paris. Bewildered by the smell, the smoke and bright lights, they were segregated immediately on arrival, and those who had been rejected as 'rubbish' were pushed naked into the gas chambers, where they died in agony, trampling, as they fought for air, on their own children. Among them were thousands of gypsies, who are said to have fought like wildcats when the guards rounded them up with their screaming women and children. On my way back to the camp gate I caught up with a church procession led by a priest, singing a hymn. I saw nothing wrong in this. But such is human nature that there are a great many Jews who resent any intrusion by the Christian church into 'their Gehenna'. Not long ago I heard a Jewish speaker at a London University seminar say that the Christian cross, as a symbol of anti-Jewish persecution, was out of place in the Oswiecim–Brzezinka death camp.

From Cracow I arrived in Katowice after dark and parked in a warehouse yard. Two policeman banged on my window soon after dawn. They burst out laughing when they saw a large toad emerge from its wrappings and stare back. By midday I was at Czestochowa, looking up at the high bell tower of the church and Pauline monastery of Jasna Gora. Here, in a screened recess behind the altar, is kept the jewel-encrusted ikon of the Black Madonna, focus of the Marian cult and centre piece of Polish national feeling and patriotism. The ikon was to be shown at 3.30 p.m. and I joined a crowd of worshippers crammed into the Matka Boska chapel. A fanfare sounded, the dark sad-faced virgin with a scarred cheek was unveiled, and the service began. But as always it was the worshippers who stirred my warmest emotions. They were ordinary people, work worn and shabby, with thick, dumpy bodies, and their smell and sweat mingled with the incense and the smoke of burning candles. As I stood among balding men and women in wrinkled stockings and head shawls, I had a feeling of special pride. For among the relics I had noticed a memorial tablet presented by the Polish Carpathian Lancers in 1980 on which their battle honours were listed. I too had been with the Poles at Cassino, Ancona and the winter siege of Bologna.

By now it was late October and I would have to hurry to visit Treblinka before winter set in. Forty miles east of Warsaw I turned off the Bialystok road into a tract of muddy fields and woodland. A peasant in gumboots, of whom I asked the way to the camp, said 'What do you want in Treblinka? Are you a Jew? Are your parents Polish?' A notice at the camp gate announced: 'Between July 1942 and August 1943 more than 800,000 were murdered here. In a prison labour camp 2 km. from here the Nazis murdered about 10,000 Poles between 1941 and 1944.'

Not far from the entrace was a ramp where the trains were unloaded. Above it was a small hill, which I climbed. When I got to the flat crest I had a shock. It was covered with an extraordinary mass of roughly chiselled, pointed stones. They gleamed repellently like filed teeth. This was the place of death, the symbolic cemetery. A split concrete slab with a candelabrum design marked the site of the vanished crematorium. As

Treblinka was an out-and-out Jewish extermination (not labour) camp, the Nazis had wasted no time with new arrivals. They were driven from the freight cars through a tunnel of leaves and branches – it was known as The Path to Heaven – stripped and thrown straight into the gas chamber, where they screamed and vomited as they struggled for air. Special *Sonderkommandos* collected their discarded clothes, the thick, shorn hair of the women, the jewellery and the gold dental fillings.

I spent the rest of the day walking round Treblinka, and visited the work camp for Poles and the enormous gravel pit they had gouged out of the earth. I met no one but two women picking mushrooms (they were very shy) and a man pushing a bicycle loaded with firewood. The sky was grey, a cold wind was blowing and, looking at the muddy fields and the leafless birch trees with scrawny white limbs, the waterlogged sand and the rooks, I was struck by the loneliness and desolation of this perverted place. The Nazis had good reason for choosing it as a killing field. Treblinka was not far from Warsaw, whence many of the victims came: it had a rail connection; and it was tucked away in the despised Jewish Pale, among frogs and foxes, in a forsaken bog-land from where the cries of the victims could not be heard.

From Treblinka I turned east to Bialystok and went on to Krynki, a mile or two from the Soviet border. The sky was dark with snow clouds, but I was anxious to visit the Jewish cemetery, of which I had seen a picture in an art book. I asked a peasant, who was loading sacks on to a cart, to show me the way. The man looked at me, and said, 'We don't want strangers here, disturbing the graves.' Then he took my hand, and added, 'Let the dead sleep in peace. Jews are humans too.' I don't think he was drunk. Clearly he meant well. Another villager guided me up a small hill to the cemetery. It was like the other Jewish cemeteries I had seen in Poland – abandoned, covered by undergrowth, sinking into the ground, the tombstones scattered as though by a great wind. A horse was tethered to a grave. With the Soviet wall only a few minutes away I felt, in this desolate and windy spot, as though I had come to the end of the world. Yet the Jews who had settled here hundreds of years ago must have had reason to do so. Perhaps they felt safer, away from the town mobs and the police.

At the end of November Lanzmann's film *Shoah* (Annihilation) was shown in three separate three-hour sessions at a Warsaw cinema to audiences of about fifty people. When the film was first shown in France it provoked protests from the Polish government for stressing the alleged involvement of Poles in the execution of the Nazi Final Solution. General Jaruzelski had given his approval for the film to be shown for one week. *Shoah* is an exhausting and merciless document; merciless, naturally, towards Germans, but heavily and unfairly biased against the

Poles, in whose midst the Nazi death camps were set up and operated. No corpses are shown. Lanzmann has filmed, not mud-spattered bodies grimacing in the agony of suffocation, but a vision of death expressed through allegory and mundane details – old rolling-stock clanking ceaselessly to the unloading ramps, watery red sunsets over Treblinka, the callous perfectionism of the murder machine and its minders. Lanzmann's German witnessess were astonishingly true to type, citing their appalling statistics with no trace of shame; and his shrewd interrogation of Polish villagers who had lived near the death camps trapped them into making the sort of damaging statements ('The Jews killed Jesus . . . They occupied the best houses . . . We're better without them') that are part and parcel of traditional Polish peasant thinking.

A few months later, when I saw *Shoah* again during the Jewish Film Festival at the South Bank, Lanzmann was there in person to discuss his film. He made it clear that he has no love for Poles ('an anti-Semitic people and much to blame for the extermination policy carried out by the Nazis on their territory'). It is true, of course, that there was no love lost between Poles and Jews. The Poles did not accept Jews as 'true Poles' – and Jews themselves, under their stubborn Rabbis, refused to be assimilated. Unarmed and vulnerable, after centuries of persecution from the medieval Rhineland to White Russia, it was their defiance that helped seal their fate.

When I got back to Warsaw snow and slush covered the streets. People had put on their fur caps and padded coats and looked like lumberjacks. It was time for me to prepare for the winter. Through Emma and her university connections I was asked to help with English-language teaching and I took part in Warsaw Radio broadcasts of English scripts. I felt happy doing this; I was no longer a drone and outsider. With my somewhat dated accent, I think I sounded on the air rather like a clergyman. Soon I had to visit Okrzei Street again to pay another instalment of my visa fees, and in view of the fact that I was now being paid regularly for teaching and translation work, my Polish friends suggested I should ask for the daily visa charge to be lifted. The blonde female director remembered me. 'So you're back again,' she said, smiling. She took my papers and told me to come back in the morning.

Next day I had an unpleasant surprise. Two solemn officials were waiting to see me – the suet-faced man who had interrogated me at the end of June, and a younger fellow with a policeman's moustache. They gave me a printed sheet to read. It was a BBC news item, extracted from the daily press report, dated 15 June 1985, in Polish. I read it with astonishment. According to the BBC, I had come to Poland to write an anti-Communist book. I was (or had been) an employee of the British

security service *(wywiad)*. I had helped Russian refugees to escape
repatriation to the USSR and I had been named in the Soviet press as
a 'Fascist agent'. I had fallen foul of Idi Amin, who wanted to shoot me.
It was the word *wywiad* that alarmed me. The slightest suspicion that
a man has had anything to do with intelligence work (or 'spying') is
fatal in a Socialist country. 'The report is nonsense,' I said immediately.
'*Klamstwo* (lies).'

There followed questioning and prodding. 'What connections have
you with the British Embassy? Whom do you know there? How have
you spent your time in Warsaw? What is this book you are writing?
You are rich – who is paying you? Why did you visit Bialystok? If the
British Government was so anxious to rescue you from Amin, you
must be an important person. What are your views on Poland?' After
an hour or so, the suet-faced official closed his pad. 'You are of course
an intelligence agent. Your own BBC says so.'

'The news item', I retorted, 'is *gowno* – shit!' He savoured the word
gowno for a moment, and repeated it. I was hoping he might smile, but
his fish-like expression didn't change. At the end of the session, Pani
Dyrektor told me to apply for a visa extension shortly before my current
permit expired (24 December 1985) and to bring receipts for my radio
and translation work. I left the building wondering if I had really been
reprieved. I had at any rate discovered the reason for my apparently
groundless expulsion in June. But who had supplied the BBC with this
malicious gossip? I had a strong suspicion as to who it was, but I could
forgive him as a foolish gasbag. It was the BBC – whose world reporting
I had always admired – who had stabbed me in the back. 'You are an
intelligence agent – your own BBC says so,' the Polish police official had
told me.

My van, parked outside Emma's flat, disappeared under a white
carapace. One had to be wary of icicles hanging over shop doorways –
they might break off at any moment like guillotine blades. In apartment blocks powerful central heating brought out the smell of cabbage,
onions and sour rubbish. I put on my balaclava, and noticed with dismay
that cracks had appeared in the toe-caps of my black plastic boots.

In December the University *Anglistyka* department asked me to take
over the English literature course after Christmas. The syllabus was
familiar to me, and I accepted. My morale now soared – I would be earning an income and could look the world in the eye. But I had to face
the visa department again. My colleagues told me not to worry – 'If the
police think you are a villain they would have thrown you out long ago.'
Six days before my visa expired I went back to the grimy building in
Okrzei Street with its creaking doors and row of little locked offices.
Pani Dyrektor took the cash receipts from my radio earnings and gave

me a visa form to fill in. I was to come back in the morning, and left in a mood of suspended elation. Next day, alas, what I had feared all along came true. Pani Dyrektor was looking particularly raddled and grim. She handed me my passport and said, 'You must be out of Poland within forty-eight hours.' I looked at the fresh stamp. It was another deportation order. My second!

I resisted the temptation to bang the table and call her a shit. 'So you are sending me off in the depth of winter, at Christmas,' I said, 'on a road journey of hundreds of miles. You must consider me a grossly unacceptable person.' 'It seems so,' she said. What angered me most was not the blonde lady's wintry smile but the BBC's nasty little news item. The police, confronted with the report, were only doing their job. The report might have landed me in a police cell. It was the BBC who were the shits.

As it was a weekend, everything was closed, including the British Embassy, and I had to leave, like a dispossessed tramp, with my van unchecked (it had been parked in the snow for weeks) and without my diary notes. I had a useless battery, a broken dynamo and no lights or windscreen wipers, so I limped slowly to Ostend via Brunswick (Ingrid was away), driving by moonlight through snow-covered fields in Poland and half blinded by snow showers on the German Autobahns. I was towed on to the ferry, towed off at Dover, moved on by the police for parking in the night off the Old Kent Road (the police gave me a push start and one of them lost his cap in a gust of wind), and pounded along the tarmac towards Warwickshire. I had just passed through Newbury when the engine gave a loud bang and died. It was Sunday. I would have to spend another night in my cold tin box. Then I remembered that David Winfield lived not far away, at Oxford. He was the very man to help a traveller in distress. A phone call, and there he was with June, in a Land Rover with tow rope. Back at a roaring fire off the Banbury road, I celebrated the end of my second Polish honeymoon.

The mystery behind the BBC report was quickly cleared up. A friend sent me a copy of an item that had appeared in the Peterborough column in the *Daily Telegraph* on 15 June 1985:

Battling on

Totalitarianism it seems holds no fear these days for Denis Hills, the British lecturer and wartime intelligence officer once sentenced to death by Idi Amin whom he had described as a 'village tyrant'. Reports reach me that Hills, now in his 80s, is living in Poland where he is writing a less than complimentary book about the communist regime.

Visitors to his rusting caravan, ironically sited between a Red

Army cemetery and Warsaw airport, are proudly shown a cutting from the Soviet newspaper *Pravda* which describes him as a 'notorious fascist agent' – a reference to his efforts after the 1939–45 War to save Russian refugees from forcible repatriation and the wrath of the Soviet secret police.

No doubt, when roused from my damp stretcher-bed, I did look like an octogenarian toad. But my camping place, though it attracted gypsies, was an authorised one; and I had no *Pravda* cutting.

When I wrote to them, the editor of the Peterborough column, the BBC foreign news editor, and the 'informer' replied that they were sorry. 'Sorry' – this must be one of the most facile and most abused words in the English language.

Epilogue

For the next three years I was busy writing and adjusting to a new life in England. I moved into a bed-sitter a few minutes from the green-painted footbridge at Richmond Lock on the Thames, and was lucky to have a landlady, Rosanne, who didn't mind the noise of my typewriter. Then in May 1990 I boarded the Warsaw coach on a train at Ostend. Poland was being liberalised, the exorbitant daily visa fee for visitors had been abolished, and I had nothing more to fear from paranoid Warsaw policemen with thick white fingers.

My first brush with Poles was in the shape of the dubious traders who, taking advantage of the new freedom to travel, were swarming over the frontiers to stock up with foreign goods. At station halts in Germany I watched husky Poles manhandling bulky packages and crates through the carriage windows to accomplices. At Essen great boxes of what I think were textiles were stacked in my compartment, with a small, wizened Polish woman to guard them like a watchdog. Frontier checks were impossible – the police and customs let everyone through unsearched. This was the Polish version of a free market economy: roguery, enterprise, and the muscles of a weight-lifter. Then, at the end of the journey, pickpockets were waiting on the dimly lit platforms of Warsaw Central Station to pluck a wallet or two from tired passengers.

Emma let me stay in her flat. She had been promoted. The British Council and Embassy had asked her to set up a new English-language centre in Warsaw and to organise premises and textbooks. This belated recognition by the British of Emma's worth was justly deserved. Warsaw's

251

face had changed under the new economic regime. Shops were better stocked, the queues had disappeared, but prices had rocketed, and the inflated currency filled one's pockets with wads of crumpled notes. A rash of street traders had invaded the pavements. They sold everything, from lumps of bloody meat (heaped on the floors of grimy vans) to kiwi fruit and Moroccan bananas, dictionaries, art books and bicycles. *Kantors* (foreign exchange dealers) operated an efficient service from cubby-holes in alleys and courtyards. 'The gypsies have done well out of the *kantor* racket,' I was told. 'They've made fortunes and gone to live in palaces in Cracow.' At Praga the big open air market was overrun by a mob of hucksters from Lithuania, Moldavia and the Balkans. Many of them were black-browed gypsy women from Romania, squatting on the dusty ground like squaws. Money changers openly flourished rolls of rouble notes. One heard voices from Minsk and Wilno. A single police car, standing quietly outside the market entrance, was the only sign of surveillance.

There were other signs of change. The Poniatowski bridge across the Vistula, which used to vibrate alarmingly, had been repaired, and the new Marriott Hotel, left unfinished for eight years, had been transformed by squads of Cuban workers from an unsightly mass of rusting girders into a shiny black tower block glittering with kitsch. The Lenin Museum had been closed down. But the Jewish cemetery at Okopwa was being tidied up and new Jewish graves had been added, some inscribed by relatives as 'symbolic graves' in memory of those 'murdered by Nazi torturers and beasts'. Other Jews were trickling back to Warsaw in small numbers – one saw them in the street, quiet and no longer obtrusive. Parties of young Israeli tourists were also regular visitors. They visited Okopwa and the ghetto monument, and took pictures of Polish guards doing the goose-step.

Through my old army friend Major Pawlak I met Hlebowicz, a retired lawyer with a straight military back and a big Roman nose. Hlebowicz took me to stay at his country house in Konstancin, outside Warsaw, where he had just been elected mayor. Konstancin was, for me, a link with the past, for I had been there with Dunia on our honeymoon when we had used the tiny *samovarek* train. Hlebowicz was a rare specimen. He was one of the few survivors of the nearly 15,000 Polish prisoners, mostly officers, whose disappearance in April 1940 from Russian camps at Kozielsk, Starobielsk, and Ostashkov was known as 'the crime of Katyn'. Only some 4,000 of the missing bodies had been traced. The rotting corpses were exhumed by the Germans in Katyn wood in April 1943. They had been brought from Kozielsk, their arms bound with cord, and shot in small groups in the back of the head. Hlebo-

wicz, then a young cavalry officer, managed to deceive his NKVD inter-
rogators in Ostashkov by passing himself off as a politically harmless
private from a small town near Poznan in German-occupied Poland. He
was segregated with 150 of his comrades and as part of an exchange of
prisoners handed over by the Russians to the *Wehrmacht* in November 1939. The other inmates of Ostashkov were listed by the NKVD
as 'dangerous pro-Allied Fascists' and kept behind to await their
gruesome fate. Hlebowicz's subsequent escapades as a prisoner of the
Germans took him for a time to Colditz, among the Allied trouble-
makers – 'a wonderful body of men [he said] whom the Germans found
it impossible to control.' At the end of the war the Americans released
him from a gaol for common criminals in Germersheim, and he returned
to Poland in 1947.

After decades of denial, the Russians had just admitted, in April
1990, that it was their own secret police who carried out the Katyn
executions. Their confession of guilt was vital news for the Poles –
even the British, to their shame, had hitherto refused to accept Polish
claims that the Russians were responsible. This was an issue that touched
Polish honour, and the press was making much of it. But what had
happened to the 10,000 missing men? Sunk in barges in the Arctic?
Mouldering in tiers in some Ukrainian bog? The Poles were still waiting
for the Russians to acknowledge their guilt for the whole of this 'act
of selective genocide'. (In October 1991 it was revealed by Nicholas
Bethell and Russian researchers that over 6,000 of the men missing
from Hlebowicz's old camp of Ostashkov were shot; the graves have
been exhumed.)

Like most Polish gentlemen who had been cavalry officers, and
owned a country house with a few hectares of land, Hlebowicz
was a delightful snob. He didn't approve of Solidarity leaders in
shirt-sleeves who spoke ungrammatically. I spent happy hours reading through his library of escape books (Polish officers have written
dozens of war memoirs) and helping Mrs Hlebowicz to pick cherries
and scare off the starlings. Her family had occupied the house for
over a hundred years. She told me that the German army officers
who were billeted in it during the war had behaved well – 'one of
them played Chopin'. The Russians were different. 'They fouled and
broke everything.' Restored and refurbished, the mansion now stands
spick and span amid the cherry trees, the cornfields and spinney,
with gleaming parquet floors, oil paintings, and shelves crowded with
books.

Before I left for England, I watched an excellent Warsaw television
film based on Boleslaw Lesmian's life as a gifted but misunderstood poet.
There were touching scenes of his family life in Zamosc, and of the shock

when he discovered that the lawyer with whom he had been associated had lost every penny of the poet's money. By now the excitement of the world football cup was over; it had kept most of Warsaw glued to its sets. I arrived back at Liverpool Street on a very hot day. The platforms had been railed off for repairs, there were no trolleys, and people were stretched out amid their luggage on the dirty ground. This was England's welcome to her visitors: 'We are sorry'. That word again!

Back in my bed-sitter near Richmond Lock, among old Christmas cards and rumpled blankets, the damp Thames air and the grey winters are, I fear, stiffening my bones. But the tow-path offers me an escape. I like the anglers with their wind-chapped faces and boxes of worms, the racing crews, the gulls and herons, and at night the comforting melancholy of the cold black river. It is the incontinent dogs and the joggers I don't care for – the latter stealing up from behind like footpads. Living in London has enabled me also to keep in touch with old friends. At literary parties I sometimes come across Michael Wharton surrounded by giggling cronies – the slight body a little more roly-poly these days, the raven hair now grey. David Thomson I last met in the bar of the Edinburgh Castle, Camden. He was wearing a rough peaked cap, like a Dutch tram-driver's. Two months later he was dead. At his funeral service, which I attended, there was an emotional reading from his book *Nairn*, and a beautiful Gaelic lament. Of the old Bucharest Follies Ivor Porter, who was parachuted back into Romania in 1943 and went on to enjoy a notable diplomatic career, has retained his looks and courtesy. Geoffrey Household is dead. Shortly before he died in 1988 he warned me in a letter 'not to get bogged down in a bed-sitter but to keep on travelling.' Not only did he enjoy a varied and exciting life: he lived to be 87! David Winfield, alas, has flown away to the sea-girt Isle of Mull. But I am lucky to have had as neighbours my old school friends Warty Bailey and Roy Lewis – and Macartney too from the days of heat and sandstorms with the Poles in Iraq. Lewis, a former assistant editor with *The Times* and the *Economist*, gives me a weekly tutorial on current affairs and his wife provides a splendid Sunday meal.

I visit Ingrid and my sons at their home in the Jasperallee, Brunswick, travelling there by motor coach with British Army families, who are dropped off at their scattered barracks. My daughter Gillian, after successful appearances in French films (she was first taken up by Vadim) and British television, has left the screen and is married. Since the death of Dunia she has gone back to painting and has her own riverside *dacha* with studio. Through Major Pawlak I keep in touch with Polish army veterans in London. When Pawlak escaped from a German prisoner-of-war camp on the Silesian border in 1940 and set off on foot on the long journey to join his Polish colleagues in Palestine, he wrote in his diary: 'To be free at last is wonderful. No barbed wire, no Germans, nothing but bird-song and the splash of streams. I and my companion walked in silence. I have never since that time felt so near to God.' To be free is wonderful! Perhaps that should be the message of these memoirs – 'madly singing in the mountains', like that ancient Chinese poet.

Index